Master Basic DIY

Teach Yourself®

Master Basic DIY

Mike Edwards/DIY Doctor

For UK orders: please contact Bookpoint Ltd, 130 Milton Park, Abingdon, Oxon OX14 4SB. *Telephone:* +44 (0) 1235 827720. *Fax:* +44 (0) 1235 400454. Lines are open 09.00–17.00, Monday to Saturday, with a 24-hour message answering service. Details about our titles and how to order are available at www.teachyourself.com

Long renowned as the authoritative source for self-guided learning – with more than 50 million copies sold worldwide – the **Teach Yourself** series includes over 500 titles in the fields of languages, crafts, hobbies, business, computing and education.

British Library Cataloguing in Publication Data: a catalogue record for this title is available from the British Library.

First published in UK 2008 by Hodder Education, part of Hachette UK, 338 Euston Road, London, NW1 3BH.

This edition published 2010.

Previously published as *Teach Yourself Basic DIY*.

The **Teach Yourself** name is a registered trade mark of Hodder Headline.

Hachette UK's policy is to use papers that are natural, renewable and recyclable products and made from wood grown in sustainable forests. The logging and manufacturing processes are expected to conform to the environmental regulations of the country of origin.

Impression number	10 9 8 7 6 5 4 3 2 1
Year	2014 2013 2012 2011 2010

Acknowledgements

Huge thanks to Doris, for Dorising throughout; to James and Lou for holding the fort; to Kate and Ben for refuge and, together with Steve, Polly and Philippa, thanks for providing the incentive. Thanks to Ian for knowing stuff and Dad for being able to spell. Thanks a million to the following organizations:

DIY Doctor Ltd (www.diydoctor.org.uk) for supplying time, content and images

Property Repair Systems Ltd (www.timber.org.uk) for content

Screwfix (www.screwfix.com) for images of tools

Wickes DIY (www.wickes.co.uk) for content and images

B&Q (www.diy.com) for content and images

UK Fire Services Resources (www.fireservice.co.uk) for advice on detectors

Towers & Sanders Ltd (www.scaffold-tower.co.uk) for images

Central Heating Repair (www.centralheatingrepair.co.uk) for content and images

The Lead Sheet Association (www.leadsheetassociation.org.uk)

Foreword

DIY can be hugely rewarding and many exciting projects can be undertaken which, if done by a professional, would stretch your budget a little too far.

The best results, however, will always be obtained with a careful, organized approach to the jobs you plan to do. A little research, using books and the Internet, on the best tools to use for your project will pay dividends. Even something as simple as using a screwdriver that is too small for the screw can result in a slip and a scratch across an expensive surface.

Building materials can be expensive. Some time spent drawing up a detailed plan of the item you wish to produce will enable you to work out exactly what you need. This will reduce wastage and can save you another 30 per cent of the cost!

Timber is the most common material used in DIY and also one of the most expensive. It comes in standard lengths so, if you are making a timber frame, for example, for a wall cupboard or rabbit hutch, you will need to cut several different lengths from the timber you have bought. Spending a little time working out which parts of your frame to cut from which lengths could drastically reduce the amount of wood you might otherwise waste. It's no good trying to cut a standard 5.1 m length of timber into lengths of 2.3 m, because you will waste 0.5 m of timber each time. It would be much better to order lengths of timber that are 4.6 m (another standard length).

Similarly, consider whether you have the right size and type of drill bit for the holes you may need to drill. An entirely different type of drill bit is used for masonry from that used for timber and steel, and they cannot be interchanged.

Using the right tools and materials, together with a well-researched plan, can make DIY both great fun and very profitable. Getting it wrong by rushing in can cost a fortune and put you off for ever!

Contents

Image credits

Front cover: © Digifoto Diamond/Alamy

Meet the author

Welcome to *Master Basic DIY*!

Trying desperately to finish a job for a valued customer late one evening, I popped into a well-known DIY store for a length of timber. When I asked a young assistant where they kept the 4 × 2 he looked at me in bewilderment. I explained I was looking for timber which was 4 inches wide and 2 inches thick or 100 mm × 50 mm. He told me where the timber was kept but said he had no idea if they had any that size.

It occurred to me that, if the store did not train its staff in the purpose or details of the products it stocked (and I knew exactly what I wanted, and what I wanted it for), then members of the general public must be wandering about in the store for hours and still not be sure, even after purchase, if they had the right tools and materials for the job they had planned. It certainly explained the many bemused faces scanning the backs of the cards the tools were stuck to.

I wrote to the DIY store and offered to put a building professional in each one of their stores for one day per week. The builder could answer any questions the public had, and would be able to point them in the right direction for the tools they needed and the materials required.

The store thought it was a good idea and the idea was trialled for a while but the financial value the store placed on this service did not match my expectations or needs.

I had, however, realized that if I could do it for one store, I could do it for everyone, using a website on the Internet.

In November 2000 DIY Doctor, the website, was born. In the year of writing, DIY Doctor, the company, celebrates its tenth year of offering completely free DIY help and advice to all 'handypersons' in the UK.

Only got a minute?

DIY can be a hugely rewarding experience which can transform a home while saving you a fortune on tradesmen's bills.

It can, however, be fraught with danger. DIY, however simple it is made to look on the television, is still building work done by non-professionals. As such care must be taken to stick to the rules which are there to protect both you and the integrity of your home.

DIY projects can, and should be fun. If a project is researched properly and advice is sought in the right places (such as this book) the outcome of your efforts can make a huge difference to how you use your home as well as giving you a great insight into why everything in the building is constructed the way it is.

Simple projects, such as fitting a shelf, can be undertaken easily and this will lead to the confidence to take on bigger projects. Many DIYers go on to be self builders, building their own homes.

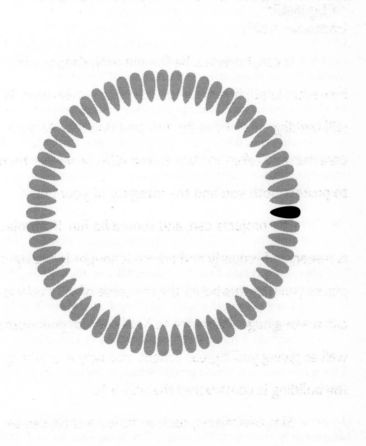

5 Only got five minutes?

As with any work or hobby which has a skills element, practice is the key to getting the best possible outcome.

DIY in a general form requires a number of skills and each one can (and should) be tried out before you embark on projects which could alter the shape, colour or structure of your home.

Most homeowners will want to decorate walls or ceilings at some time. These surfaces will probably have taken some knocks from normal living and, when you come to paint, you will notice little dents and scratches. Painting over dents and scratches gives a bad finish. As the light reflects on the walls they will show and, as you paint, you will wish you had filled them.

▶ Filling holes, dents and scratches is a job which, although one of the most basic DIY tasks, still requires practice. Fillers generally advertise that they do not shrink back, but they almost always do. Practising using filler on the wall long before decoration is a good idea. See how much filler you need. See how flat you can get it with the filling knife and see how long it is before it can be sanded back to blend in perfectly with the wall surface. With practice, filling should be invisible.

This is one idea of a simple project which is not quite as easy as it seems.

To build up to larger DIY projects, there are many simple jobs which can be tried first. The simple jobs listed here will give you the basic skills required for the larger ones and will allow you to move on to bigger jobs with confidence.

▶ Putting up a shelf will teach you how to secure things to different surfaces. It is an entirely different job fixing something to a masonry wall from fixing it to a plasterboard wall.

▶ Building a barbecue in the garden will give you access to the skills required to build walls.
▶ Constructing a simple wooden toy box will teach you the basic carpentry techniques you need to make your own cupboards.
▶ Using a plastering float to flatten out the top of a children's sandpit will show you how difficult it is to get a concrete or plastered surface smooth.

This book contains many projects that will give you the confidence and skills required to tackle jobs you would previously have paid to have done.

10 Only got ten minutes?

DIYers make mistakes. It is the nature of DIY, and one can learn valuable lessons from these mistakes. However, aside from the common DIY errors, one look at the accident figures shown in this book will show you that some of the mistakes made by DIYers are very dangerous indeed. Most of these mistakes are unnecessary.

▶ DIYers should never attempt electrical repairs and installations unless: a) they are allowed to by law (a list of allowable jobs can be seen in this book) and b) they are absolutely sure they know what they are doing. Electricity is very dangerous indeed.

▶ Working at height (even quite low heights!) is also dangerous. Accidents involving ladders and steps are at the top of the accident statistics. Ladders should be placed on a firm surface and tied at the top to stop them slipping sideways. They should be placed at the correct angle and the correct height. It should always be possible to hold the ladder when working. Even small stepladders must be placed on a flat surface. The merest hint of a wobble can cause the DIYer to overbalance and fall off.

Many DIY mistakes, and many very poor jobs, are produced as a result of using incorrect tools for the job in hand. Without the correct tool any job will be many times more difficult and the results disappointing. If you do not have the right tools, hire them. This money is very well spent if you want to produce work you can be proud of.

The most common DIY mistakes are all as a result of poor preparation and planning. This often involves some research to find out the most effective, easiest or even cheapest way to do the job.

A common example of this is the number of people who paint over wallpaper which is already showing signs of falling off the wall.

Only if the wallpaper is very securely stuck down (and not always even then) should it be painted. The moisture from the paint can dissolve the wallpaper adhesive and the wallpaper can come unstuck in places, causing unsightly bubbles to appear all over the wall. It is far better to strip the wallpaper and paint the wall wherever possible.

If, after stripping, the walls are seen to be uneven and pitted, it is usually a good idea to replaster them with a coat of skim plaster. This plastering leads to another very common DIY mistake.

As a result of the many DIY programmes on the television which show rooms being plastered in minutes, it is a common misconception that plastering is easy. It is not. Many DIYers have found out, sometimes to their extreme cost, that plastering is something which should only be undertaken after much practice.

The cost of a piece of plasterboard and a bag of Multifinish plaster is absolutely nothing compared to the cost of calling in a plasterer to put right a bodged DIY attempt.

▶ The practice board can be used over and over again, with one coat of plaster being applied over the last one, until you are sure you have enough technique and speed to attempt the walls in a room. Research the project by using books and websites such as www.diydoctor.org.uk to find out the best plaster to use for any given surface or how to stop the surface being too porous and allowing the new plaster to go hard too quickly.

Another very common mistake is to build walls in the garden without adequate foundations. The ground moves!

Ground movement accounts for settlement cracks in buildings which have been constructed using the strongest foundations possible, so a garden wall, with inadequate foundations, stands little to no chance of survival.

This is also an extremely dangerous mistake as heavy DIY walls have fallen on people many times due to a lack of research into the correct way to build foundations.

Another very dangerous, yet often undertaken project is removing walls from the house to make rooms larger. Many of the walls in your house are holding up the floor above, but the number of people who just start hammering away at a wall, without a thought about the integrity of the building, is quite frightening. It is not just the outside walls which keep your building upright.

▶ At DIY Doctor we advocate drawing a plan of every room in your house, showing walls, pipes, cables, sockets, radiators etc. and undertaking the research which will tell you what every part of your house does and how (and why) it does it.
▶ Spending a little time reading about your chosen project, using websites and joining Internet DIY forums will give you the answers that you will need. It will also give you access to the hundreds of tips and tricks available to tradesmen enabling them to produce a fine job without compromising the construction of the property.

Introduction

Why do we DIY?

The obvious answer to this question is to save money, but it goes far deeper than that for some people. The DIY Doctor website (www.diydoctor.org.uk) surveyed some 10,000 DIY enthusiasts: 38 per cent wanted to save money, 22 per cent just wanted to see if they could do it, 9 per cent could not get a builder when they wanted one so went it alone, 6 per cent said that they started doing it to protect themselves from the shoddy workmanship of 'cowboy builders', and 25 per cent had reasons which could be described as a mixture of all the above.

Most of the answers were expected, but a surprising one was using DIY as protection against shoddy workmanship. Why does a completely inexperienced person believe they can take a giant leap into a construction minefield and produce results better than a 'professional'? As many of the 1 million questions DIY Doctor has answered show, the reality is that, in the main, they cannot. DIY can be difficult, with the degree of difficulty depending on the task to be tackled. However, with the right tools and the right guidance and information it is within the reach of many would-be DIYers.

Why are builders so expensive?

▶ Builders need a great many tools to complete all the tasks asked of them. Putting up a shelf requires a completely different set of tools from laying a patio. Fitting a bathroom necessitates different tools from fitting a kitchen. Builders' tools need to be robust and can be very expensive. They also have to be replaced periodically. A general builder's tool kit can cost over £3,000.

(Contd)

> ▶ *Due to the climate in the UK, builders can only work outside for approximately nine months out of the year. Builders have to take this into account, and the remaining three months have to be covered by the work they do in that time. Although it is possible to book 'inside work' for the (historically) most inclement months, it very rarely works out like that. The weather can be unseasonably hot in December and pouring with rain in June.*
>
> ▶ *Builders also spend a lot of time quoting for work and working out prices from very complicated drawings. This, together with ordering and collecting materials, is all unseen and unpaid work that has to be built into the hourly rate.*
>
> ▶ *Finally, most building work is very skilful and carries a lot of responsibility. People do not think twice about paying huge sums to solicitors and accountants, and good builders may have trained for twice as long as them.*

Apart from the obvious dexterous skills involved in many of the trades, there are the less obvious problems of how to bend bricks round corners, or stop a retaining wall falling on your patio table because the foundations are not strong enough. To do a job safely and properly, especially in the building trade, it is important to know why you do it in a certain way: why bricks are laid at half bond, why plaster should be the same thickness for the whole area of the covering, and many more technical things that tradesmen – at least the good ones – study for years. It is for this reason that the first few chapters in this book focus on how your house works and endeavour to give you a greater understanding of why a house is constructed in the way it is.

A good example of this is to be found in the Chapter 4, about foundations. It is essential for even the most amateur DIYer to know about the principle of a solid foundation: a strong base of a uniform thickness and consistency. This leads not only to rigidity, but also to flexibility. Houses move after they have been built, either because their component parts settle in, or the ground on which they are built moves, or both. If the foundations were not flexible enough to accommodate this movement, the settlement cracks we experience would soon be settlement passages! If the foundations were not rigid enough to support the building in an inert state, then the building would collapse. To see this working, take an ordinary pencil and hold both ends. Pull down gently on both ends (putting them in compression) and you will see a slight bow or flex in the top of the pencil (in tension). This bow is even and stable and, up to a point, bending will not ruin the integrity of the pencil. Now take a hobby knife and cut a small nick out of the underside of the pencil. This nick only needs to be a couple of millimetres deep. Now repeat the experiment and you will see that, because the thickness of the pencil is no longer uniform, it will break at this thinner, weak point. This will also occur if the nick is placed at the top of the bow in the pencil.

This principle applies to every area of the building trade and hence is an important one for the DIY enthusiast to be familiar with. If a foundation strip or floor slab thickness is inconsistent, if plaster on a wall is uneven, or the base under a patio, garden shed or barbecue is uneven, it will dry out at different speeds or lose integrity and strength. This can easily cause damage to a job that looked perfectly all right to start with.

Another example might be found when fitting a new bathroom. Say you have decided to move the position of the hand basin but you need to cut just a little out of one of the floor joists to get the waste pipe back to its original position. If you do this incorrectly, you may weaken the joist and, consequently, the floor. Think about the pencil example. No wonder it creaks a bit now!

Using these examples you can easily see how the same construction principles apply from the lowest level of your property to the highest, so don't just follow 'How to...' instructions – read this book to find out why.

Using this book

DIY is essentially building work (including decorating, plumbing and so on) done by non-professionals. The many DIY television programmes tend to make it all look much easier than it actually is when, in truth, some areas require specialist knowledge and skills. For example, plastering a wall is not simple and, since it takes a tradesman two years of training and practice to become skilled at the task, it is reasonable to suggest that you too will need to practice before tackling the lounge ceiling. This does not mean, however, that a DIY enthusiast cannot learn a great number of the techniques required to complete many DIY tasks successfully.

This book is divided into two parts:

▶ *Part 1 aims to provide a sound base of background knowledge that will stand you in good stead for embarking on your DIY journey. It provides lots of useful information and advice on what you should know about your home before you take on any significant DIY projects. The first few chapters provide guidance on the tools you are likely to need, discuss the jobs most commonly tackled by DIYers, and suggest a logical and practical sequence of work, which will particularly apply to any larger jobs, such as building an extension. The following chapters then go on to outline what is involved in the construction of the 'shell' of a building, from the foundations to the roof, including specific chapters on electrics, plumbing and plastering.*

▶ *In Part 2 the focus moves from the general to the specific, providing step-by-step guidance on how to complete particular DIY projects. The scope of this book cannot cover every type of building work that may need to be carried out on your home at any given point, but it does include many of the projects most commonly taken on by DIYers and those for which DIY Doctor has received the most queries over the years.*

This book is written not only to help you tackle jobs which you may not otherwise have undertaken, but also to try and keep you, and your property, safe while you are doing the work. In time, anyone can be taught to lay bricks, plaster a wall or rewire a property, but in that teaching not every problem can be foreseen and explained. It is the ability to deal with unforeseen problems (which will most certainly arise) safely, and to lasting and aesthetically pleasing conclusions, that differentiates a good tradesperson or DIYer from a bad one.

Tip: builders' merchants

If you are an avid DIYer, it may pay to wander down to your local builders' merchant, where you can chat with the manager about getting some reduced rates for materials. It is unlikely you will be able to open an account, because merchants are primarily for trade customers, but if you use the same merchants a lot, you can receive preferential rates. The personnel in builders' merchants tend to know a little more about the construction industry than DIY store staff. Another huge bonus is that builders' merchants are always full of builders. Builders generally are happy to pass on a little wisdom, and getting to know three or four builders, plumbers and electricians is always useful when there are projects at home that it is just not safe for you to complete on your own. The staff at builders' merchants may even be able to help by recommending tradesmen they know to be reliable.

Part one

The basics

1

Tools

In this chapter you will learn:
- *what tools it is useful to own*
- *about hiring larger tools*
- *what to look for when choosing power tools.*

Introduction

Good tools are essential to DIY success. Even what is deemed to be a simple operation, like sawing a piece of timber square and straight, is impossible with a blunt, bowed saw and with no means of accurately measuring a right angle. Many failed DIY projects are the result of trying to do a job with inappropriate or cheap tools. The main reason most people carry out DIY jobs is to save money, but this will prove to be a false economy if you try to assemble expensive products with the incorrect tools. This chapter offers some advice on the tools you are likely to need in order to carry out a range of DIY tasks.

Insight
For most basic jobs we use Jack (of all trades) saws, which are multipurpose saws for all timber sawing.

There is a tool for just about every job in the building world. If you lever the lid from a paint tin using a wood chisel, then you must expect that the chisel may be damaged and may not be in good working order the next time you need to use it. Good tools are expensive, but looked after properly they will serve you well.

Insight

Even fairly cheap chisels can be sharpened regularly to give a good clean cut.

Most tradesmen's tools have a less expensive DIY version and generally these are perfectly adequate. Do ask yourself, however, why a set of chisels from the market costs only £3.99 when a set of chisels from a dedicated tool supplier, such as Screwfix.com, costs £23.99. Tools are not an area where you should economize too much – good tools are expensive but, handled correctly, produce good work time and time again. Cheap tools, no matter whose hands they are in, produce a shoddy finish.

Tool requirements

If you want to DIY and be proud of what you produce, then buy the right tools for the job and make sure they are the best tools you can afford. You can 'kit out' a basic tool box for around £100, and the list below contains the essentials that you will use on just about every DIY job.

Essential tools:

- *5 m tape measure*
- *20 oz claw hammer*
- *Stanley knife*
- *600 mm spirit level*
- *medium-size adjustable spanner*
- *junior hacksaw*
- *set of crosshead and flathead screwdrivers*
- *insulated electrical testing screwdriver*

- *insulated pliers*
- *radiator bleed key*
- *set of masonry drill bits, from 3 mm to 7 mm*
- *set of HSS drill bits (3 mm to 7 mm) for drilling through wood, plastic and plasterboard*
- *wood chisels – 13 mm, 19 mm and 25 mm*
- *general-use 20-inch professional quality Jack saw (a timber saw which can be used to cut across the grain, down the grain and at any angle to the grain)*
- *electric drill, minimum 600 watt with hammer action.*

Hiring larger tools

Insight

Hiring larger tools gives you access to top-quality equipment without a huge outlay.

You may occasionally need to use larger, more expensive tools. For example, cutting a hole through a wall for a new dishwasher waste pipe will be slow and laborious with a hammer and chisel, but will take only five minutes with the correct drill and a 50 mm diamond-tipped drill bit. The job is neater, quicker and much less frustrating! You can hire this sort of equipment from tool-hire shops, which are found in just about every town and where the staff are always willing to help you choose exactly the right tool for the job. In real terms it is the difference between a small project taking two hours or a whole weekend.

Choosing power tools

The three most commonly used power tools, in addition to the electric drill mentioned above, are the jig saw, the power sander and the battery drill/driver.

JIG SAW

The more powerful a jig saw is in terms of watts, the faster it will cut and the deeper the material it will get through. An average wattage for the DIY enthusiast is 650 watts. Look for a variable-speed jig saw as some materials (Perspex, for example) get very hot when cut at high speed. A good selection of blades is essential and all DIY stores sell packs containing multipurpose blades for different materials. Jig saw blades are classified (as are hand saws) using the number of teeth they have per inch of length (TPI). The greater the number of teeth, the finer the cut.

POWER SANDER

Power sanders are also measured in watts. The higher the number of watts, the greater the power. An average 250-watt sander is fine for most jobs, and variable speed is an advantage but not a necessity. A ½-sheet orbital sander is perfectly adequate for most DIY jobs. These use half a sheet of sandpaper clipped to the backing pad of the sander, and they sand in small orbits rather than rotations. Different grades of sandpaper can be interchanged to give a coarse, medium or fine finish to the work. Other types of sander include:

▶ *rotary sanders, which can do a job more quickly but with which it can be harder, without experience, to get an even finish*
▶ *detail sanders, which are smaller, with a pointed end for getting into awkward corners*
▶ *belt sanders, which work by running a loop of sandpaper over rollers driven at high speed.*

Insight
We always keep a vacuum cleaner running for 30 minutes in the room after sanding.

Look for a sander with a dust collection bag or, even better, the ability to connect the 'exhaust' to a vacuum cleaner.

Usually a piece of work is sanded in order to paint it; if there is sawdust in the air for hours after sanding, the paint finish will be poor.

See Project 42 on stripping paint.

Is there still lead paint around and is it dangerous?

Paint in houses built in the 1960s or earlier is likely to contain lead and, in all honesty, extensions and alterations built as late as 1970 may also contain lead paint as unscrupulous builders and decorators used up their stock. Lead paint can be removed safely simply by taking a few precautions. Do not burn off with a blowlamp or heat gun as fumes are produced. Do not sand down, especially with an electrical sander, as this produces dust. Use a (preferably) solvent-free paint stripper and scrape the paint into a plastic bag for safe disposal.

BATTERY DRILL/DRIVER

If you do a lot of DIY, a cordless drill/driver is one of the most useful tools you can buy. The power in a cordless drill comes from the battery. Generally speaking, the larger the battery the more powerful the drill. A 12V drill is average for DIY work, although 14V will allow you to drill larger holes through more dense materials. If possible, pay a little extra for one with two batteries – it's a real nuisance if your battery runs out half way through a job and you have to wait three hours for it to recharge.

Most cordless drills have keyless chucks, which means you can change drill bits quickly and easily. Look for a 14V drill/driver with two speeds and a keyless 10 mm chuck. This is the largest diameter drill bit the drill can accommodate. A drill with a variable clutch is an advantage as, should the drill bit get stuck or 'bind' in a material, the clutch will disengage and stop the drill motor from turning the drill bit. This saves the drill kicking in your hand and causing sprained wrists and broken thumbs!

Most cordless drills can also be used as electric screwdrivers but are best used only to screw or unscrew crosshead screws. The screwdriver head or 'bit' will not easily slip out of a crosshead screw, whereas a slotted driver bit can slip very easily at speed and cause all sorts of expensive damage to the work surface.

Tip: skip hire
Many DIY jobs produce a lot of waste, and travelling backwards and forwards to the council waste disposal site can take up valuable time (not to mention energy!). Hiring a skip is one option.

▶ Skip hire prices have increased in recent years because of the new emphasis and legislation on recycling.
▶ Skip hire charges are usually for three weeks' hire but always check with the hiring company.
▶ Domestic skips range in size from a mini skip (2 cubic yards and about 2 ft 6 in high, 4 ft long and 3 ft wide) to a builder's skip at 8 cubic yards. This skip is about 4 ft high, 12 ft long and 5 ft 6 in wide.
▶ Skip companies will not accept items which cannot be recycled or sent to landfill. These include car batteries, fridges/freezers, asbestos, tyres, paint, computer monitors and food.
▶ Skips placed on public highways need permits. These are almost always organized by your skip hire company.

10 THINGS TO REMEMBER

1   *Talk to builders at builders' merchants about the tools you need.*

2   *Talk to the tool hire shop about the best tools.*

3   *Buy the best tools you can afford.*

4   *Look after your tools. Sharpen chisels etc.*

5   *Plan and research each project thoroughly.*

6   *Draw a plan whenever possible.*

7   *Remember the principle of uniform thickness.*

8   *Find a way to practise each new skill you try.*

9   *Use a vacuum cleaner when sanding.*

10 *Talk to builders' merchants about buying materials at discounted rates.*

2

Top ten DIY jobs for homeowners

In this chapter you will learn:
- *how to recognize some common problems*
- *how to deal with these problems.*

Introduction

The main concern for most homeowners is electrical safety, which is tackled separately in a chapter of its own (see Chapter 7). The top nine concerns after this are:

- ▶ *rising damp*
- ▶ *condensation damage*
- ▶ *woodworm*
- ▶ *dry rot*
- ▶ *burst pipes*
- ▶ *blowing light bulbs*
- ▶ *drilling through pipes and cables*
- ▶ *radiator problems and maintenance*
- ▶ *fire, carbon monoxide poisoning and gas leaks.*

In this chapter we will look at each of the above in turn.

Rising damp

WHAT IS RISING DAMP?

The term rising damp is used to describe water that seems to be rising up through the ground, being soaked into brickwork and blockwork foundations. From there, it is sucked up by the masonry to levels that allow it to evaporate inside the property. This evaporation leaves salt deposits on the surface of the walls (see the section on efflorescence in Chapter 5) and/or mould on the plaster. Rising damp is often wrongly diagnosed when no real investigation has been carried out. The reality is that genuine rising damp is a rare occurrence. If there is rising damp, in all but the most extreme cases it is extremely rare that it will reach more than 1.2 m above floor level. It is at this point that gravity takes over from the capillary action which makes the water rise (capillary action or capillarity is the rise or fall of a liquid in a tube or other confined space, such as the very fine air pockets and cracks in masonry and mortar). The narrower the passage, the higher the liquid rises. Some fissures in masonry and mortar are indeed very small, but most are too large for capillary action to take place and it is overcome by the force of gravity pulling the liquid down again.

Insight

If rising damp has been diagnosed always get a second, third and even fourth opinion from recognized companies.

DEALING WITH RISING DAMP

In Chapter 4, on foundations, you will read about damp proof courses and damp proof membranes. These are installed to stop moisture rising to a level where it could potentially get inside your house. This being the case, and despite many scientists' attempts to prove that rising damp is a myth, the fact remains that water does, quite often, manifest itself on walls and skirting boards.

Of course rising damp exists, but it is not as bad as is widely thought. The remedies for rising damp are, for the most part, expensive, so anyone suspecting that they have rising damp should make absolutely sure that this is the problem, rather than any number of other possibilities, before resorting to remedial work of this nature. It is no good, either, to apply damp proof paint over a damp spot on the wall. Covering it up is only dealing with the effects of the damp. You need to deal with the cause first, then the effect.

Many people think they have rising damp when they find damp patches on the inside of external walls. This is generally not the problem, however – there are many possible causes of damp within a building, and all of the areas listed below should be checked before embarking on the major project of injecting a damp proof course or tanking the walls. (Tanking is a construction technique of covering the affected walls of a building in a waterproof and water repellent rendering material.)

- ▶ *Check for a damp proof course. In most houses you can see a thin black line around the perimeter of the property, in between two bricks at about 150 mm from the ground (see Figure 4.6). If you do not have one at all, think seriously about getting one installed.*
- ▶ *If the damp is at floor level, check for evidence of old doorways being bricked up without a damp proof course having been inserted. Check every bit of masonry for defective mortar joints or, if the walls are rendered, for cracks. With older stonework, look for cracked and broken stones.*
- ▶ *Is your patio too high or running towards the property? No part of your garden, even paths, patios and decking, should be higher than 150 mm below the level of the damp proof course. Constant rain splashing up the wall from paths, patios and decks that are too high can cause damp spots.*
- ▶ *Look for white, salty deposits on the brickwork. This is called efflorescence, and is a sure sign that there is an excess of moisture within the structure. When the moisture evaporates from the wall, it leaves behind the salts it has extracted from the masonry and/or mortar. How is it getting in?*
- ▶ *Check above and around windows/doors for a bad seal; water can get in and trickle through joints to find a weak spot.*

- Check all ground levels, paths, etc. close to the house. Are they at least 150 mm (6 in) below the damp proof course? If they are not, dig them back. If this is impossible, look at the section on land drainage in Chapter 4.
- Check roof tiles for damage. Water can get in and run down the roofing felt, collect in the bottom of the felt where it meets the external walls, and rot through the felt. This will allow water onto the top of the walls, which can then trickle down through masonry joints and come in through a weak spot.
- Check all gutters for leakage, blockages and overflow. A constantly damp wall will suck moisture in. Check the gullies where your washing machine, dishwasher, downstairs sinks and basins discharge. Also check your overflow pipes.
- Check any abutments to the wall and the joint it creates. If a garden wall butts up against a house wall, water can become trapped in the joint and soak through to the house masonry.
- Check for holes drilled in walls for hanging baskets, etc.
- Have your drains checked for broken or blocked pipes and manholes.

See Project 36 on unblocking toilets and drains.

- Check all lead or other flashings for correct sealing at the point where they are cut (chased) into the wall. Check also for adequate coverage to the surface and joint they are protecting.
- Check outside taps for leaks.
- Outside flues can sometimes cause condensation on the external wall they rise on; check the masonry in this area. (Make sure the boiler is turned off for this check.)
- Once you are absolutely sure the moisture is not getting in from the outside, check all internal pipe and waste connections to washing machines, sinks, basins, dishwashers and so on.
- Check all toilet waste pipes and cistern connections and look for condensation on the cold feed pipes to all taps and valves.
- Once you are sure these internal pipes and connections are not the cause either, condensation is the most likely cause of the problem (see the next section for more information about this).

Do not attempt to decorate by sealing these damp spots in the wall. Moisture must be allowed to evaporate and the cause of the damp must be found. Sealing moisture in will lead to larger, more expensive problems.

Damp will sometimes remove the adhesion between plaster and wall, leaving the area 'hollow'. This is easily detected by simply tapping on the wall. A wall should make the same or a very similar sound throughout, but a hollow wall will sound totally different. It is better to remove the plaster from this section and replaster it once the source of the damp is dealt with.

Damp plasterboard will swell and lose its insulation and decorative qualities. This is also better replaced. Mould can be treated by many fungicidal solutions on the market today, and fungicidal protective paints are available for areas of high humidity. Kitchen and bathroom paints are generally oil-based eggshell, which will not allow the absorption of water.

Tip: decorating over a water stain

When decorating over an area that has been water stained, once the cause of the staining has been addressed, apply a coat of oil-based paint or stain block first. If you do not, the stain will bleed through no matter how many coats of emulsion you apply. The cheapest method of blocking water stains is to mix up some oil-based undercoat with some oil-based topcoat.

Insight

We use stain block in spray form. It is a great deal quicker to apply and dries more quickly also.

Remember, buildings must breathe. There is natural water content in all building materials. If this is sealed in by a waterproof coat on the outside, and similar applications on the inside, it can turn to mould easily.

See Project 39 on blocking stains.

Condensation

CAUSES OF CONDENSATION

Condensation is an extremely underestimated cause of damage to our homes. It is also one of the very last causes of damp to be diagnosed. It is responsible for rot in rafters, joists and window frames. It can cause mould and fungal growth on walls and ceilings. If not dealt with, it can damage our health.

All air contains water vapour. The amount it contains depends on the temperature of the air. This ratio is called the relative humidity. Hot air is able to carry much more moisture than cold air. As the temperature of air rises, in broad terms, it expands and attracts a greater volume of vapour. At a given temperature, the air can carry no more moisture until it is warmed up – this is called the dew point, at which the air is saturated. If the temperature drops while the air is saturated, the vapour is released.

▶ *If this happens near the ground, to a small layer of air, dew or frost will be formed; if a larger amount of air is involved, mist or fog will arise.*
▶ *If this happens to air that is rising in the atmosphere and expanding, clouds will form.*
▶ *If it happens in the home, it's called condensation!*

As soon as warm air, containing vapour, hits a cooler surface, it will condense. This is most obvious on windows, cold water pipes in warm rooms and wall tiles, but it is happening on the walls and ceilings a lot of the time. It might be thought that if a house is insulated and warmed thoroughly then this should not happen, but it will. The air temperature will rise until it finds a cooler surface, unless we let out the warm air and let in some cooler air.

Ventilation is the answer to condensation. There are many ways to deal with the symptoms or effects of condensation, such as dehumidifiers, but only one way to deal properly with the cause – ensuring that the home is adequately ventilated.

Condensed moisture soaks into the walls and invites fungicidal spores, which develop into mould. This can cause breathing problems if not checked. Sometimes irreparable damage to walls and furniture can occur.

DEALING WITH CONDENSATION

▶ *Open all windows at least once a day, even for five minutes. Change all of the air in the house.*
▶ *Wipe down walls and other surfaces regularly.*
▶ *Place proprietary absorbent strips or condensation tubs (available from most DIY shops) on windowsills and other problem areas.*
▶ *Place silica (a substance that absorbs moisture, available from chemists and some double-glazing stores) in strategic places around the home.*
▶ *Do not hang washing on radiators, or at least confine this to one room with the door closed. Afterwards, ventilate the room well.*
▶ *Keep the kitchen door closed when cooking, and open the windows.*
▶ *If security permits, leave top windows open, especially at night when the outside temperature drops and the indoor temperature rises as the heating kicks in.*
▶ *Keep furniture a little further away from the walls so the air has a free flow around the room.*
▶ *Do not fill cupboards to bursting point; again, allow the air to flow.*
▶ *Make sure the insulation in the loft is not blocking the ventilation provided by the gap between the facia boards and the house wall or, as in a lot of cases these days, purpose made vents. (See Chapter 6 for more about this.)*
▶ *Install cavity wall insulation (if permissible through building regulations).*
▶ *Have the heating thermostatically controlled wherever possible.*
▶ *Ventilate tumble driers externally, or invest in a condensing tumble dryer.*
▶ *Install extractor fans in the kitchen and bathroom. They are available with humidistat control.*

► *Install trickle vents in windows. This is not a difficult operation. The vents come in two halves for inside and outside the window. Several holes are drilled through the top of the window head to allow the passage of air into and out of the room. Flaps are fitted so the vents can be closed, and insect grills keep all the creepy crawlies on the outside! Trickle vents can be bought from any double-glazing merchants.*

Insight

A fan heater in a room, even on the cool setting, can keep air moving in a room and help stop condensation.

Why do I get mould behind/inside my wardrobes?

This is usually as a result of condensation. Condensation is prevented in most rooms because of a constant movement of the air caused by an open door or some other form of ventilation. However, if the air is not moving, e.g. behind a wardrobe, moist warm air will deposit its moisture on the cooler wall. Keep rooms well ventilated to avoid condensation.

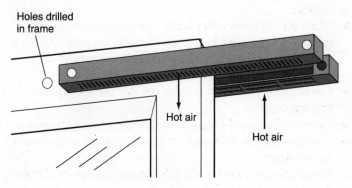

Holes drilled in frame

Hot air

Hot air

Figure 2.1 A trickle vent before installation at the top of a window.

> **Insight**
>
> Two-part anti-mould agents can now be bought, with the
> first part being applied directly to the wall and the second
> part mixed with the paint you choose.

A premium-quality, low-odour, anti-mould coating can be used to
protect against unsightly and unhygienic black mould, even when
there is persistent condensation. This is achieved by combining
modern paint technology with highly advanced, proven biocides.
The anti-mould biocide is combined throughout the paint film,
which is formulated to impart toughness, elasticity, water
resistance and durability to the finish. Anti-mould emulsions can
be bought from most good decorators' merchants and the larger
DIY stores.

ANTI-CONDENSATION COATING

A high-quality coating is recommended for use on areas not subject
to abrasion or washing. Typically this means ceilings, the underside
of roofing sheets, ducting, steel building frames, pipework and
inside cupboards. Anti-condensation coating inhibits condensation
by absorbing moisture and improving insulation. It also contains
a biocide for the sole purpose of protecting the paint from mould
growth. This paint can be bought from decorators' merchants and
most stores.

Woodworm

Very little is known about woodworm by the general public, and it is a
problem that is frequently encountered. A word of advice, then – if you
live in an older house and haven't done so already, go and check
your rafters now. There are three types of woodworm in the UK:
the common furniture beetle, the house longhorn beetle and the
deathwatch beetle.

FURNITURE BEETLE

Symptoms and habitats
The furniture beetle is the most common of all woodworms. Damage by the furniture beetle is identifiable by a peppering of tiny holes in the surface of the wood. These are in fact emergence holes through which the adult beetle has left the timber after tunnelling through it as a grub. This beetle attacks softwoods, leaving 1–2 mm exit holes in most softwood. It prefers damp rather than dry wood and the grubs will head for, and stay in, plywood for longer than any other timber.

Insight

If laying new boards, leave them in the room for up to two weeks to acclimatize them to the conditions in that room.

Damp floorboards, damp loft timbers and old furniture where the polished finish has worn off (the furniture beetle prefers unfinished wood like old floorboards and loft rafters) are good targets for the beetle. It lays its eggs on the timber and the grubs do the burrowing and tunnelling in the timber. With active woodworm there is a scattering of tiny dust piles on the timber. These are called 'frass'.

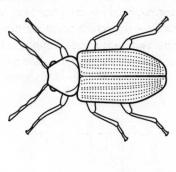

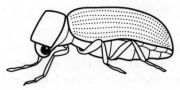

Figure 2.2 An adult furniture beetle.

Effects and implications

Structural weakening is rare with the furniture beetle except in timbers where the cross-section is small and there is a lot of damp. This occurs in older houses, for example, where the floor joists are near the ground and ventilation may have been blocked.

Recommended treatment

Treatment for this beetle can be bought from most DIY stores in the form of a spray or liquid preservative. Building societies will insist on a specialist company making repairs if structural timber has been affected.

HOUSE LONGHORN BEETLE

Symptoms and habitats

The house longhorn beetle is not common in the UK except in certain areas of north Surrey, where the coniferous areas and warmer summers suit its development. Strict building regulations have been introduced in these areas to stop the spread of this beetle, which is now quite rare in British buildings. It is principally found in roof timbers where it attacks the sapwood of exclusively softwood timbers.

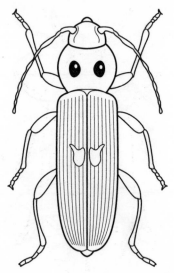

Figure 2.3 An adult house longhorn beetle.

Effects and implications

Attacks by house longhorn beetles often result in structural weakness of the roof timbers. The holes and tunnels of this beetle are significantly larger than those of the furniture beetle.

Recommended treatment

Treatment for this beetle can be bought from most DIY stores, as for the furniture beetle. Building societies will insist on a specialist company making repairs if structural timber has been affected.

Buildings in the area affected by the house longhorn beetle must have all new timbers treated, to comply with building regulations.

DEATHWATCH BEETLE

Symptoms and habitats

Deathwatch beetle attacks large hardwood timbers such as elm and oak. These timbers are usually found in the old churches, stately homes and other ancient buildings that are more common in southern and central England. Northern parts of Britain are not affected except where timbers have been imported.

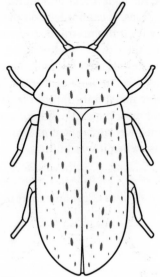

Figure 2.4 An adult deathwatch beetle.

The beetle, having started in these hardwoods, may move across to neighbouring softwoods in a kind of feeding frenzy! This beetle much prefers very damp conditions, particularly when there is some kind of fungal decay or 'wet rot' in the timbers. The beetle needs these conditions to develop rapidly.

Recommended treatment

Treatment, as with the other two, can be applied in the form of a paste, spray or paint-on preservative. It is recommended strongly that you call in a specialist if you think you have deathwatch beetle.

Dry rot

WHAT IS DRY ROT?

Named dry rot because of its apparent ability to grow in dry areas, this clever fungus has developed the ability to soak up moisture from timber, totally drying it out, and then develop strands which can travel across and through bricks and mortar to other timbers in unventilated conditions. It cannot feed on the masonry but carries the moisture with it in the strands to allow it to spread. Every property carries the risk of developing dry rot, but building regulations and the materials used in modern properties make it less likely to occur in these. In older properties, however, where kiln-dried timbers were not specified, roof tiles were generally clay and more porous, and most materials did not carry any British Standard specifications, wet timber and masonry could be found on all levels of a house when it was built.

Insight
Never ignore dry rot. Always get an expert to check if you are not sure.

DEALING WITH DRY ROT

DIY detection of dry rot is now considerably easier, and dry rot sensors can now be bought. These sensors are wooden dowels impregnated with a detector dye that are inserted into 8 mm holes in the 'at risk' area. The dye detects the presence of oxalic acid (present in all dry rot), turning the dowels yellow. DIY treatment of dry rot is possible, but most mortgage companies will insist on professional certification, together with insurance-backed guarantees. It therefore pays to contact a reputable damp proofing company to carry out repairs and treatment.

Burst pipes

WHY PIPES BURST

A burst pipe, especially when you are away from the property, is a homeowner's nightmare. An unprotected water pipe will often freeze during the winter months. Frozen water expands quite dramatically and, if contained in a pipe where no expansion room is available, the pipe will split. This in itself is not the problem, however – the problem occurs when the ice thaws!

DEALING WITH A BURST PIPE

Tip: lagging pipes

Pipes can be protected with the correct lagging and insulation in order to minimize the chance of them bursting. The minimum recommended thicknesses of pipe insulation are:

15 mm pipe:	25 mm insulation
22–28 mm pipe:	19 mm insulation
35 mm pipe and above:	9 mm insulation.

See Project 32 on fixing a burst pipe.

Blowing light bulbs

Many people experience light bulbs blowing at regular intervals and fear that they have a dangerous electrical short circuit. This is not the case.

Myth versus fact

Myth: Regular blowing of light bulbs means you have a major wiring fault.

Fact: Regular blowing of light bulbs does not imply a major wiring fault. Any wiring fault in your circuit will be picked up by fuses and miniature circuit breakers (MCBs) long before it reaches the bulb.

WHY LIGHT BULBS BLOW

There are a few reasons why bulbs can blow.

▶ *Cheap bulbs – the elements in cheap bulbs are very thin and any surge of power, however slight, simply breaks them. Always go for more expensive light bulbs; it's cheaper in the long run.*
▶ *A loose connection in the lamp holder can also cause bulbs to blow. This is because the circuit is not completed as tightly as it could be and the electricity may have cause to 'arc', or jump, across the contact, rather than simply flow through it. When this happens it produces more heat in the fitting than is expected or catered for by the bulb, and the bulb can blow. The same can happen if the spring-loaded connection in the bulb holder is slightly loose. This will cause electricity to arc across the contact, causing too much heat and so blowing the bulb. This can often be diagnosed by looking at the contact on the bottom of the bulb to see if it is pitted – arcing electricity effectively melts the metal it is arcing onto (this is how arc*

welding works), so if the bulb contact is being subjected to arcing, tiny little indentations occur, called pitting.

▶ It is sometimes possible, if the live connection in your light switch is a little loose, for this to happen here also. Heat will be generated and it is possible, though very unlikely, for the bulb to blow as a result of this. When a bulb blows, 99 per cent of the time the circuit breaker for the lighting circuit will trip also. This makes the problem seem worse than it actually is. The reason for a blowing lamp tripping a MCB (miniature circuit breaker) is that the lamp element becomes thinner during its life until it breaks at the thinnest point; this point will melt just before failure. The resistance of the overheating element will momentarily be very low and a current surge is caused which is picked up by MCBs but not usually by fuses.

DEALING WITH BLOWING LIGHT BULBS

So, there are three things to look into if your bulbs keep blowing:

▶ the quality of your bulbs
▶ the wire connections inside your bulb holder, and whether the spring-loaded connectors are working properly inside the bulb holder
▶ the tightness of the connections in your switch. It is a good idea, wherever possible, to use dimmer switches. Dimmers that switch on at the lowest brightness are a big help in extending the life of a bulb, but a dimmer switch will reduce very slightly the maximum amount of light available.

Drilling through pipes and cables

This is a common problem for the DIY enthusiast, but it can be avoided. Having decided where you want to drill, check above and below for electrical sockets or water outlets. If there are any in the area, there is always a chance of hitting a pipe or cable. Always ascertain the type of wall you are drilling into. Pushing hard with a large drill on a plasterboard wall can send you straight through the plasterboard and into a pipe or cable in the void.

> ## Insight
>
> Never assume pipes and cables travel only horizontally or vertically. They should of course, but many DIYers – and even builders – have been known to run service pipes and cables diagonally.

Pipe and cable detectors can be bought at all DIY stores for a few pounds and they are well worth the investment.

Radiator problems and maintenance

Radiator and heating problems figure highly in the list of things homeowners are concerned about. The thought of spending either a few winter days without heat or a vast amount of money repairing a system motivates many DIY enthusiasts to find out as much as possible about their heating system. The following instructions are for the most common open-vented heating system only. See Chapter 8 to check your system before attempting any of the following.

RADIATOR PROBLEMS

Top of radiator cold, bottom hot

This is usually a result of air getting into the radiator and rising to the top, preventing any more hot water filling the radiator. The problem can be resolved by 'bleeding off' the air from the top of the radiator by opening the bleed nipple (a small square peg at the top of the radiator, usually protected by a round cast in the radiator body) and allowing the air to escape. Hold a cloth close to the bleed nipple – when water starts to come out the air should have gone. If your radiators need constant bleeding then too much air is entering the system and the problem is a bigger one that requires investigation by a central heating engineer.

Top of radiator hot, bottom cold

Rust and sludge has probably built up in the bottom of the radiator and this will displace any water, leaving the bottom of the radiator cold. Follow the instructions for draining down the system and then flush out the radiators. Proprietary sludge removers can be used to clean systems through. These are available from all plumbers' merchants, but read the instructions before use.

Radiators hot downstairs, cold upstairs

This generally means that the feed and expansion tank in your loft has run dry, which can indicate a problem with the valve. This needs addressing quickly and a change of valve is usually in order. This is not a huge job and, as long as you have turned off the water, is well within the capabilities of a DIY enthusiast.

Radiators hot upstairs, cold downstairs

This may indicate a faulty central heating pump and should be checked by an engineer.

No radiators getting very warm

This indicates a build-up of rust and sludge. Follow the instructions for draining down the system.

Radiators warmer nearer the boiler

This shows that your system needs balancing. This can be done by turning the valves down on the radiators nearest the boilers to restrict the flow to them thus allowing those furthest away to receive a greater share of the hot water. See Chapter 8 to find out how the system works and to see this process in more detail.

DRAINING DOWN THE SYSTEM

Insight

There are many 'Drain-Easy' kits available now. These enable you to drain radiators and heating without the fear of spillage.

The thought of draining down a central heating system is quite daunting, but it is not a difficult process. Sometimes it is necessary to drain down a heating system to introduce an agent to clean it and flush it through, removing sludge, or simply to change a radiator. In all events it is necessary to turn off the boiler. Turn off the gas or electricity supply to the boiler or, in the case of a back boiler or solid fuel, make sure it is out.

In your loft you will have a tank called a feed and expansion tank. This is recognizable by a pipe coming in at the top, which is the expansion part of the equation. This allows the water to expand (in the form of steam) if it gets too hot. The steam can condense, via the pipe, into this tank.

The water is fed into this tank from the mains via a ball valve. This valve is the same as the one in your toilet cistern. When the water rises it lifts the ballcock. The ball is attached to an arm, which closes the valve when it is lifted. When the tank is full of water, no more can get in because the valve is closed. When some water is drawn off, the ball drops, the valve opens and water rushes in to replace it. To ensure that no water comes in while you are draining the system, place a piece of timber across the tank, lift up the valve arm and tie it to the timber. This will close the valve and prevent it from opening when the water is drained from the system.

Now connect a hosepipe to the drain nozzle, which will be on or near one of the downstairs radiators, and run it outside to a suitable point. Make sure, especially in winter, that the water does not run onto the road or pavement where it could freeze and cause accidents. Open up the drain valve and let the water drain from the system.

The water will run faster if you open any bleed valves on the radiators, starting with the radiators at the top of the building. As the water level drops you can open the bleed valves in the downstairs radiators also. When no more water comes out of the hose you must check that the system has finished draining before you remove radiators or start work. There is a chance that some air has got into the system and locked the water from escaping. Go into the loft and fill the tank with about six inches of water by loosening the arm you have tied up. This should, in a few seconds, start running out of the hose. If it does not, you have an air lock and should connect the other end of the hose to the cold tap and send a short blast of water back into the radiator you are draining from. Make absolutely sure the hose is well attached to the radiator drain nozzle and close any open bleed valves before you turn on the tap.

REFILLING THE SYSTEM

Close the drain valve on the radiator and all the bleed valves you have opened. Untie the piece of wood in the feed tank and let the water fill up the system via the tank. Wait until the tank stops filling and go downstairs to bleed the bottom-level radiators. Repeat with the upstairs radiators. This should ensure that your system is properly filled.

Double-check the work you have done to ensure you have retightened all nuts, etc., turn on your power supply and relight the boiler. As the water heats up, you may hear some knocking sounds as any air in the system expands. The radiators will probably need bleeding again once the system is fully heated.

Fire, carbon monoxide poisoning and gas leaks

It is essential that all homes are fitted with fire and smoke alarms and carbon monoxide detectors.

FIRE

Insight

Get into the habit of changing fire alarm batteries regularly. Do not leave it until the battery is dead.

Wherever possible, alarms should be fitted to the mains with battery back-up. Every year the Fire Service is called to over

600,000 fires, which result in over 800 deaths and over 17,000 injuries. An unbelievable 50,000 (140 per day!) of these happen in the home and kill nearly 500 people. Over 11,000 people are injured in the home. Many of these injuries and deaths could be prevented if an early warning system had been put in place.

There are three types of smoke alarm currently on the market: ionization, optical and combined. The optical type is often described as photo-electronic.

▶ **Ionization:** *These are the cheapest form of detection and cost very little either to buy or run. They are very sensitive to small particles of smoke produced by flaming fires, such as chip-pan fires. They will detect this type of fire before the smoke gets too thick. They are marginally less sensitive to slow-burning and smouldering fires, which give off larger quantities of smoke before flaming occurs.*

▶ **Optical:** *These are more expensive but more effective at detecting larger particles of smoke produced by slow-burning fires, such as burning foam-filled upholstery and overheated wiring. They are marginally less sensitive to free-burning flaming fires.*

▶ **Combination:** *As the name suggests, these are a combination of both of the above and can also include an emergency escape light. These units are usually a little more expensive but give greater peace of mind.*

The different types of detector look similar to each other and are powered by battery, mains or a combination of both. Some are inter-connectable, so a fire in one part of the home can set off the alarm in another. Some have additional functions, such as emergency lights.

Buying and fitting smoke alarms and ensuring that they are properly maintained could give you that extra few seconds in which to execute a safe escape. Plan an escape from your home in advance and talk about it with your family. If a fire occurs and you have to get out in the dark, make sure you have a system for letting others know you are safe, such as all meeting in the same place in the garden or other safe place.

CARBON MONOXIDE POISONING

Insight
Be sure you know what the symptoms of carbon monoxide poisoning are. See www.diydoctor.org.uk/projects/carbonmonoxide.htm

Carbon monoxide is produced as a result of the incomplete combustion of fossil fuels. This includes gas, oil, coal and wood, all used in the home. Carbon monoxide is poisonous to humans and is particularly dangerous as it is colourless, odourless and tasteless. Carbon monoxide detectors can be bought from all DIY stores and are an extremely worthwhile investment given the poisonous properties of this gas and the impossibility of detecting it any other way.

If one of your fossil fuel-burning appliances at home is not working properly there are telltale signs for you to watch out for, such as soot or other stains and discoloration at the joints of flues and gas water heaters. This indicates that the flue is blocked or partially blocked and the dangerous fuel residues are not escaping.

GAS LEAKS

Natural gas is a very safe means of heating your home. If leaks occur they can usually be smelled quite easily, giving some warning that there is a problem, but fitting a detector for gas leaks can certainly do no harm. Gas detectors are not as widely available as other detectors but can be found, together with installation instructions, on the Internet.

10 THINGS TO REMEMBER

1 Check all potential (listed within this chapter) damp causes regularly.

2 Rising damp will very rarely rise above 1.2 m.

3 Always seek specialist advice if you suspect rising damp.

4 Safeguard your home against condensation.

5 Woodworm can be prevented, not just cured.

6 Use dry rot detectors in older properties.

7 Lag all pipes to prevent freezing.

8 Do not buy cheap light bulbs.

9 Service boilers regularly.

10 Buy and install smoke and carbon monoxide alarms.

3

···

Sequence of work

In this chapter you will learn:
- *about planning permission and building regulations*
- *what other formalities should be carried out before you start work*
- *what work to do when and in what order.*

Introduction

One of the first questions you may ask as you embark on a new project is, 'What do I do when, and in what order?' This chapter should help to answer this question. Most of the procedures outlined below are covered in more detail in subsequent chapters, but an overview is required at this stage, and the easiest way to provide this is to outline the entire sequence of building a house or an extension.

1 Check planning requirements and building regulations

PLANNING PERMISSION

First, you must establish that you are allowed to do what you plan to do. Check with the Planning Department and the Building Control Department of your local council to find out if you need planning permission or approval under the building regulations. This can sometimes even apply to work indoors, such as knocking two rooms into one (although it is unlikely to apply if you just want to put up some shelving!). It can certainly apply if, for example, you are building a raised deck in your garden.

Insight

We always get an appointment with the local building inspector just to introduce ourselves and start a relationship. It makes future meetings easier.

See Project 13 on basic decking.

Parliament has given the main responsibility for planning to local planning authorities. While the government has tried to outline the principles of the rules, local authorities will have differing interpretations of these, and you should always check with them if you are in any doubt. It is vital that you **never assume that you do not need planning permission** to carry out work on your home. It costs nothing to check, but can be very expensive to undo work that has already been completed. Most councils will provide planning and regulation booklets free of charge.

The purpose of the planning system is to protect the environment and its amenity in the public interest. It is not designed to protect the interests of one person over another. Councils will try to ensure that development is allowed where it is needed, but that the character and amenity of the area are not adversely affected. Local authorities are concerned with the visual aspect of any building and its impact on the surrounding area, and also on the appropriateness of its intended use. Applying for planning permission is sometimes a complicated and lengthy process, so it is as well to seek professional advice, first from the local council, then from an architect.

Tip: tell the neighbours!

It is always a good idea to inform your neighbours of what you intend to do, even if you do not need planning permission. They have a right to request that this decision be checked, which can delay proceedings. If you do need permission, the council will ask your neighbours for their views anyway.

Another little-known fact is that when you decide to make alterations to your home and hire a skip to throw your rubbish in, part of the fee the skip company charges is to pay for a planning permission permit should the skip need to be placed on a public right of way.

BUILDING REGULATIONS

Building regulations exist to keep you, and those using the property, safe. The house in which you carry out the work may not be your home forever, and those who follow have a right to be safe. Also, you have a duty of care to keep yourself, and those entering your property, safe. In addition, there is an obligation to save as much energy as possible through adequate insulation. This applies particularly to one of the most popular DIY projects, that of turning a garage into living accommodation.

Insight

A good architect can save you days of searching through different regulations. They will know immediately which parts of your alterations will need permission.

All building work has to comply with the building regulations, which are part of the Building Act 1984 (amended by the Building Regulations Act 1991). The regulations are updated, amended or changed from time to time and your builder and/or architect should be fully conversant with the changes. The regulations only affect any new work undertaken when done as an addition to an existing building or on a 'stand alone' basis. It is not necessary to bring any existing structure into line with the current regulations, unless stipulated by the local authority.

Even when no planning permission is needed, building regulation approval may be required. **Always seek advice from your local authority before starting work.** Where building regulations have to be complied with, the Building Control Office of your local council will appoint a Building Control Officer to inspect the work at regular intervals to make sure it complies with the regulations.

It is also possible to arrange with the NHBC (National House Building Council), who are licensed to inspect building control, to do the same job. The NHBC also operate a ten-year guarantee on the work they approve. The building regulations come in booklet form and can be purchased from Her Majesty's Stationery Office:

> *HMSO Publications Centre*
> *PO Box 276*
> *London SW8 5DT*

---

2 Carry out other preliminary formalities

FIND YOUR ARCHITECT – IF YOU NEED ONE

If you get the go-ahead for your project, you may need to employ an architect to produce some working drawings for you. When structural work is carried out on a building it obviously has to be safe, and items such as lintels, joists, rafters and insulation must meet certain specifications. It is the responsibility of the owner to prove that the materials they plan to use meet all of the specifications required. The knowledge and, sometimes, the mathematical ability required to do this can be complicated, and employing the services of an architect can make the process much simpler.

The number and content of forms that have to be filled in to gain planning permission is pretty daunting in itself, and mistakes can put your application back to the beginning of what is already a fairly lengthy process. At the time of writing, the average time for a planning application to be approved in the UK is eight weeks. One mistake in a form and that could become 16 weeks.

Employing an architect is no different from employing a builder or any other professional. They will come to your home, where you will explain exactly what you would like to achieve. They will then supply a free quotation for their services. You should try to get quotes from at least three architects before choosing the right one for your job.

SITE INSPECTIONS

Once your permissions have been granted, you will receive approval documents, which will include information on site inspections. Site inspections are carried out by a Building Control Officer at different stages of the build, and are a legal requirement. You should give the Building Control Officer as much notice as possible of when an inspection is due. You are required to inform the Building Control Office when you start work, and inspection visits are required:

▶ *when foundations are excavated to the depth you intend to pour concrete*
▶ *when foundation concrete is poured but before it is covered up*
▶ *when you are ready to cover up any damp proof courses and membranes (i.e. before pouring the ground floor slab)*
▶ *before and after any drains are backfilled*
▶ *before occupation*
▶ *before completion.*

Insight

Always check with your local council as the number of visits may alter at any time.

EMPLOYING BUILDERS AND CONTACTING SERVICE PROVIDERS

If you are employing a builder to do any of the work it makes sense to have a written, formal contract with that builder. Suitable contracts can be found on the Internet easily and it is as well to withhold at least a percentage of the final payment until the completion certificate is signed by your Building Control Department. This is called retention and is usually 5 per cent of the total contract value.

When your plans have been passed and you have the necessary permissions, you should get in touch with any providers of services to which you will need to be connected. For example, if you are connecting to the mains drainage, or you require a change of water main, this is the time to organize it.

---

3 Plan and build foundations

▶ *Once you are ready to start, you must set out the lines and levels for your foundations. If you are using a digger, make sure you will be able to dig the trenches at the back first, so the digger can get out when all the trenches are done. Make sure, if using ready-mixed concrete, that any lorries can get in and out of the site.*

▶ *Once the foundations have been inspected and passed, you can start the foundation masonry, which is built up to damp proof course level.*

▶ *If there are any drains or services to go into or come out of the building, this is the time to make provision for them.*

▶ *Next, damp proof courses are laid and the floor slab is poured (again, after the inspections detailed above).*

---

4 Build up from the foundations

Masonry can then be continued up to first floor level (if more than one floor is being built) and first floor joists installed. Ground floor windows and doors can be built in as work progresses but it is usual, to avoid damage, to leave gaps for these with all lintels built in as you go.

Insight

Scaffolders will prefer to do as much as possible in one visit and you can save a lot of money by organizing this.

When the masonry is up as high as you can sensibly reach, the scaffold is erected. You can at this point, if you wish, erect the scaffold to full height and even extend it over the building so a temporary roof can be put on. This will allow you to carry on working in inclement weather, and is especially useful if you have to take off any part of an existing roof covering to join it to your extension.

Internal masonry then continues up to roof level, where a wall plate is fixed around its perimeter, on which to sit the roof joists or rafters. External masonry is built up when these rafters or joists are in place, and then the external skin can be built around them.

5 Fit the roof, windows and doors

Insight

We prime or treat all timber before it is fitted. It makes painting a great deal easier and you know that any hidden edges have at least one coat of paint on.

The roof is fitted and covered, along with any eaves ventilation, sofit boards, fascia and barge boards, guttering and lead or other flashings. As much high-level work as possible is done while the scaffold is up.

When all is waterproof and the scaffold has gone, the windows can go in, although many builders prefer to board up the gaps and leave the insertion of windows and doors until as late as possible in the build. This makes good sense while people are wandering around with planks of wood and wheelbarrows!

Why do my doors and windows stick sometimes?

There are two possible reasons for this if it happens regularly. Houses move (all of them!) due to expansion and contraction

(Contd)

of a lot of different materials, at different rates, in changing temperatures. Some of this movement can twist items such as door and window frames very slightly so the door or window will catch on the frame. The most common cause of sticky doors and windows, however, is that when the air is damp, either through increased humidity or heavy rainfall, unprotected timber can expand as it soaks up some of the moisture.

The remedies are different for each situation. Once you have determined why your door or window is sticking you can rectify the problem. A twisted door or window frame is unlikely to regain its original position, so the door or window must be altered slightly to adapt it to the new shape of the frame. This can be done by planning, filing or sanding off the area where it is sticking. Where a door or window has expanded due to moisture, it will regain its original shape when it dries out, so it is not sensible to remove any of the timber. Simply wait for it to dry and protect it with suitable paint or varnish so it does not happen again.

Insight

Sometimes a mildly binding door or window can be made to open and shut more easily by rubbing the offending edges with a wax candle.

6 Carry out first fix

The plumbing, heating and electrics work can now start. This type of work is almost always done in two stages: first fix and second fix. This is because much of the work will be hidden from view in the finished version of your extension, and it is easier to get these in place before things like floors, ceilings and plaster obstruct the work.

ELECTRICS

In the case of electrical work, the first fix involves:

▶ *running all wires to and from the outlets (sockets, lights, cooker, immersion heater, etc.) and source points (meter, fusebox, generator, etc.)*
▶ *cutting (chasing) walls (and floors, if necessary)*
▶ *fixing in the boxes to which the wall and floor sockets will attach. The appropriate wires are fed into these boxes (pattress boxes) during first fix and left loose with enough cable sticking out (tails) for connection later.*

PLUMBING AND HEATING

For plumbing and heating, all gas and water pipes are positioned and secured, meters, tanks and valves are fitted.

CARPENTRY

Insight

Use only dry timber. Even if the timber is only slightly damp it will shrink as it dries out. This will leave you with unsightly gaps.

Carpentry first fixing is also done now and any internal door frames are fixed together with any boxing framework (studding) required to hide larger, or clusters of, pipes and cables. The external windows and doors also need to go in now. Stud walls are built and plasterboard is fixed to walls and ceilings. Loft hatch and access panels to valves, switches and other controls are fitted.

See Project 22 on sawing timber, Project 23 on countersinking, Project 24 on boxing in pipes, Project 25 on working with skirting boards, architraves, coving and dado rails, Project 26 on hanging a door and Project 27 on fitting a mortise latch.

How do I cut timber in a straight line?

Drawing lines and cutting timber in any form can cause the novice a great deal of problems. The answer to the question above is to let your hand saw do the work.

▶ *Make sure you are looking at the saw from directly above it and not from the side. If your body is leaning, the chances are the saw will be leaning too, giving you a cut that is far from square.*
▶ *Hold the saw with your finger down the handle, pointing to the work, and make sure the timber is totally secure. Any movement in the timber will make the saw judder and go off line.*

Insight

We buy a new saw at the start of every job. The cost of a saw is very much less than a crooked, jagged cut caused by a blunt saw.

7 Finish floors, walls and ceilings

When the first fix is complete, floor screeds can be laid, plaster put on the walls and new ceilings fitted. The floor can go down onto the first floor joists. Internal insulation should also be added at this point, making sure that no electrical cables are trapped under the insulation. Care is taken (usually!) not to fill the new pattress boxes with plaster.

Can I paint ceramic tiles in my bathroom?

Because of their high glaze, paint will not stick well, or for long, on ceramic tiles without a special primer coat. The tile primer, or tile paint, can be bought from most DIY stores. Tiles should be cleaned well (usually using a degreasing agent such as white spirit) before applying a coat of tile primer. When this is dry you can then paint over it as desired.

See Project 40 on ceramic tiling and Project 41 on wallpapering.

My wallpaper overlaps at corners and will not stick down

If using washable or vinyl papers, apply a special overlap adhesive. If using ordinary paper, use some more of the original paste and go over the joint with a seam roller.

The wallpaper has blisters all over it

The paste may not have soaked into the paper for long enough or is not completely pasted. Check also that the walls are not damp or greasy.

8 Carry out second fix

When plastering is complete electricians, gas fitters, plumbers, central heating engineers and carpenters can complete their second fix. Socket faceplates can be wired and fixed, light roses and pendants can be fitted, and final connections can be made to the electricity meter. Bathroom suites can go in, kitchen units can be installed, walls tiled, taps and showers fitted and connections made to the mains water, tanks and drains. Radiators and boilers can be fitted and skirting boards, doors, architraves, handles, latches and door knobs completed. All that is left is decoration.

Insight

You will need to clean the plaster out all of the electric back boxes (pattress boxes) before the electrician can wire up the face plates.

Anything you may have forgotten is dealt with in the next few chapters, but the above sequence shows you how your house was put together. This will hopefully make it easier to understand when you find something you are not sure of while undertaking any DIY.

See Project 28 on making shelves, Project 29 on building a cupboard and Project 43 on painting timber.

Case study: knowing how your house works

A woman recently contacted DIY Doctor with an electrical query. She had moved into a new home and wanted to add an electrical socket in her lounge. She had read an article on adding a 'spur' socket, which is simply an extra socket wired into the back of an existing socket. The regulations state that a spur socket can be added to an existing socket, but no further sockets can be added to that spur.

The nearest socket to where she wanted to add her new socket was a surface-mounted socket, in a big white surface socket box. Having read DIY Doctor's 'sequence of events' paper, she knew that socket boxes are usually placed behind the plaster, not on the surface, which led her to ask if she was still allowed to spur from this box. DIY Doctor told her to follow the wiring back as far as she could and was able to ascertain that the surface socket was already a spur, meaning she could not safely use it as a source for a new socket.

Knowing how your house works is invaluable for any DIY practitioner.

10 THINGS TO REMEMBER

1 *Check with local authorities to see if your intended project(s) need planning permission or building regulation approval.*

2 *Tell your neighbours what you intend to do.*

3 *You are legally obliged to keep your home safe for all those who enter it.*

4 *Research your intended project thoroughly allowing plenty of time to introduce the required safety measures.*

5 *Always use a contract when employing professionals and retain a percentage of the contract value until it is fully complete.*

6 *Have a detailed plan of the way the project should proceed.*

7 *Keep all glazing until the last possible moment.*

8 *Dry all timber before use.*

9 *Protect all unseen timber with rot preserver or paint.*

10 *Never attempt scaffolding yourself.*

....

From foundations to the ground floor slab

In this chapter you will learn:
- *about load-bearing foundations*
- *why different types of foundations are used*
- *about laying underground service and drainage pipes through foundations*
- *how and when foundation masonry is built*
- *about preparing to lay the ground floor slab*
- *how and when a damp proof course and underfloor insulation are added*
- *how and when the floor slab is added.*

Introduction

Why do you need to know about foundations? You will be able to undertake DIY tasks much more effectively if you have this essential background knowledge. For example, if you know how the foundations of your home are constructed, you will know whether, after a heavy rainfall, the water disappearing under the foundations will cause damp.

For the purposes of this book, foundations are considered to be everything from the concrete in the bottom of the foundation trench, right up to the damp proof course. A house is designed so that every part works together. The foundations will be a certain size, depth and strength of concrete because of the load they will carry. This load includes everything from the roof down.

Load-bearing foundations

Load-bearing construction has become the most popular form of construction in the United Kingdom, with load-bearing strength masonry walls being built onto concrete foundations. These are constructed so as to spread the load (weight) of the building over the entire footprint of the property. The weight of the roof is spread, therefore, via the load-bearing walls of a property directly to the foundations. If too much weight is placed on part of a building that is not directly connected to the foundations, collapse can occur.

Tip: load-bearing in cavity walls

It is worth noting at this point another important but little-known fact that, in most domestic cavity wall constructions, it is the internal skin of the wall that bears the weight of the building. The external skin, however solid and heavy it may seem, is simply there to look good and stop the weather getting in!

Insight

Whatever you build will only be as strong as the foundations you have built it on.

Every wall that can be considered structural, i.e. holding something up, or retaining something, needs a foundation. If you are simply putting a few bricks in a circle to provide a garden feature, no foundation is necessary. In all cases, the wall you are building is only as strong as the surface it is placed on. A wall built on soil will not stay in position long even if it is only holding back a few inches of gravel in your driveway.

How deep should foundations be?

Foundations of any kind are designed in relation to the load they have to carry and the type of ground they are in. The minimum thickness of any type of foundation is 150 mm, the most common thickness, in solid ground, is 225 mm. However, these days foundation trenches are often filled to the top with foundation concrete as much as 1 m deep (see the explanation of trench-fill foundations later in the chapter). Tables giving foundation requirements can be seen at www.planningportal.gov.uk, the government website for planning permission and building regulations.

If you are in any doubt about what type or thickness of foundation is applicable to a project you are embarking on, you should contact the Building Control Department of your local council for advice. The ground conditions will determine which foundations you should use.

There are many types of foundation. Differing ground conditions, proximity of trees, backfilled land, soil types, proximity of drains and wind speeds all dictate the type foundations required. This book explains a little more about strip foundations than other types of concrete foundations as they are the most common and widely used.

Strip foundations

Insight

If mixing concrete for foundations remember that wet concrete is much easier to level than dry concrete.

A strip foundation is quite simply a strip of concrete placed in a trench. The absolute minimum thickness of this strip is 150 mm, even for DIY work. Although a foundation of only 100 mm may be enough to carry the weight of your garden wall, it will not be thick enough to stop it cracking when the ground moves.

There are occasions, such as when a garden wall is to be placed on sloping ground, where it is impossible to achieve the required thickness of concrete on a level plane for the required length. It is then permissible to place a step or steps in this foundation, which then becomes known as a stepped foundation (a strip foundation that has steps in it when required). The depth of the step is usually dictated by the rise or fall of the wall, but the same rule applies as for strip foundations: the concrete must be a minimum of 150 mm deep, so from the top of one step to the bottom of the next step must be at least twice the thickness of the concrete, or a minimum of 300 mm, whichever is greatest.

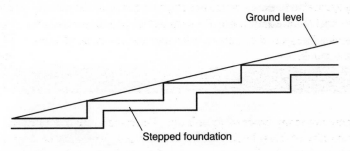

Figure 4.1 Stepped foundations in sloping ground.

When a stepped foundation is required, you should consider the size of brick or block you will be laying for the wall. It is much easier to construct a step that is in accordance with the thickness of the brick or block course (see Figure 4.2). The following information may be useful when you are planning your stepped foundation:

▶ *A standard brick is 65 mm deep and is usually laid with a 10 mm joint.*
▶ *A standard block is 215 mm deep and is usually laid with a 10 mm joint.*
▶ *A block laid flat is 100 mm or 150 mm deep, with a 10 mm joint. Blocks come in thicknesses of 100 mm, 150 mm and 215 mm. The depth will obviously depend on the thickness of the block you are laying flat.*

It is also possible to lay a combination of bricks and blocks to get the height required for an easier job.

Insight

Just because foundation masonry is underground doesn't mean any less time should be spent making sure all joints are full of mortar and the correct bonding is used for strength.

Using a combination of bricks and blocks, as long as the joints are still staggered (more about that later), steps can be constructed to build a level wall into any type of sloping ground. DIY enthusiasts will usually only encounter foundation problems where a garden slope is to be levelled using a retaining wall, or where a garden wall is to be built. In these cases, follow the foundation rules in this chapter and ensure that the depth of the ground to be retained does not exceed four times the thickness of the wall (see Figure 4.3).

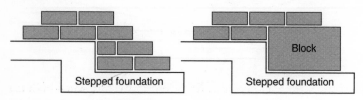

Figure 4.2 Use of bricks and blocks in stepped foundations.

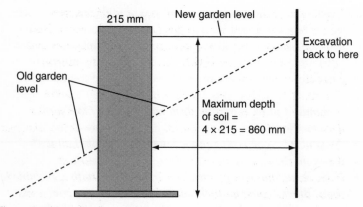

Figure 4.3 A retaining garden wall.

Building regulations give a clear list of conditions that must be met in order for strip foundations to be suitable. This list is conditional upon the walls the foundations will support being placed centrally on their respective strip of concrete. The conditions apply as much to an extension as to a house, but do not apply to garden walls or garden retaining walls, as these are exempt from building regulations (although, in many cases, planning permission will be required for them).

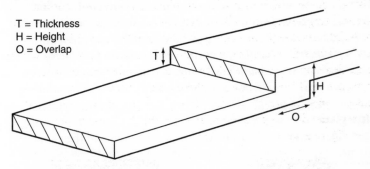

T = Thickness
H = Height
O = Overlap

O = 2 × T or 1 × H or 300 mm, whichever is the greatest

Figure 4.4 Stepped foundation overlap.

There are also other considerations to bear in mind when building foundations.

- ▶ *Existing trees draw a considerable amount of moisture from the ground, particularly in clay soils. The roots from trees can also be very damaging, and this should be considered when putting in garden ponds. Roots can easily puncture pond liners.*
- ▶ *The depth at which your foundations start may need to be determined by the local authority, which will make the decision based on ground conditions in the case of foundations for a wall that is required to meet building regulations.*
- ▶ *Again, in the case of an extension or other structural foundation, once the ground conditions have been ascertained, the weight of the load to be placed on the foundation (walls, etc.) is calculated and foundation widths are decided.*

The depth of concrete must also be worked out. This is a complex procedure for the layperson and employing the services of an architect is strongly recommended.

▶ When digging foundations for any form of strip foundation construction, it is as well to remember (unless you plan to fill the trench with concrete) that you will have to stand in the foundation trench to build the walls. Most foundations are excavated to a width of 600 mm. This will cover almost all eventualities in a domestic build. The marking out, or determining the exact position, of a building, garden or retaining wall is made a great deal easier if the foundations are wider rather than narrower. This allows for a margin of error in excavation. It is also worth noting that 600 mm is a standard size for a digger bucket!

Insight

When hiring a digger always ask for a lesson and then practise driving before digging up your garden!

▶ The choice of filling the foundation trench with concrete is now given in most cases, and it is usually much cheaper to do this. This type of foundation is imaginatively called a trench-fill foundation. The cost of the labour involved in laying bricks and blocks to ground level, together with the materials, is usually greater than the cost of pouring concrete to the required height. Steps can still be introduced in a trench-fill foundation.

▶ The walls constructed below the ground are subject to pressure from the earth in both directions and are treated as retaining walls. In most domestic builds, therefore, any cavity must be filled with a weak concrete mix – normally 8 parts ballast (sand and small stones pre-mixed) mixed with 1 part cement – up to finished ground level, and in all cases up to 150 mm below the level of the damp proof course. More details are given in the foundation masonry section that follows.

See Project 12 on concreting fence posts.

Underground drainage and services

Pipes passing through the foundation concrete (even the concrete for your garden wall foundations) must pass through a purpose-made duct, allowing the amount of room indicated by the local authority, to remove the possibility of pressure from any other surface coming to bear on the pipework. These pipes are likely to be the drains taking away your foul waste (everything from your toilet, bath, shower, bidet and all hand basins) and/or surface water (rainwater from the roof and ground). This principle applies to service pipes (gas, electricity and water) which are inserted (or at least the ducts are inserted) at this stage. Laying pipes and cables through foundations should not be undertaken by the DIY enthusiast, so this book will not go into detail about the thousands of regulations governing underground drainage. It is assumed that what you really want to know is what to do when something goes wrong. For this reason the book focuses on how the drains work until they are off your property, where they become someone else's problem. Drains and drainage will be dealt with in more detail in Chapter 8, but this section will deal with ground water and land drainage.

GROUND WATER AND LAND DRAINAGE

You may be lucky enough to live in an area where natural drainage takes care of all surface water. The garden, if it is not rock or clay, may allow the rainwater to soak down to the water table, where it then drains to natural water courses, streams and so on, using gravity as its pump. (The water table is water collected underground in voids or porous rocks, usually in a layer. The depth of water table can vary greatly, depending on the porosity of ground.) On the other hand, you may suffer from a surplus of surface water caused by impermeable ground and your garden may be very boggy.

DO YOU NEED TO IMPROVE LAND DRAINAGE?

If your garden tends to become boggy in bad weather, you may want to think about inserting some additional drainage to take water away from the parts of the garden used most often. Laying a land drain or a French drain is the easiest method of dealing with surplus water in your garden. The water can be taken to a natural drainage point, like a stream or ditch, but more often it will be taken to an artificial drainage point like a soakaway.

See Project 7 on installing land drainage.

If you move into a newly constructed property, you may find that little attention has been paid to the garden and that just under the surface there are the discarded broken bricks and other rubble the builders have left there. Before you dig it all out and dispose of it, wait for a while to see if your garden drains well. If not, you can use the broken bricks and other debris in your new soakaway.

See Project 8 on building a soakaway.

Insight

A water level (an easy to use device for checking the levels of your land over fairly long distances) can be hired to check where the low spots are in your garden. These are the areas that will naturally collect water.

Drainage is dealt with at this point because, in the case of an extension, for example, this will be the last point at which access to the garden is relatively easy and the raw materials for a soakaway are available. Once you are happy that your garden will drain well it is time to start building.

Foundation masonry

Having got a solid level base to work from with the foundation concrete, the underground masonry is built up to a level 150 mm above the ground surrounding the property. This is the level at which a damp proof course (DPC) is installed to stop any moisture, which may have soaked into the masonry below, rising up and soaking through into the habitable parts of the building.

Points to note:

▶ *The underground masonry should not be laid, or treated, differently from the brickwork or blockwork.*
▶ *It should be laid to the correct bond (see Chapter 5) and all joints filled properly.*
▶ *The cavity should be filled with a weak concrete mix to ground level to stop the ground pressure collapsing the wall.*
▶ *The cavity wall should be insulated from this level according to specifications outlined by the architect and/or the building inspector.*

Preparing to lay the ground floor slab

1 *When the foundation masonry is complete and solid, the trench either side of the new masonry can be filled back up (backfilled). The backfill must be compacted in layers. The compaction is done on both sides of the wall at the same time to keep the pressure even. Compaction is done 'to refusal', meaning that it will not go down any more.*
2 *The area inside the building is then covered with a layer of hardcore (the hardcore bed, as it is called), usually between 150 mm and 300 mm deep. This too is compacted to refusal. Most faults with ground floor slabs (subsidence, cracking, etc.) are due to poor laying of the hardcore bed. Hardcore, historically, is broken bricks and concrete rubble but, although both are excellent as hardcore, they are not that easy to shovel, work with and level. Crushed rock, broken chalk and gravel all make excellent hardcore and are much easier to work with. Road planings (the top few millimetres of tarmac which are shaved off a road when it is resurfaced) also make excellent hardcore and bind together really well under compaction. The compaction is achieved using a vibrating plate or vibrating roller, both of which can be hired locally from a tool-hire shop.*

Insight
It is sometimes possible to collect enough hardcore simply by placing a sign outside your house which says 'Free Hardcore Tip'.

> **Tip: using hardcore beds in DIY**
>
> All of these hardcore bases can be used for many DIY projects such as laying a patio, building a shed base and laying drives or paths, so the principle of a solid house base is again extended to DIY jobs. The hardcore should not contain any timber or building materials (paper, plaster, plasterboard, etc.), which will not compact at the same rate, or are likely to break down or rot and cause voids in the bed.
>
> It is common for patios to sink, paths to 'tilt' and drives to develop huge holes, most of which can be avoided by simply hiring a vibrating plate or roller for the day and compacting the base properly.

See Project 14 on building a shed base.

3 *A thin (25 mm) layer of sand, called a blinding layer, is placed on top of the compacted hardcore. The purpose of this is to ensure that the damp proof membrane under the concrete floor slab (see Figure 4.6) cannot be punctured by any sharp bits of hardcore.*

4 *A thick, polythene damp proof membrane is now laid on top of the sand. Building regulations say that a floor should resist the passage of moisture to the inside of a building, hence the introduction of the membrane beneath the concrete, which could soak up ground moisture if the membrane were not there. The membrane should be spread up the sides of where the slab will be, and tucked into the internal skin of masonry to avoid any moisture being squeezed between slab and wall, thereby forcing its way into the building.*

> **Insight**
>
> Do not attempt to be a miser with the polythene. Use more than you need and cut it off afterwards. You will be surprised how much gets pushed into corners when the heavy concrete is placed on top of it.

Damp proof courses and membranes

WHAT IS A DAMP PROOF COURSE?

A damp proof course (DPC) is a layer of non-porous material, usually polythene, bitumen or plastic these days, which stops water passing between the sections either side of it. Polythene membrane can be bought in rolls from builders' merchants. It is always laid in a continuous layer around the perimeter of a building at a minimum height of 150 mm. Damp proof courses can be formed by layers of impervious slate or very dense bricks called engineering bricks, but the effectiveness of these is determined more by the mortar which joins them than the materials themselves. If the joints are very porous, the DPC is far less effective.

HORIZONTAL DPC

The horizontal DPC prevents water that has soaked into the masonry from the ground from rising up the wall to a height where it could cause problems. Of the problems this water could cause, one is particularly visible on outside walls, where the face of the bricks or stone is 'blown' off. This problem is called freeze-thaw action and it occurs because the water in the tiny pores of the masonry freezes in very cold weather. When it freezes it expands as ice does. This expansion causes tiny fractures in the masonry which, in turn, let in more water. This freezes, and so on. Eventually the masonry is more crack than brick and it falls apart.

A DPC will not stop this process entirely because most bricks are slightly porous anyway and will still get damp, but it will prevent it from concentrating at a lower level where gravity will take any moisture that has not evaporated.

VERTICAL DPC

DPCs are also used at every point where a cavity needs to be closed (see Chapter 5). This is usually a DPC placed vertically to stop moisture passing from the damp external skin to the inside skin.

Another use for a DPC is to transfer moisture which has made its way into the cavity through masonry faults, condensation or structure damage, back to the outside of the building. This is done using a cavity tray DPC, which simply acts as a slide and shoots any water in the cavity towards the outside skin where it escapes through vertical joints in the brickwork which have purposely been left empty. These are called weep holes. This situation is found mostly over windows and doorways where, if it was left to settle on top of the frame, the water would soon rot the wood or, in the case of PVCu frames, would stagnate and harbour mould spores. It would also soak into the inside skin of the building causing internal damp. Cavity trays over windows and doors are often in the form of specially shaped lintels (see Figure 4.5b). If these are not used a simple, extra-wide length of DPC is built into the appropriate courses of masonry (see Figure 4.5a).

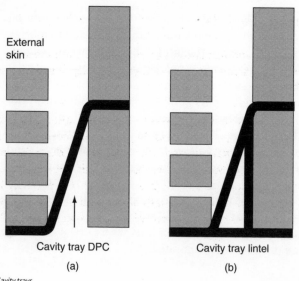

External skin

Cavity tray DPC

Cavity tray lintel

(a)

(b)

Figure 4.5 Cavity trays.

Underfloor insulation

In 2002 new building regulations were introduced which stated, in brief, that the heat loss from ground floors must be improved. This meant, in most cases, increasing the thickness of insulation placed under a floor slab. (In some cases this insulation is placed on top of the slab and under the floor screed.) The insulation has a high thermal resistance and an added benefit is that it also improves the resistance to sound. Tables are available in the building regulations (Document L1) that show you how to calculate the required amount of insulation for your extension or conservatory.

Of particular importance to the DIYer is the insulation placed at the perimeter of the slab, which stops the cold external temperature being transferred via brickwork and concrete to a 'cold spot' inside the room. Cold spots are areas where warm air can condense, introducing unwanted moisture and subsequently possible mould into the room. There is more about cold spots in Chapter 5.

The ground floor slab

Once the DPC and insulation (if it is going beneath the slab) have been laid, a concrete slab of a specified depth is then poured carefully on top.

A concrete floor slab is very likely to have sand and cement floor screed placed on top of it. Unless they are sealed correctly, concrete floors are not hardwearing and will cause a lot of dust; this is one reason for a screed. Secondly, because of the size of aggregates used, it is virtually impossible to get a concrete floor slab perfectly level, so a finely grained material, usually sharp sand or flooring grit, is mixed with cement at proportions of 4:1 to provide a perfectly level and smooth floor finish.

See Project 1 on mixing concrete.

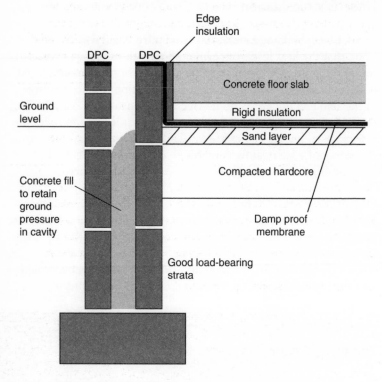

Figure 4.6 Foundation construction to ground floor slab.

If the floor screed is laid within a couple of hours of the floor slab, allowing the two to go hard, or set, together (bonded screed), then the screed only needs to be 12–15 mm thick. If, as in most cases, the screen is laid well after the floor slab (semi-bonded screed), then a minimum of 40 mm should be laid.

Figure 4.6 shows the insulation under the concrete slab. In some designs insulation is placed between the slab and the floor screed, in which case the screed should be a minimum of 65 mm.

Floor screeding looks easy, but is a very difficult process. Project 16 on floor screeding, although only short, gives invaluable advice regarding laying a flat, level floor screed. This project is not just useful for screeds; the principles can also be applied to laying garden paths, patios, shed and garage bases, drives and so on.

See Project 16 on screeding a floor.

Can I tile over my existing floor covering?

DIY Doctor receives many questions asking if is acceptable to tile over existing lino/vinyl tiles/quarry tiles. Good building practice would advise you not to do this. You are relying totally on the perfect adhesion of the covering below and, while your new floor make be stuck good and fast, if the one below is not then you may have problems. There are huge handheld floor scrapers available from tool-hire centres and builders' merchants which make removal of vinyl and vinyl tiles much easier. There are even electric chisels. One thing that is worth repeating time and time again is that every single job in the building (and DIY) trade is only as good as the preparation done for it.

(Contd)

- ▶ If you insist on doing it, then make sure that the original surface is absolutely stuck down, with no loose or floppy edges and no cracked tiles.
- ▶ Prepare the surface well by scrubbing any grease or dirt with a solution of sugar soap.
- ▶ Remove any loose or flaking material and vacuum up any dust.
- ▶ Scratch vinyl surfaces with a wire brush (an attachment on a drill is ideal).
- ▶ If you are applying vinyl to vinyl, use the adhesive straight onto the original surface.
- ▶ If you are applying quarry tiles to vinyl, then coat the vinyl with an undiluted coat of SBR latex adhesive first.
- ▶ If you are laying vinyl on quarry tiles you will need to smooth the floor with a self-levelling floor compound.
- ▶ If you are laying quarries on quarries, then a coat of undiluted SBR latex adhesive is a good idea as well, and make sure the joints of the new tiles are staggered with the joints of the old.

Please note, **we do not advocate any of the above applications** and prefer to see a job started on 'solid ground'.

Insight

Imagine putting a sheet of newspaper on the wall with four drawing pins, then sticking a tile to the newspaper. The newspaper would tear off the wall. This is what happens if the existing covering is not firmly stuck down.

See Project 17 on tiling floors.

10 THINGS TO REMEMBER

1   Research and plan your intended project thoroughly.

2   Create suitable access to avoid damage and accidents.

3   Use a concrete mixer to ensure an even mix of ingredients.

4   Ensure a uniform thickness and the correct depth of foundations.

5   Be aware of proximity of existing drains, service pipes and trees.

6   Use adequate insulation in floors and walls.

7   Use the correct masonry bonding and fill all joints.

8   Ensure all damp proof membranes retain their integrity.

9   Avoid internal cold spots.

10 Use correct adhesives for different types of floor covering.

5

Brickwork and blockwork

In this chapter you will learn:

- *about cavity walls*
- *what types of brick are available and how to use them*
- *about different types of brickwork and blockwork bond*
- *what types of block are available and how to use them*
- *what sort of scaffolding to use*
- *about efflorescence and how to treat it*.

Brickwork

Once the foundations are complete and you are 'out of the ground', going upward, you need to know how to build walls. The most common type of domestic wall is the cavity wall.

CAVITY WALLS

The actual construction of a cavity wall can vary. In general, a cavity wall is two individual walls built parallel to each other with a gap (cavity) in between. In all cases (building regulations, Approved Document A) the individual walls (also known as skins, or leaves) of a cavity wall must be a minimum of 90 mm thick, with a minimum 50 mm cavity in between. The two skins of a cavity wall are held together by wall ties built into the mortar bed of the bricks and blocks.

Wall ties

▶ *If the cavity is between 50 mm and 75 mm wide, the ties should be placed at a maximum spacing of 900 mm horizontally and 450 mm vertically.*

▶ *If the cavity is between 76 mm and 100 mm wide, the ties should be positioned at maximum intervals of 750 mm horizontally and 450 mm vertically.*

▶ *The ties should always slope very slightly towards the outer skin to stop any moisture in the cavity being able to travel towards the inner wall.*

▶ *The wall ties are often used to hold sheets of cavity insulation in place, and the type and thickness of this insulation will be dictated by the Building Control Officer.*

What does a cavity wall do?

The cavity in a cavity wall is there to prevent moisture from travelling from the outside skin to the inside skin. The cavity also, in almost all cases, is used to insulate the internal wall against heat loss from inside.

Even a dropped trowel of mortar can collect on a wall tie and transfer moisture and cold temperatures across the cavity. Damp and cold spots on walls in an otherwise warm room are usually the result of a transfer of cold temperature from the outside wall to the inside via what is known as a 'bridged cavity'. This can be particularly noticeable at the sides of windows and doors (reveals), where the cavity is closed to allow the fixing of the frame.

Insight

Use a timber baton, the same thickness as the cavity width, to clean the cavity of loose mortar as you build.

Cold spots on a cavity wall

Figure 5.1 shows what can happen when two very common things occur during the construction of a cavity wall. First, a lump of mortar has fallen from the trowel into the cavity. This has obviously gone unnoticed and, when the insulation has been added to the cavity, it cannot get down to the required DPC level.

The mortar has bridged the cavity allowing moisture and cold temperatures to pass between the skins of the cavity wall. At the same time, while the garden was being dug, a heap of spoil was left against the cavity wall. The top of the heap was above the height of the DPC.

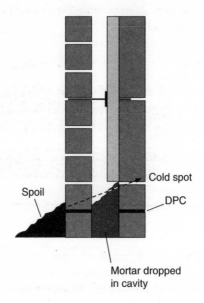

Figure 5.1 A bridged cavity.

The combination of these two occurrences can cause problems. Ground water can rise up into the spoil heap, which is probably already damp anyway. This moisture can then soak into the brickwork above the DPC and, via the mortar in the cavity, soak into the internal wall. This makes a section of the internal wall cold and even damp, allowing the warm air in the room to condense in this 'cold spot'. Because the wall is covered by very porous plaster, this damp cold spot can be home to any number of mould spores which will soon show as a dark mouldy patch which, no matter how hard you scrub, will not go away.

Figure 5.2 shows, in plan view (looking from above), how a cavity wall is 'returned' to close the cavity when meeting a door or window opening. (Return is the term used to describe when a wall, or part of a wall, changes direction in order to meet, or join up with, another part of the building.) It is at this point that there is least insulation and cold temperatures can travel through the walls. A vertical DPC inserted between the two walls will stop any damp from getting in, but the cold spot inside can still lead to condensation forming on the wall.

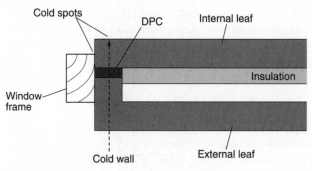

Figure 5.2 Cold spots around a window frame.

TYPES OF BRICK

Most bricks are made from clay and imaginatively titled 'clay bricks'. Clay bricks (and tiles) are very durable and extremely versatile. In days gone by, when bricks were shaped and fired by hand in small batches, different coloured clays, of different compositions, from different areas were used, and brickwork was as much of a visual delight as it was practical. With the increasing demand for housing, larger and larger automated factories are producing more and more standard bricks leading, for the most part, to purely practical construction. Experimentation with different clays is advancing brick technology to keep up with the demands for increased durability standards from the EU.

However, architects and planners are beginning to insist on redeveloping traditional styles of house (and other) building, using techniques and appearances that are sympathetic to existing local styles. This may mean that the demand for clay bricks will rise again as, in the 30 years between 1974 and 2004, it dropped by just over half, from 5,000 million to 2,750 million. This huge drop in the production of clay bricks is accounted for by the huge rise in concrete products used today, together with a massive increase in timber and plasterboard internal wall construction.

Common bricks

The term 'common brick' comes from the fact that, although they are fired hard enough to use for most load-bearing brickwork, these bricks are of a lower quality than facing or engineering bricks (see below). No attempt is made to control their colour, and their composition is such that they should not be used below ground.

Common bricks are used mostly for indoor partitions and for parts (or skins) of walls that will not be seen. They are lighter in weight than facing and engineering bricks. Their use is, as described above, being overtaken somewhat by the use of concrete and lightweight blocks for internal partitions.

Insight

Wear gloves when handling or laying bricks. The coarse surfaces of the bricks can wear the skin off your fingers in no time.

Engineering bricks

An engineering brick goes through a more elaborate process of clay selection, careful crushing, firing and moulding to make it a very hard brick indeed. The process delivers a brick that combines very high compressive strength with very low water absorption. Engineering bricks can be used underground and are often laid as a damp proof course. They are rated in two classes, A and B, with A being the strongest and least absorbent.

Facing bricks

There are a number of different types of facing brick, but generally they are the 'face' of the building. They are hard burnt to give them the strength and durability which they need to withstand the hugely varying temperatures and climate found in the UK, not to mention the acid attack from smoke and soot from any number of furnaces and cars.

▶ **Stock facings,** *or stocks, are a soft, irregular facing brick produced by pressing wet clay into sanded moulds. It is the use of sand to release the stocks from the mould that gives them their soft texture and slightly irregular shape.*

▶ *Most facing bricks in the UK are* **wirecut** *(shaped by wire cutting). The tightly packed clay is pushed through a mould, from which it gets its perfectly rectangular shape. The block or column of clay is then wirecut into individual bricks and fired in a kiln.*

▶ **Waterstruck** *bricks are released from the mould by water. They contain no holes and have smoother edges.*

▶ **Handmade** *bricks are made using an extremely expensive process which, as the clay is folded by hand into the moulds, produces distinctive creases (smiles) in the brick. Handmade bricks are used in the most prestigious of buildings.*

▶ **Reclaimed** *bricks also do exactly what it says on the tin. They are reused bricks that can be a variety and mixture of the other styles of facing bricks. The fact that they have been used once and reclaimed gives them creases and marks which will add something to any building they are used on. Because reclaimed bricks tend to come from older buildings, they are often in imperial rather than metric sizes. This makes it difficult to integrate them into larger, modern walls, so special reclaimed 'panels' are often inserted.*

▶ **Special** *bricks are so called because they are made to fulfil a specific task. An example of a special is a bull-nosed brick (see Figure 5.3). This type of brick is used, for example, to finish off the top of a wall or to make a windowsill. Other commonly used specials include plinth bricks, copings and arch keystones. Brick companies can make a brick into almost any shape that's required, at a price.*

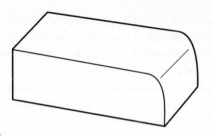

Figure 5.3 Bull-nosed brick.

All bricks have different uses but all need to withstand a certain amount of wear and tear. Bricks are crush tested to determine their usability – the crush-testing result for each brick type is an average figure based on the crushing of 12 bricks of that type. Crushing strength is measured in Newtons per square millimetre: the softer facing bricks will have a crushing strength of about 3–4 N/mm^2, whereas engineering bricks can withstand up to approximately 145 N/mm^2.

Insight

If you are trying to find a brick to match the existing bricks of your house, brick matching companies exist to help you.

As different bricks are used for different conditions, and in different walls, so different ways of laying them are employed in different situations. Some walls are laid so you can see only the ends of the bricks, some in a way that only leaves the sides visible. These different ways of laying bricks are called 'bonds', and the most popular are discussed below.

See Project 10 on laying edging stones.

Brickwork and blockwork bonds

Bonding, or tying together individual bricks and blocks, can be done in a number of ways. Whichever method is used, it is imperative that the maximum strength possible is obtained for the task of the wall. Brickwork or blockwork bonding should be laid out dry before you start, to make sure the bond works. Sometimes a brick should overlap the brick below it by half of its length (half bond). At other times a quarter bond is used, where one brick overlaps another by a quarter of the width of a full brick.

Tip: practise bonding

Buying a pack of dominoes and practising brickwork bonds with them can save you a great deal of time and money when it comes to building a retaining wall in the garden.

STRETCHER BOND

The long face that you can see in a brick wall is called the 'stretcher face'. The shorter ends are called 'headers'. Stretcher bond is the type most commonly used in house construction, because of the economy of bricks it allows and the speed at which it can be laid in most constructions, which only require a single (half-brick) skin. Stretcher bond is formed by laying one stretcher on top of another, making sure that the end of the top stretcher face finishes halfway along the stretcher face below it.

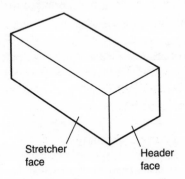

Stretcher face

Header face

Figure 5.4 Brick faces.

Two stretcher walls can be built back to back and tied together using wall ties to form a double skin of two single-brick walls. This type of tie is called a collar tie and is a way of getting an attractive face on both sides of the wall, but it is not the strongest method of producing a single-brick wall as the ties between the skins are a weak point.

Stretcher bond uses 60 bricks to the square metre in a half-brick or single-skin wall. This is obviously doubled to construct a double-skin or one-brick wall.

You can see clearly in Figure 5.5 how each brick in the stretcher bond overlaps the one below it by half of its length. Turning corners with stretcher bond is simply a matter of placing one brick at right angles to another. This automatically continues the half bond. To finish off the ends of the wall a brick is broken in half (half batt) and laid to keep the end of the wall in line vertically.

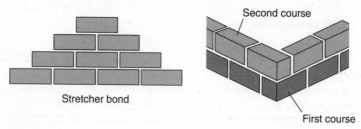

Stretcher bond

Second course

First course

Figure 5.5 Stretcher bond.

Stretcher bond is not the strongest of bonds, however, and if a wall of any length is built, piers must be inserted to maintain strength.

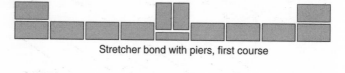

Stretcher bond with piers, first course

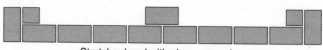

Stretcher bond with piers, second course

Figure 5.6 Stretcher bond with piers.

There are two ways to end a stretcher wall with piers. The first, in Figure 5.6, shows the use of a half batt in alternate courses (the name given to a horizontal row of bricks), while Figure 5.7 shows the use of a three-quarter batt.

 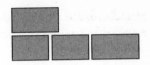

Figure 5.7 Alternative first and second course.

In some brickwork bonds, a gap develops which is not the same size as a full or half brick. In these cases, a brick is cut to fit the gap and this cut brick is called a closer. Some bonds do not work at all without closers, and the same size and type of closer is used in every (or every other) course. Where the closer has common usage it is often named – 'King' and 'Queen' closers, for example, are common closers, as are half and three-quarter batts.

Insight

If a 'closer' is required do not be tempted to fill the gap with mortar. The wall will lose a lot of strength.

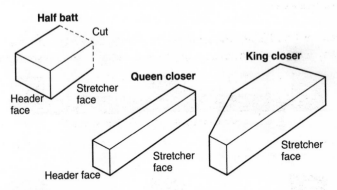

Figure 5.8 Types of closer.

Laying bricks correctly

Most bricks used for home construction in the UK have indents in the top of the brick. This indent is called a frog and, if bricks are laid to British Standards, as they should be, the frog should be laid upwards and filled with mortar. British Standard Code of Practice BS 5628-3 states: 'Unless otherwise advised, lay single-frog bricks with frog uppermost and double-frog bricks with deeper frog uppermost. Fill all frogs with mortar...'. This maximizes strength, stability and general performance of the brickwork.

When the frog is laid upwards, the load is evenly spread throughout the width of the brick all the way down to the foundations. If the frog is laid downwards, the load is forced to the outsides of the brick (see Figure 5.10).

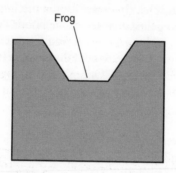

Figure 5.9 A frog.

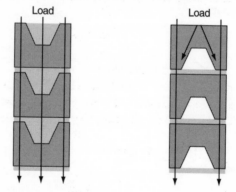

Figure 5.10 Spread of load in frogs.

The recommended maximum number of brickwork courses to lay in a day is 16. This equates to a height at which the wall can remain stable without support and, except in the worst conditions, can withstand wind pressure. Coming back to work in the morning to find your beautiful new wall leaning over at an angle is not a good moment!

OTHER TYPES OF BOND

English bond

English bond (also known as 'ancient bond') requires quarter-bond work in its construction of a course of stretcher bricks and a course of header bricks laid alternately. It is the strongest brickwork bond. It is, however, one of the most expensive because of the labour involved. The Victorians, when building many of their classical gardens, introduced a variation on English bond, called 'English garden wall bond', which introduces the course of headers in between five courses of stretchers. This maintains the strength, looks attractive and is cheaper and quicker to build.

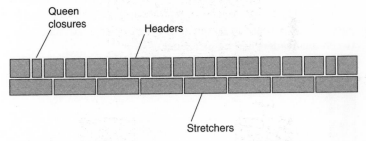

Figure 5.11 English bond.

It can be seen from Figure 5.12 that English bond requires closures on each course to maintain the bond. This type of closure, a brick cut down the middle of its length, is called a Queen closer (see Figure 5.8).

English bond

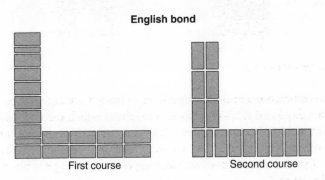

Figure 5.12 Closures in English bond.

Flemish bond

Flemish bond – elevation

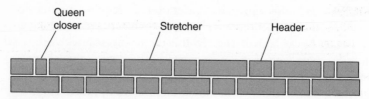

Figure 5.13 Flemish bond.

Not quite as strong as English bond, but used for its visual effect, Flemish bond is laid using stretchers and headers alternately in each course, to give it a quarter-bond finish. Flemish bond also has a 'garden wall' variant in so much as the number of stretchers in between the headers can be increased.

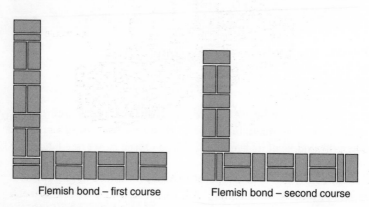

Flemish bond – first course   Flemish bond – second course

Figure 5.14 Closures in Flemish bond.

Quetta bond

This is a brickwork bond designed specifically for industrial use for retaining and load-bearing support. This bond can be adapted easily for garden use where a very strong, attractive retaining wall is needed.

The wall is built, as shown in Figure 5.15, using stretchers and headers. The voids created by this bond are filled with concrete.

The first course of this type of wall is built laying the bricks onto the concrete foundation before it has set.

Insight

Allow the brickwork to dry completely before introducing concrete.

Steel reinforcing rods are driven into the concrete foundation, through the voids, and further courses built up around these rods. When the voids are filled you are left with a very attractive, very strong garden wall which will retain pretty much anything you throw at it! The steel reinforcing bars (12 mm high-tensile bars are recommended) can be bought at any builders' merchants and easily cut with a hacksaw.

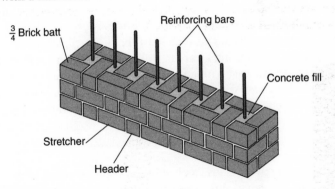

Figure 5.15 Quetta bond.

For extra strength in any type of wall, a galvanized steel mesh can be laid into the mortar course. A little like chicken wire, this mesh is called expanded metal lathing and is available from builders' merchants in sheets or rolls. For the DIY enthusiast it is far more useful in rolls, which come in various widths ranging from 50 mm to 450 mm. The mesh can be cut with a hacksaw or tin snips and can virtually double the strength of some walls.

Honeycomb bond

This bond is used for decoration in garden walls, as shown in Figure 5.16, but it serves the useful purposes of allowing some visibility while also creating less resistance to strong winds.

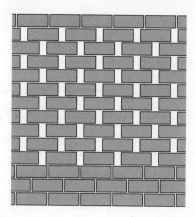

Figure 5.16 Honeycomb bond.

Tops of walls

To finish the top of a wall, a course of bricks is often laid on one of their stretcher edges. This is called a 'brick-on-edge' course. Another way of finishing a garden wall is by using coping stones. Coping stones are cast with an angled top to allow the water to run off and, as with windowsills, usually overhang the brickwork slightly so the water does not run down the face of the brickwork and stain it.

> **Insight**
> Sometimes paving slabs can be used as coping stones. They offer an attractive, and sometimes cheaper alternative.

As stated before, the bond used most commonly today is stretcher bond, and for DIY purposes this is perfectly adequate, especially for use in the garden. The problem with single-skin stretcher bond is that it has very little strength when pushed from the back or the front. Despite this, it is often used as a retaining wall, with the result that it is likely to buckle and fall over under the pressure of soil. Last year, DIY Doctor received nearly 5,000 questions regarding building retaining walls. Over 50 per cent of those questions were sent because the retaining wall which was already in the garden had ceased to retain!

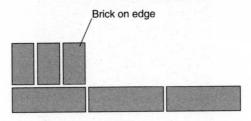

Figure 5.17 A 'brick-on-edge' course.

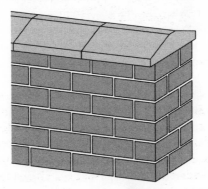

Figure 5.18 Coping stones at the top of a wall.

Why is it so hard to get a course of bricks level?

Most DIYers lay a course of bricks and tap each brick down with the tip of the trowel, or even a hammer, as they have no-doubt seen professional bricklayers do on the television or on building sites. What they do not see, however, is that bricklayers only do this when absolutely necessary and even then, far more gently that it may appear. The reason for this is that as soon as you tap a brick a little too hard, the one underneath it moves as well. The result? An uneven wall. Always lay your bed of mortar and gently press the bricks into it rather than dumping them on it and trying to level them out afterwards.

Blockwork

See Project 2 on laying bricks and blocks.

Concrete and lightweight blocks are widely used in all areas of building and DIY. They can be bought with a 'fair face' for work which is seen. They are much quicker to lay, given that one standard block is equivalent to six bricks. (For buying purposes, there are ten blocks to the square metre when the block is 440 mm × 215 mm.) These dimensions are the same as two bricks and one mortar joint wide, by three bricks and three mortar joints high. This allows blocks and bricks to be used (and bonded) together simply, as shown in Figure 4.2.

Blocks come in various thicknesses (the distance from the face to the back side of the block). They can be laid flat, and walls built using flat blockwork stretcher bond are incredibly strong. Special blocks are used for various applications and one of the most common of these is the 'hollow' block. The hollow block can be laid as it is and the voids can either be used to provide insulation, or they can be filled with concrete to make a very strong wall.

Concrete blocks are almost always used in foundation walls as they are so much cheaper to lay in terms of labour time.

See Project 9 on brick and block paving.

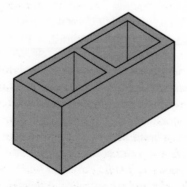

Figure 5.19 Hollow block.

Tip: laying blocks

A word of warning: blocks are not easier to lay than bricks.
Getting a block level, on a flat, level mortar bed is every bit
as difficult, if not more so, than laying a brick. Bricks can
be picked up and lightly pushed into a bed of mortar with
ease. A block, however, may take some 'persuading' with a
hammer (using the handle of the trowel is not recommended).
Because of its surface area, hitting a block in one place will
make it move in another and then the block will start to rock,
and because of its weight, hitting a block will cause the one
underneath to move also. So, laying a block wall, even though
the blocks are heavy and cumbersome, requires a light touch.
It is not recommended to lay more than five courses of blocks
in one go, for the same reasons as only laying 16 courses of
bricks, given on page 74.

Insight

Practise brick and block laying before you start a project.
The wasted sand and cement will be worth it to get a great
job on the real thing.

LIGHTWEIGHT BLOCKS

Lightweight blocks can be used for most types of building. The blocks
have all of the qualities needed to satisfy the building regulations, both
inside and outside, load-bearing and non-load bearing.

Advantages of using lightweight blocks:

▶ *The strength of lightweight blocks is very deceptive and their
  compressive strength, needed to form the load-bearing inner skin
  of a cavity wall, is far more than is required. The lightweight
  nature of the blocks allows them to be picked up and laid with
  one hand, a huge bonus when you are laying blocks, and your
  back will thank you for using them at the end of a long day.*
▶ *Thermal resistance (U) values are met much more easily with
  lightweight blocks and their ability to deaden sound makes*

them perfect for modern domestic internal use. The thermal resistance qualities alone can save a great deal of money on other insulation.

▶ Cutting lightweight blocks could not be easier. They can be cut to any shape or size using an ordinary carpenters' saw (buy a cheap saw at the DIY store for this purpose). Lightweight blocks can be drilled as easily as wood and the only real problem is getting a strong fix to them for shelves, cupboards, etc. However, special lightweight fixing plugs can be bought from builders' merchants that are literally screwed into the blocks and then normal screws fixed inside these.

▶ Lightweight blocks are considered to be non-combustible, giving them a great rating in the fire resistance section of the building regulations.

▶ Their ability to withstand sulphate attack makes them suitable to lay in the ground, and their resistance to frost has been proven time and again. Similarly, they have shown no tendency to lose compressive strength under the conditions associated with freeze-thaw action (mentioned in the DPC section of Chapter 4).

▶ Lightweight blocks have millions of tiny air pockets in their structure, but these are not connected, making them able to withstand damp conditions well.

Generally, lightweight blocks are more expensive than other types of block and are rarely used in commercial construction where cheaper blocks will accomplish the job just as well.

GLASS BLOCKS

Glass blocks are now widely used. These can be laid as normal blocks, i.e. with sand and cement joints, or by using special frames and spacers, which usually come in kit form with the blocks. If laying glass blocks with sand and cement, it is as well to remember that glass has no porosity at all and, if care is not taken, a wet mortar mix will very soon squeeze out all over the face of the blocks. Glass blocks can be laid indoors or out and are an excellent way of letting light into a space while still keeping that space separate from others. They come in a variety of sizes, with a clear or frosted finish for maximum privacy. Glass blocks are tested to see how long it takes before fire makes them unstable and they are also tested for their thermal insulation qualities. This, if the correct block is chosen, will keep them within building regulation guidelines. Other than for aesthetic reasons, glass blocks are rarely specified except when light is required through an otherwise solid wall.

Insight

We use glass blocks with lights behind for a great effect, indoors and outdoors.

See Project 5 on pointing brickwork.

Mortar

Mortar is used in many DIY projects and needs to be mixed to different specifications for different purposes. The table below outlines the ingredients and their proportions for mortar mixes for different jobs. It is only a guide and is prepared from general mixes used. You may prefer to build retaining walls, for example, using sharp sand and cement alone.

See Project 11 on repointing a patio.

Application	Cement	Builders' (soft) sand	Lime (if chosen)	Sharp sand
House walls – bricks	1	5	2	
House walls – blocks	1	5	1	
Retaining walls – bricks	1	3	2	1
Retaining walls – blocks	1	3	1	1
Coping stones and sills	1	2	½	2

(Contd)

Application	Cement	Builders' (soft) sand	Lime (if chosen)	Sharp sand
Chimneys	1	5	2	
Haunching for chimneys	1		1	4
Joints for paving	1	3		
Beds for paving slabs	1			6
Pointing brickwork	1	3	2	
Floor screed	1			4
External render – first coat	2	3½	1	3½
External render – second coat	2	4½	2	4½

WHY MORTAR IS MIXED IN PARTICULAR WAYS

Brickwork and blockwork need to be tough. For maximum strength they need to be bonded (as already described) and held together with one of a variety of mortar mixes.

The mortar used for any particular type of work or material must be as close as possible to the crushing strength of the material itself. It is no good laying blocks to hold up a roof if the mortar in between them will be crushed the moment the load is applied.

Other requirements, particularly for face-work (that is, work built as the finished article), are that the mortar should be fairly flexible to accommodate some movement in the wall, and be resistant to weather. One material that has fitted this description for thousands of years is sand.

▶ *Sand comes naturally (unwashed) mixed with a little clay and is soft to the touch. The type of sand usually used for mortar is called builders' sand or soft sand.*

- *When washed, sand becomes much coarser and feels like sharp grit to touch. This type of sand is called sharp sand.*
- *Soft sand is much smoother and has a more plastic texture, making it easier to work with, which is why it is used, in most circumstances, for laying bricks and blocks.*
- *The sand alone will not go hard, so something must be used to bind all the particles or grains of sand together.*
- *There are two types of mortar used for laying masonry: cement mortars and lime mortars. Both cement and lime can be used individually, or together, to bind the grains of sand together.*

See Project 3 on mixing mortar.

LIME MORTAR

When limestone or chalk is burnt, quicklime is produced. When quicklime is mixed with water, heat is generated as a chemical reaction takes place. This chemical reaction makes the lime expand to about three times its former volume and, by the time the reaction has finished, the lime has become hydrated or has no further capacity or thirst for water. The material is then known as hydrated or slaked lime.

When a further mixing of hydrated lime and water takes place, another chemical reaction occurs, but this time between the lime, the water and the carbon dioxide in the air. This reaction turns the lime into a solid mass which can bind the sand in lime mortar.

Lime mortar has advantages and disadvantages when used as a mortar for laying masonry. Its advantages are that it is relatively cheap and easily available. It has the ability to allow any moisture it absorbs to evaporate from it, enabling the mortar to breathe. However, this particular advantage can turn into a disadvantage over time as, if lime mortar is constantly allowed to get damp, it can lose its binding properties and the mortar begins to crumble and become weak.

Pre-mixed lime mortar can be bought, in drums, from builders' merchants.

Lime adds plasticity to the mortar, making it very workable, but it is messy to use, harder to mix than cement mortar and takes much longer to go hard. Most of the work done on heritage sites and older listed buildings uses lime mortar at the insistence of the surveyors in charge, as it is more in keeping with the integrity of the original buildings and allows the structure to breathe. This stops, or at least arrests, damp build-up in the buildings.

CEMENT MORTAR

The use of modern building materials in house construction relies a great deal on the external skin of the building being waterproof. Older buildings did not have damp proof courses, which meant the walls became damp and it was imperative to allow them to breathe and any damp to evaporate out.

The word cement means a substance that hardens to act as an adhesive, and the first 'cement' was wet clay used to build huts and shelters. The modern building material that we know as cement is itself some 5,000 years old, first used when the Egyptians found that mixing burnt lime with gypsum and adding water made a very firm material. The Portland cement, as we know it today, was invented, or reinvented, in about 1800 and a patent was granted in 1824.

Cement production began in earnest in 1840, and by 1870 there were a number of small companies manufacturing cement in north-west Kent. Kilns were improved and the bottle and rotary kilns became very popular, raising the temperature at which chalk could be burnt. Smaller companies could not afford the investment for the larger kilns and several got together to form a co-operative, known as the Associated Portland Cement Manufacturers Ltd or, locally, The Combine. This is how the Blue Circle Group originated.

Cement can be mixed with sand to give a high-strength mix which can be, for the most part, waterproof. Lime can be added to aid workability and breatheability. A lime cement mix will go hard fairly quickly while still allowing moisture to evaporate through it. Cement, lime and sand mixes for various jobs can be seen in the table on page 83.

MATCHING MORTAR COLOURS

There are many times during DIY projects when matching mortar to an existing colour is important. You may be replacing a damaged brick or would like your new garden wall to match your house, or you may need to repair brick or block walls. While it is relatively easy to match the bricks and blocks, matching the colour of the sand and cement, or mortar, is no easy task.

Insight
If using a dye to change the colour of your mortar, the dye should be mixed with the cement before it is added to the mix.

There is no science involved in matching a sand and cement mix to that of your existing wall or property, it's just a question of trial and error; even a little research is necessary sometimes.

There are many types of sand and each type will produce a different coloured mortar when mixed with cement. Your property may have been built using local sand or using sand imported from a quarry further afield. If your house is relatively new it may be worth talking to the local builders' merchants to see if the development was built using materials ordered through them. You can try to contact the developers or even the actual builders. Life will certainly be easier if you can track down the sand used.

See Project 4 on matching mortar colours.

If you cannot locate the sand, then talk to the builders' merchants and even the local quarry to find out how many local building sands are available. Ask if you can have a small sample of each and do the experiment outlined in Project 4 on each of the different sands. It's boring and time consuming, but if you do not want your repairs to stand out like a sore thumb, it has to be done!

Scaffolding

Tip: scaffolding warning

Scaffolding, in the tube and fittings form, should not be attempted by any DIYer. There are many reasons why a normal tube scaffold should not be put up in a DIY context, the main one being that it is a highly skilled job that, if done incorrectly, can also be very dangerous.

Tower scaffolds can be bought, or hired, to complete jobs at home safely. Scaffold towers are easily portable and can be carried, in lightweight sections, directly to their place of use. Most have lockable wheels, so once a job like cleaning out gutters is started, the scaffold can simply be pushed further down the line, allowing safe access to all parts of the project.

Insight

Never work at height on your own, even if you only have a family member checking on you every 15 minutes. A fall from even a few feet can be disabling.

The tower shown in Figure 5.20 is called a micro-podium. It is designed for work at between 1.2 m and 4 m, so is ideal for most work around the home. Platforms sit at heights from 1.2 m to 1.6 m, bringing most first-floor operations within easy reach. These towers, or podiums, can be erected by one person, but two people should work together to erect higher towers.

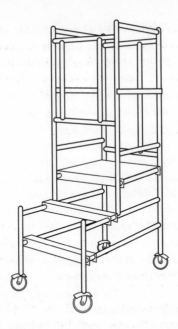

Figure 5.20 Micro-podium.

Scaffold towers of all kinds can be purchased, but it is more usual, in a domestic/DIY situation, to hire them.

Tip: working at height

In 2005, regulations were brought in to cover working at height. A copy of these regulations can be found on the website of the Health and Safety Executive: www.hse.gov.uk/pubns/cis10.pdf

Efflorescence and mortar stains

Efflorescence (the salty white deposit found on masonry) is a problem that can occur in brickwork and blockwork after they have been completed. It is formed by water and natural salts within the construction material reacting with each other and the mortar.

These salts dissolve in the water and are carried to, and deposited on, the surface by the natural evaporation that occurs by air coming into contact with the surface of the masonry.

Under normal circumstances, efflorescence occurs in relatively new buildings because the brickwork was not protected during construction and has got wet. This water will find its way out, through evaporation. In this case the salts can be brushed off and should not reoccur. However, if a lead flashing is damaged, or joints are missing and water is allowed to continuously enter the construction material, efflorescence will continue to form.

TREATING EFFLORESCENCE

- *Once you have discovered the cause of the efflorescence, and resolved this if necessary, the most effective treatment for efflorescence is Mother Nature and time. Natural weathering of the surface, if maintained, will remove the efflorescence.*
- *For a build-up of deposits on a wall, a good scrub with a dry, stiff brush will remove the worst, but make sure you follow it with a soft brush to move the salts away from the wall entirely. They could stay in the pores of the brickwork and dissolve again when it is wet.*
- *Treatments, such as acid, can work. Mortar stains are best dealt with by using a brick cleaning (phosphoric) acid. These are available from most DIY stores and all builders' merchants. Follow the instructions on the tub to apply the acid in diluted or undiluted form, then wash off. Take precautions with gloves, goggles and masks – acid is dangerous.*
- *Do not try to remove large lumps of mortar with acid. Instead, gentle persuasion with a chisel will take them back to the surface of the wall, where a quick rub with a wire brush will take you down to the stain, which the acid should remove.*
- *The same method can be used when cleaning patios of mortar stains; however, patio cleaning can be assisted with the use of a power-washer.*

Tip: handling muriatic acid

Use of phosphoric acid masonry cleaners is recommended before resorting to the very strong, very dangerous, muriatic acid. Muriatic acid is a hydrochloric acid and should be handled with the utmost care. Gloves, goggles and masks must be worn and the acid should not be used indoors if at all possible.

See Project 6 on replacing a damaged brick or tile.

10 THINGS TO REMEMBER

1 *Use a brick matching company to be sure of a good match.*

2 *Keep all cavities clean.*

3 *Place wall ties at correct intervals.*

4 *Ensure ground level is a minimum of 150 mm below damp proof course.*

5 *Use the strongest possible masonry bond in all walls.*

6 *Do not fill big gaps with mortar – cut a closer.*

7 *Practise laying bricks before you start a project.*

8 *Use the correct mortar mix for the project.*

9 *Do not bang bricks down with a trowel or hammer – it will move the bricks below.*

10 *Use only professionally built access platforms or scaffolds.*

6

Roofs, roof coverings and loft conversions

In this chapter you will learn:

- *about different types of roof*
- *about tiles, slates and roofing felt*
- *some causes of roof leaks*
- *how roof trusses are used*
- *how to insulate your roof*
- *why lead is used for flashing and other roof fittings*
- *about some of the requirements for loft conversions.*

Introduction

Roof design is quite a complex field and involves many calculations regarding the strength of the materials used. A roof has to:

▶ *carry the weight of the covering (e.g. tiles) that it needs to support*
▶ *withstand very high wind speeds and snow loading.*

Each roof is designed specifically for the purpose it will serve: the part of the building it will cover and the materials used to make it. For example, a conservatory roof, designed with clear plastic (polycarbonate) roofing sheets, would not be able to carry the weight of concrete or clay roof tiles. It is important to realize that a roof is constructed the way it is for many reasons and it is not safe to alter that composition in any way without consulting an architect.

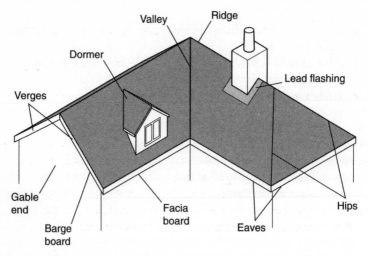

Figure 6.1 Parts of a pitched roof.

Roofs are categorized as being either pitched (sloping) or flat. This book will consider pitched roofs only. Flat roofs are not covered because, generally, repairs to a flat roof do not last very long. In most cases, when a flat roof starts to leak, a new covering is required. This is seldom a DIY job.

Pitched roofs

A pitched roof can be constructed in three ways: trussed, traditional or a combination of the two.

► *For a trussed roof, pre-made sections called trusses are placed on top of load-bearing walls or supports.*

▶ *For a traditional roof, sections of the chosen material, usually timber in domestic construction, are built together in situ.*

Most pitched roofs have an equal pitch on both sides of the ridge (a symmetrical pitch), but there are many variations on this theme, such as:

▶ *a mono-pitch may have only one sloping side coming down from a wall*
▶ *an inverted pitch or 'butterfly' roof has two sides sloping inwards to a valley at the bottom of the pitches*
▶ *an asymmetrical pitch has one side of the roof slope at a different angle from the other.*

A lean-to roof (a type of mono-pitch roof) is the type most commonly constructed by the DIYer. Although this is a much smaller project than building a main roof, the principles are exactly the same: the timbers must be the right size to support the structure; the tiles must be put on in the correct way; and the top of the roof must be sealed against water penetration.

Whatever the roof, it should be designed to give the inside of the property the best protection possible from the weather.

Roof coverings

TILES AND SLATES

Roofing in the UK is generally covered with small sections of material, like tiles and slates, because these are easier to get up onto the roof, safer to handle when you are up there and are small enough to allow for contraction and expansion in the dramatic temperature changes experienced in the UK.

The covering is usually fixed onto battens, which are spaced out up the slope of the roof. The battens are fixed at regular intervals according to the gauge (distance between battens) specified by the tile manufacturer. This in turn will vary according to the angle, or pitch, of the roof. Each batten is nailed to every rafter it passes over (see Figure 6.3).

The sections of covering are laid overlapping each other, much the same as bricks. However, in this case it is not for strength, as with the bricks, but to ensure that the roof is watertight (if two joints fall on top of each other the resulting gap will allow water penetration).

Tip: matching tiles

If you are building an extension or porch, and wish to match the tiles but are unsure which tiles you have, zoom in on them with a digital camera and take the picture to your local builders' merchant, who will be able to identify them for you. They will then be able to tell you how much overlap each tile must have and at what gauge the battens should be put on.

ROOFING FELT

Underneath the battens is a rooting felt. There are various makes of felt, but they all serve as a vapour barrier in that they stop warm air inside the roof space from hitting the cold underside of the tiles, where it may condense. Water condensing on tiles has historically been the most common cause of rot in the roof space through gaps between the tile surfaces. Roofing felt also acts as a secondary waterproof layer but it is not designed to be so. The main roof covering should be maintained well so it stays waterproof; if it does not the underlying felt should not be relied on to keep you watertight.

LEAKING ROOFS

When a roof leaks, it is almost impossible to tell where the leak is, bearing in mind the felt under the tiles and the pitch of most roofs. The water can get through a broken tile or slate and run down the felt until it collects in a sagging bit of felt, or it can simply drip through an unnoticed puncture in the membrane. Water can get in through a broken ridge tile but may not be evident until it is seen running down the far wall in the bedroom. This makes leak diagnosis on a roof an expensive job and can result in many people trying to find the leak themselves. Given the dangers of working on a roof and, in 99 per cent of cases, the impossibility of mending a leaking roof from the inside, it is highly recommended that you leave the roofing to a professional.

Tip: working on a roof

Never attempt to work on a roof without a scaffold. Tiles and slates are constantly exposed to the vagaries of the weather, so can be very slippery even on the driest of days.

Insight

Roof ladders have 'hooks' built into them which fit over the apex of the roof. These ladders allow you to get to the top of the roof safely.

Roof trusses

The word truss means 'tied together'. Roof trusses are sections (again, usually of timber) fixed solidly together to form the angled shape required for the pitch of the roof.

Most ordinary house roofs in the UK are formed using roof trusses. These are designed for each particular type of dwelling and, as many houses in Britain are built to the same style, there is one very popular truss type, the Fink truss. The Fink truss is a duo pitch truss: it has two sloping sides meeting in the middle. Roof trusses are placed on top of the external load-bearing walls of a building. They are placed at regular, equal intervals to suit the type of load they are to carry. The heavier the load, the narrower the spacing or the larger the timbers used to make the truss. A normal spacing for a roof truss in a domestic situation is 600 mm.

What is a load-bearing wall and how can I identify one?

A load-bearing wall is one that is supporting part of a structure. It is therefore a wall that, if removed, would cause other parts of the structure to collapse. A downstairs wall may continue through the first floor and go right up to the roof. This wall, as well as supporting the roof, may also be supporting the first floor. A wall that stops at ceiling level on the ground floor may be supporting the ceiling and the floor of the level above, even if it is a plasterboard wall. Identification of a supporting wall is best left to the professionals.

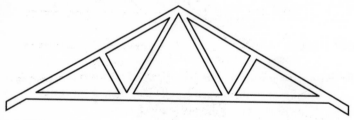

Figure 6.2 A Fink truss.

Roof trusses remain upright because they are linked together by binding timbers, which are fixed to the underside of each truss. The end truss, or couple of trusses, is fixed to the inside skin of the gable-end wall to make sure that the trusses do not achieve the 'domino' effect, i.e. if the end trusses were not fixed rigidly to the building in some way, if one truss started to lean over it could push them all over. Battening the roof for tiling also helps to join the trusses more firmly together.

The bottom, horizontal timber of a roof truss is also a ceiling joist. As far as its load-bearing capacity is concerned, it is only designed to hold up the ceiling of the room below and perhaps a few empty suitcases in the attic. It is not designed to be walked on or slept on, and neither is it designed to carry lots of heavy boxes full of unused possessions. See the section on loft conversions on page 102, which covers what you may and may not do in the loft.

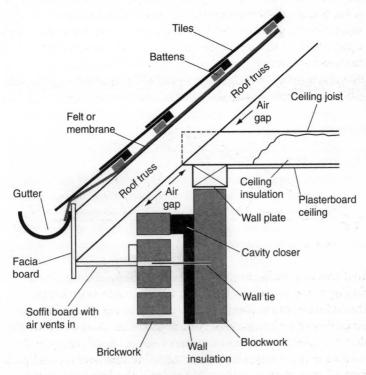

Figure 6.3 The gable end of a pitched roof.

Water tanks in the loft are placed on strengthened platforms, which spread the weight over a number of trusses and joists.

Insulation

A roof space is not designed to be hot (unless, of course, it has been converted). The heat is meant to stay in the building and now, with the latest amendments to Part L of the building regulations (The conservation of fuel and power) it is expected that (when all condensation and boarding out problems are considered) your existing loft insulation is topped up to at least 200 mm. This is to be placed between and over the ceiling joists and will stop heat from the building rising up and escaping through the roof.

Insulating a roof in this way means that the loft space itself is always quite cold. It is therefore necessary to insulate water tanks and pipes as, in this 'cold roof' design, it can often be as cold in the roof space as it is outside. This is why many burst pipe situations originate in the loft (see Project 32).

Tip: insulation
- ▶ When a roof is designed as a cold roof, as most roofs are, it is important that the roof is adequately ventilated to avoid problems caused by condensation (see Chapter 2).
- ▶ As mentioned on page 42, it is important not to cover cables and light fittings with insulation.

The insulation in the loft, then, should be stopped short of the edge, or eaves, of the loft floor, leaving a gap as shown in Figure 6.3. Roof construction, in cold roof scenarios, allows cold air to pass through the eaves into the loft. This should keep the loft at a constant temperature, thus avoiding condensation. The air is admitted through air vents, known as soffit vents, which are placed in the soffit board between the facia board and the external wall of the house.

Do not place insulation under the cold water tank in your loft.

Lead flashing

When any part of a roof meets a vertical surface or abutment, as it would with an extension, a roof window or a dividing wall between two terraced properties, the joint between the vertical surface and the roof covering needs to be sealed against leaks. Lead is usually used for this, and when lead is worked and installed in this way it is called lead flashing.

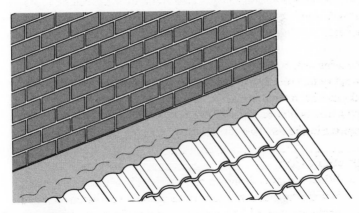

Figure 6.4 Lead flashing.

There are several advantages to using lead flashing.

▶ *Lead is used because it is a very durable material which has the ability to expand and contract with varying temperatures. This is essential on a roof, which is quite obviously exposed to the elements.*
▶ *Lead can also be worked into the most complicated of shapes. When lead is worked into different shapes to suit different roof (or other) applications, the process is called 'dressing'.*
▶ *Lead will not catch fire (but will melt at 327 degrees Celsius).*

- *As well as providing flexible cover for joints in the roof, lead can be used for gutters and complete roof coverings.*
- *Lead is extremely resistant to atmospheric corrosion, is a great sound-proofer, protects against radiation and offers protection against the effects of lightning.*

Insight

Bending and hammering lead into different shapes is called dressing and different types of dressing hammers can be hired from local tool-hire shops.

The drawbacks of lead are that it is extremely heavy and expensive. With regard to safety, the DIY user is perfectly safe as long as a couple of basic precautions are followed:

- *do not sandpaper or use wire wool to clean lead without wearing a protective breathing mask*
- *do not heat lead in a way which may produce fumes*
- *always wash your hands thoroughly after handling lead.*

You can download a health and safety booklet on working with lead from www.leadsheetassociation.org.uk.

Loft conversions

Loft conversions are subject to many regulations and permissions. Each conversion is unique and depends very much upon the condition and structure of the existing property. The majority of lofts can be converted, and can often provide a very attractive and large living area. Done properly, a loft conversion will also add to the value of a property. However, do not take any chances with loft conversions. Ceilings are designed only to hold what is already there, so loft conversions really are a specialist job that will require input from building professionals.

Check with three or four estate agents to see if the cost of your proposed loft extension will add the same value to your home. Very often it does not.

There is no doubt that you will need to gain building regulation approval if you plan to convert your loft. You will also certainly need the services of an architect. For each designed load you intend to place on an existing floor, a calculation will need to be made to prove that the floor is capable of withstanding it. You will also have to comply with fire regulations at every point in the construction of your conversion.

Some properties may not require planning permission, provided the loft conversion is the first extension and does not exceed 40 cubic metres on a terraced property, or 50 cubic metres on others. This condition only applies when properties are not located in a conservation area, and are not at the junction of two public highways. You should always check whether you need planning permission before going ahead with a loft conversion. A future buyer's solicitor will, or should, check that permissions were gained for the conversion, and that it complies with the relevant regulations.*

All flats require planning permission.

*These conditions were correct at the time of publication. Please check for alterations in regulations.

10 THINGS TO REMEMBER

1 *Research and plan your project thoroughly.*

2 *Check with local authorities that your intended work has the required permissions.*

3 *Check all load-bearing calculations.*

4 *Use only treated timbers in the roof.*

5 *Check you have the correct tiles for the angle of the roof.*

6 *Check the sizes of all roof timbers.*

7 *Insulate all loft spaces correctly allowing free circulation of air.*

8 *Wash your hands after working with lead.*

9 *Never undertake a loft conversion without the required regulation permission.*

10 *It is 99 per cent impossible to mend a roof leak from the inside.*

7

Home electrics

In this chapter you will learn:
- *what electrical work you can do yourself*
- *how electricity works in the domestic context*
- *about installing electrical wiring*
- *about the different types of electrical circuit and what they are used for*
- *how to check for faults*
- *the importance of earthing.*

Introduction

As outlined in Chapter 3, if you are undertaking major work such as an extension, once the roof is on and everything is watertight, the internal work can begin. This starts with the first fix, including skeleton parts of the electrical circuit, plumbing and heating systems.

The government has introduced legislation in the form of an additional section (Part P) to the building regulations, which states that any electrical installations must be carried out by a competent person. Competency, in this case, means a fully qualified knowledge of electrical installations and the ability to issue a minor works certificate as a self-certified 'competent person'. Failure to follow these guidelines may invalidate your house insurance, so before you start any electrical work please check with the Building Control Department of your local council that it is okay to proceed. The table below provides some initial guidance. (Note: this legislation does not apply in Scotland.)

Work type	Notification required? (areas outside of bathroom, shower room and kitchen)	Notification required? (within a bathroom, shower room or kitchen – special location)
New installation or complete rewire	Yes	Yes
Consumer unit change	Yes	Yes
Installation of a new shower circuit	Yes	Yes
Installation of an additional socket	No	Yes
Installation of an additional light	No	Yes
Addition of fused connection unit to ring final circuit	No	Yes
Installation of a new cooker circuit	Yes	Yes
Connection of a cooker to an existing connection unit	No	No
Installation or upgrade of main or supplementary equipotential bonding	No	Yes
Replacing damaged cable for a single circuit	No	No
Replacing damaged socket outlet	No	No

Work type	Notification required? (areas outside of bathroom, shower room and kitchen)	Notification required? (within a bathroom, shower room or kitchen – special location)
Replacing light fitting	No	No
Installation or fitting a storage heater, including final circuit	Yes	Yes
Fitting and final connection of a storage heater	No	No
Installation of extra low-voltage lighting (not CE market sets)	Yes	Yes
Taking a new supply to a garden shed	Yes	N/A
Installation of a socket in a garden shed	Yes	N/A
Installation of a light fitting in a greenhouse	Yes	N/A
Installation of a pond pump, including supply	Yes	N/A
Installation of a hot air sauna	Yes	Yes
Installation of a solar photovoltaic power supply	Yes	Yes
Installation of ceiling or floor heating	Yes	Yes
Installation of a small-scale generator	Yes	Yes

Domestic electricity supply

To understand how to deal safely with electrical problems, you need to understand how electricity works in the domestic context. Electricity is delivered to your home via your electricity meter, which measures how much you are using. This meter, although on your property, is owned by the electricity company that delivers it. This meter must not be tampered with at any time.

The electricity is then delivered to the heart of the electrical system, the fuse box or consumer unit. A fuse box is exactly that: a box full of fuses. The fuses are rated in amperes, which refers to the rate of · flow (current) of the electricity. The higher the amperage, the more current an appliance can use before blowing a fuse.

CONSUMER UNITS

Consumer units are more modern (and more sensitive) fuse boxes. Instead of fuses they contain a mixture of miniature circuit breakers (MCBs) and residual current devices (RCDs).

An MCB is basically a fuse with a switch. When the MCB detects a fault, such as a light bulb blowing or someone accidentally cutting or piercing a cable, it turns itself off (trips) and breaks the circuit. It is easy to see when this has happened because the switch on the MCB will be in the 'off' position (or, if it is a button MCB, the button will be extended).

Insight

Compare prices of electrical components in DIY stores and professional electrical suppliers. Quite often the professional suppliers will be cheaper.

An RCD is a very sensitive device which detects any kind of earth fault anywhere in the circuit it is protecting. It detects them in a fraction of a second and isolates the supply virtually instantly.

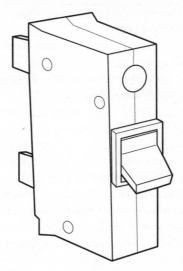

Figure 7.1 A miniature circuit breaker.

For example, if you run over the cable and cut the supply to your electric lawn mower, the RCD will trip instantly. RCDs can protect more than one circuit in a consumer unit.

Regulations state that any socket which can potentially supply power to an outside appliance must be protected by an RCD. This effectively means that every socket, certainly on the ground floor, needs to be protected by an RCD. Split-load consumer units are installed in most homes these days. These units protect your sockets either with an MCB or, where required, an RCD.

ELECTRICAL SAFETY

If you have any doubt whatsoever about the safety of carrying out electrical work, you should consult a qualified electrician. As mentioned earlier, there is a legal requirement to obtain a completion certificate from a qualified electrician for any work you do that requires a mains connection. For any work within circuits a minor works certificate should be obtained.

In general, the following points need to be observed.

▶ *Turn off the power and remove the fuse from any circuit you are working on.*
▶ *Make sure no one can turn the power on by mistake.*
▶ *Use only approved materials.*

FIXED WIRING

Fixed wiring is done in cable, i.e. a cable contains the individual conductors (wires) sheathed separately in insulating material to prevent leakage. The earth or 'ground' wire is normally bare. The wires are then jointly covered by the outer sheath. The wires in a cable are colour coded: red for live, black for neutral and green/yellow striped for earth, where this is covered. Modern cables are sheathed with PVC, which has an indefinite life; older cables were sheathed with rubber with about 20–30 years' life. If your home has these cables, do not attempt electrical extensions with them. When installed, bare earth wires should be covered with an 'earth sleeve', which can be bought in all sizes at electrical stores or most DIY stores.

In March 2006, new legislation came into effect which harmonizes the wire colours with flexible cables (used for lamps, light fittings, etc.) and European standards. The red (live) cable became brown, the black (neutral) cable became blue and the earth sleeving is now yellow and green. Houses built after March 2006 must be wired with the new colours, and any electrical work done on properties built prior to this date must be done in the new colours, with a label affixed to the fuse board or consumer unit stating that the wiring in the property contains a mixture of old and new colours. For more information on the new wiring legislation visit: www.theiet.org/publishing/wiring-regulations/colour/index.cfm.

Types of cable
▶ *The most common size (the dimension of the cross-section the cores of the cable cover) of cable used in lighting circuits*

is 1.5 mm. When installed it must not exceed 110 m in length and must carry a fuse rating of 5 amps (or 6 amps if used in conjunction with a miniature circuit breaker). It is acceptable to run 1,200 watts on this cable, the equivalent of 12 × 100 watt bulbs. Lighting circuits are normally run independently on each floor of your house. This means that an overload is very unlikely and if a fuse blows or trips on one level the lights will still work on the other.

Insight

Always use the correct cable for the current you are working with.

▶ *The most common size of cable used for the installation of power sockets on a ring main is 2.5 mm. The circuit uses a 30 amp fuse at the consumer unit (32 with an MCB).*

▶ *'Three-core-and-earth' cable (cable containing three current-carrying wires and an earth wire) is used to interconnect switches with more than one operation. An example of this is a light or lights you can turn off with two switches. This is seen most often in a hall or landing where a light can be turned on and off from both upstairs and downstairs.*

▶ *The term 'core' refers to the conductor part of the cable. In a cable used for lighting and sockets there is a live core (red), a neutral core (black) and an earth cable. In these cables the cores are solid wires but in larger cables used for cookers, showers, etc. a solid core would be too thick to bend properly, so the core is divided into strands, which are twisted together.*

▶ *Flex is simply an abbreviation of 'flexible cable'. Flex is used for connecting appliances. The colour coding in flex was, prior to March 2006, different from fixed wiring cable, using brown for live, blue for neutral and green/yellow stripes for earth.*

▶ *There are many more fixed wiring cables for connecting cookers, etc., but these are generally run directly from the consumer unit and require a professional electrician for their installation.*

See Project 30 on stripping cables and wires.

Fuses

Fuses are placed into a circuit as a deliberate weak point. If anything goes wrong within your circuit, the fuse will 'blow' and stop any current reaching its destination, thus warning you that there is a problem. With modern RCD boxes, the trip switch will go off, but **before you switch it back on it is essential that you check why is tripped.** Whenever you are working on an electrical circuit, turn off the power and remove the fuse, MCB or RCD to that circuit. If you do not do this and (let's imagine you are working in the loft) someone else comes into your home they may think that a fuse has just tripped. If they simply flick the switch back up you may well be electrocuted.

Installation

Wherever possible, an electric cable is run in a place where it has the maximum protection. A floor/ceiling void or hollow wall is ideal. Sometimes the cable has to be mounted in solid walls and it is then pushed into channels or 'chases' cut into the wall and protected by conduit, which is a tube (usually PVC) placed in the chase. The conduit allows protection of the cable while also making it a great deal easier to remove the cable if required.

The end of the cable is fed into a box, which is cut into the wall. This box is called a pattress. The cables are then stripped of enough insulation to enable them to be screwed to the appropriate terminals on the faceplate and the faceplate is fixed to the pattress. Special boxes are available for hollow walls (walls that are made of timber frames [studwork] covered with plasterboard).

Where it is not possible, or practical, to cut out chases or pull up floorboards, sockets, fittings and switches can be placed, or mounted, on the surface. Surface-mounted fittings also need to be protected, and this is done using mini trunking. Mini trunking can be bought with a self-adhesive backing strip, making it easy to mount on a wall or ceiling. The 'lid' of the trunking clips on and off, and there are various sizes to allow for more than one cable. There is no legislation to stop you mounting surface cable wherever you like, and in any direction you like, but if not using mini trunking it makes a great deal of sense to clip the cable into naturally protected places such as the top of skirting boards or to the sides of architraves around doors. However tempting it may be to fix cable to the face of these timber mouldings, it can be dangerous as you are leaving the cable open to damage by moving furniture and even vacuuming.

Cable clips can be bought to match every size of cable and these should be used frequently to keep any slack in cables to an absolute minimum.

Electrical circuits

The electricity in your home is used in two ways. One type of circuit supplies the power points or sockets while another supplies the lights. The principle is exactly the same. The lighting may be wired into two or more circuits for different areas of the home (usually upstairs and downstairs), while the power circuit is made up of different circuits to feed the sockets. Items such as electric cookers, electric showers and immersion heaters have a circuit of their own. The consumer unit channels the power, via various safety breakers, to the required circuit.

The cables that take the electricity from the various breakers in the consumer unit (or fuses, in the case of a fuse box) to the various rooms are arranged in different ways. One type of circuit used for the supply to the sockets is called a 'radial circuit'. In a radial circuit, a number of outlets are fed, but unlike in a ring main (the most common type of circuit used), the power terminates at the last outlet.

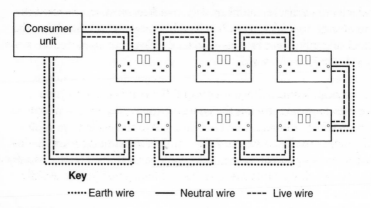

Key

······ Earth wire   —— Neutral wire   ---- Live wire

Figure 7.2 A ring main.

RING MAINS

> **Insight**
>
> A 'plug in' socket tester can be bought to test completed
> sockets. The better ones will indicate where a fault is, should
> there be one.

A ring main is a cable looping around the house, taking electricity
to one socket, then out of that socket to the next and so on, back
to the consumer unit. It is protected by a 30 amp fuse or MCB,
and the power is distributed via a 2.5 mm twin-core and earth
PVC-sheathed cable. A home is usually wired with two ring main
cables, one for upstairs and one for down, although legally there is
no limit to the number of sockets you can place on a domestic ring
main, provided that the floor area does not exceed 100 m² (this is
worked out by assessing how many heaters would be required to
heat that area). However, by using more than one ring main in the
home you are pretty much guaranteeing that, even if one trips, you
will still have power from another.

It is possible to add sockets to a ring main, increasing the total number
of sockets in the home. This is done by connecting an additional
socket, called a spur socket, to one of the existing sockets. Note that
only one additional socket (spur) can be added to any existing socket,

which means that the number of spur sockets must never exceed the number of original sockets. It is possible, however, provided that the floor-area rule is not broken, to extend a ring main to add sockets and rejoin the loop afterwards.

In modern houses with solid ground floors it is usual to have ring-main wiring leaving the consumer unit, going up into first floor/ceiling void and then travelling down the walls to provide the power to the downstairs sockets. It is important to realize this when hanging pictures, etc. The power sockets upstairs are usually fed from below, while the lighting and light switches are usually fed, on both floors, from above.

LIGHTING

Lighting in the home falls into three categories: general, task and specific.

▶ *General lighting provides overall space brightness with no concentration on any part of a room.*
▶ *Task lighting, as you would expect, provides light for tasks, such as reading and sewing, for which general lighting may be inadequate.*
▶ *Specific lighting is intended to highlight specific features, such as work surfaces under kitchen units.*

When thinking about lighting for any particular room it makes sense to think about the function of that room and what will be done in there. Most rooms will require a level of general lighting which, by the use of dimmer switches, can be transformed into various moods.

Insight

If running wires or cables in a wall or ceiling always think about someone else possibly wanting to hang pictures or coat hooks, etc. Do not put cables in the obvious places for these later additions.

The most common form of lighting circuit is the loop, in which the cable is fed from the consumer unit to the first light via a ceiling rose, as shown in Figure 7.3. The switch for that light is also wired into the ceiling rose. The live wire to the bulb is interrupted by the switch, which is why the switch wires are shown as dashed. When the switch is turned on, live current is flowing through both wires. The cable then passes onto the next ceiling rose and so on, until they are all connected.

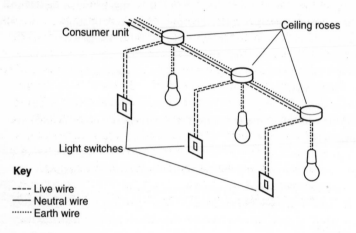

Figure 7.3 Loop lighting circuit.

Another type of circuit used for lights is the junction box circuit, in which the lighting cable comes from the consumer unit to a four-terminal junction box. The existing feed cable continues through one junction box to the next, while cables for the bulb holder (pendant) and switch are wired into the junction box. Although still used, this type of lighting circuit is less accessible than the loop system, where all wires can be placed at the ceiling rose.

I changed a light fitting and now it will not work.

Most people assume that changing a light fitting is such a simple operation that they do not make a note of where all of the wires are connected in the old fitting when they remove it. When they fit the new light they assume all the neutral wires go together, all the live wires go together and all the earth wires go together. Not so! The live wire to the light has to be interrupted by the switch, or switches, and this switch wire is hard to trace when they are all undone. Unfortunately the switch wire, although a live wire, often comprises a live wire (red or brown) and a neutral wire (black or blue), because that is the easiest cable for the electrician to use for the job. The black or blue half of the switch wire should have a red sleeve, or some red tape, placed on it to indicate that it is a live wire, but it often doesn't. If you do not know which wire is which you will find full diagrams at www.diydoctor.org.uk.

Insight
Although you may be allowed to alter an existing circuit, unless you are qualified you should never add a new one.

Bathroom and kitchen lighting
Bathrooms have strict regulations as to the type of light fitting that should be used, and where. Under the regulations, a bathroom is sectioned into four separate zones. Each zone of the bathroom is related to the position of the water source, i.e. bath, shower, basin, etc. Bathroom lighting is given an IP rating, which indicates the level of protection a light fitting has against the ingress of water. The IP rating is given as a figure and is followed by a number, and the higher both numbers are, the better. If you are unsure about the position of any light fitting you should consult a qualified electrician. Kitchens are also subject to special regulations, and advice should be sought as to the placing of lights here.

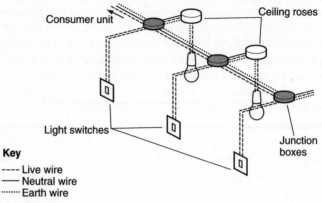

Figure 7.4 Junction box circuit.

CIRCUIT-WIRED APPLIANCES

In addition to sockets placed on a ring main, appliances such as wall heaters and electric radiators may be permanently wired to the circuit.

There is no limit to the number of appliances that can be connected, as long as they are wired into fused connection units (FCUs). These units can be seen in most properties, in the kitchen especially, and are used to turn off appliances such as the washing machine and fridge at the wall, rather than having to hunt under the worktop for the sockets.

FCUs can also be used correctly to provide protected supply for a 'sub-circuit' where a wall light, towel rail or extractor fan can be added. When the FCU is used to wire an appliance directly into the circuit, the flex from the appliance is wired directly into the FCU through a hole in the faceplate. A small fuse compartment, also in the faceplate, carries the appropriate fuse for the appliance. FCUs may be switched (for washing machines, etc.) or unswitched (for appliances which may be timed or turned off by some other means).

As mentioned before, large power users such as cookers and showers must have their own supply and these are generally switched by means of a double-pole (DP) switch. An ordinary, or single-pole, switch interrupts the live current when the switch is off, but a double-pole switch interrupts and breaks both the live and neutral sides of the circuit.

OTHER CIRCUITS

Besides the mains and lighting circuits in your home, there are other, generally more powerful (and therefore dangerous) circuits to be aware of.

Electric cookers

The largest user of electricity in the house is likely to be an electric cooker. Because of this it must be connected directly to the consumer unit or fuse boards on a radial circuit of its own. A large cooker with everything on for Sunday lunch could demand as much as 60 amps. It is unlikely that everything will be on at once, and 'diversity' calculations are made to ascertain the correct protection for a given wattage of cooker. As you should never work on a circuit where connection to the mains is required, you must seek professional advice on this.

The cooker is connected to the consumer unit via a double-pole cooker switch, which should be easily visible and accessible and no more than 2 m from the cooker. A cooker connection unit sits between the switch and the cooker, to allow you to connect the cooker cable to the supply cable.

Immersion and water heaters

Another item placed on its own circuit is an immersion heater, when used as a back-up for a hot water system. The heater is also switched via a double-pole switch placed close to the heater, and connected to it by a heat-resistant flex.

Water heaters over 1.5 kW should also be run on their own circuit fused from the consumer unit.

Electric showers (which are, of course, water heaters) need to be wired directly from the consumer unit on their own circuit. For safety reasons a shower should have RCD protection and be switched by means of a double-pole switch, which also has a neon indicator light as well as a mechanical on/off indicator flag.

Insight

Kitchen taps can now be bought which serve boiling water. The water is heated by a plug-in heater placed under the sink and this can be done DIY.

Storage heaters and outside lights/sockets

Storage heaters and outside lights/sockets must also be placed on separate circuits and again, because connection of these to

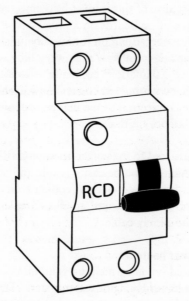

Figure 7.5 An RCD (residual current device).

the mains is required, you must seek the services of a qualified electrician. Specific information on cable sizes and fuse ratings are not given in this book as it is, in a great many cases, a direct contravention of the building regulations to attempt electrical work in the home without the proper certification or approval.

Extra-low-voltage circuits

Finally, another type of circuit is the extra-low-voltage circuit usually referred to simply as low voltage. Extra-low-voltage lighting consists of small tungsten halogen bulbs producing two or three times the light of conventional bulbs of equal wattage. They are powered by a 12 volt electrical supply rather than the 230 volts needed to power conventional lighting and are therefore fed through a (concealed) transformer. Through the use of this transformer, energy consumption may be reduced by up to 60 per cent, although this only really becomes apparent when several conventional lights are replaced. Additionally bulb life is increased by about three times.

Insight

Keep a supply of low-voltage bulbs handy. The cheaper ones do not last too long.

The halogen bulbs are fitted into special multifaceted mirrored reflectors with sealed fronts so they can be used safely in bathrooms and kitchens. They are described as dichroic reflectors, which means that the majority of the heat generated by the bulb is reflected backwards and not into the room. The light, as a result, stays relatively cool.

If you are using low-voltage lighting for a complete room, the general rule of thumb is one 20 W wide beam light per square metre or one 50 W light per 1.5 square metres. This rule starts half a metre in from the edge of the room.

Generally, low-voltage lighting transformers are placed in the floor or ceiling void and it is very important to ensure they are in a well-ventilated space. Do not cover them with insulation – remember, the heat comes out backwards. Never position transformers near central heating pipes. Most transformers are fitted with a safety cut-out which will operate if the transformer core temperature gets too high. The cut-out will automatically reset when the temperature cools.

Checking for faults

If a fuse blows or trips in your home, it is as well to find out why. It may be that a light bulb has blown (see Chapter 2), but it may be that you have a faulty appliance. Electricians have special equipment for checking faults, but there are some simple checks you can do yourself. First, make sure that there are no appliances such as a lawn mower being used outside and that no cables have been compromised or cut.

See Project 31 on wiring a plug.

▶ *Turn off the power to the circuit that has tripped, or on which the fuse has blown and, as mentioned on page 112, put the fuse in your pocket or leave a note on the fuse board warning others not to turn it on.*

▶ *Unplug everything possible from the circuit, push the trip switch back on or replace the fuse and turn the power back on.*

▶ *If the circuit still trips, take the fuse out again and check behind each socket outlet and light switch for obvious signs of a loose wire or connection. Look for black marks on wires that are touching each other, or close to terminals, and stray strands which may have worked loose. If you cannot find an obvious fault, call an electrician.*

▶ *If the circuit is fine when you turn it back on, this usually means there is a fault in one of the appliances that is plugged into the circuit. This fault is causing the circuit to trip. Plug each appliance back in, one at a time, and see which one causes the trip.*

Make a check list as you go round as it is easy to forget
which appliances have been turned off.

Is it worth fixing broken appliances?

Very rarely, because most regularly used home appliances are so
cheap that the parts are very difficult to get. Manufacturers keep a
supply to fulfil guarantees on larger items like washing machines,
fridges, etc. but getting a new element for a specific kettle is
rarely cost effective.

Earthing

Electricity can be compared to the flow in the water supply of your
house. This is ideal to explain the principle of the earthing system
in a house. The water supply travels round your home supplying
taps and tanks where required. When a tap is opened or a toilet is
flushed, water flows into the basin, bowl, etc. Electricity flows in
the same way, supplying lights, sockets, cookers and so on when
you flick on the switch. Electricity does not like to be contained
or harnessed so, if there is a fault or leak, the 'leaking' electricity
will simply travel to the ground by the easiest route, as water does
when it leaks from its pipes.

Electricity goes to ground (just take a look at a bolt of lightning)
because there is little voltage there, and it will always travel from
the place where there is the highest voltage to the place where there
is the lowest. This is called a difference in potential, and it is the
job of the domestic earthing system to equalize the potential
between conducting surfaces as much as possible.

You will notice in your home that on many pipes and cables there is a green and yellow cable fixed by means of an earthing clamp. These clamps (or the cable) should not be removed under any circumstances as they 'bond' together any conduction surface to equalize the potential between them. This means that if there is a 'leak', the electricity will not travel round the house before going to ground, as everything that can conduct within the house is at the same potential. That is, everything except you of course, so be careful. If you see any earth clamps or cables in your home that are not connected, call an electrician. Electricity always finds the easiest passage through the easiest conductor and, as human beings contain a great deal of water in one form or another, we are very often the easiest route. This makes us particularly vulnerable to electric shocks which, of course, can kill.

10 THINGS TO REMEMBER

1 *Check, plan and research your project, especially Part P of the building regulations.*

2 *Never undertake electrical work you are not allowed to do.*

3 *Use only approved cables, fittings and equipment.*

4 *Never work on a live circuit.*

5 *Make sure others know when you have turned off the power.*

6 *Use only the correct sized fuses for each circuit.*

7 *Protect all cables in walls and floors.*

8 *If a circuit keeps tripping, get it checked by a professional.*

9 *Never leave earth cables or wires loose.*

10 *When in doubt, call a professional.*

8

···

Plumbing, central heating and drainage

In this chapter you will learn:
- *how domestic hot and cold water are supplied*
- *about the different types of boiler used*
- *about the different central heating systems available*
- *how waste water is taken from your home*
- *how surface water is drained away from outside your home.*

Introduction

Plumbing, central heating and drainage really are different subjects, but they are closely linked. Having dealt with some of the major heating issues in Chapter 2 and some drainage issues in Chapter 4, these are linked together with plumbing to give an overview of all of them in this chapter.

Hot and cold water supplies

The domestic water system is divided between hot and cold, and obviously all water coming into your property starts out cold. It therefore needs to be heated somehow to give you hot water. The most conventional way of heating water is through a direct boiler system. If water is to be heated for the home, it makes sense to use the same heating for both the hot water and the central heating. Although the water for both is always kept completely separate, the boiler can provide the heat for both.

Insight

When we are working on a customer's water system we draw a diagram explaining to the customer how everything works. You can draw such a diagram yourself as you work your way through understanding your system.

Why is my tap dripping?

A dripping tap is one of the most common problems in the house and yet one of the most misunderstood. When we have a dripping tap we are invariably led to believe we need a new tap washer when, in fact, 99 per cent of the time it has nothing to do with the washer which, because it is rubber, is as good as the day it was installed. The problem is normally the valve seat, which the washer sits on when the tap is closed.

Water is held back by the valve until you open the tap. When the valve is closed, water is 'pressed' up against it until it is opened. It is prevented from getting to the spout by a rubber washer, which presses down on the metal that surrounds the water inlet, sealing it off. As the point where the water presses up against the valve is usually the weakest point of the valve, quite often water forces its way into the valve mechanism, between the rubber washer and the metal (brass) seat, and erodes part of it. This allows more water in, which erodes more of the valve, and so on until the mechanism is undermined by a tiny channel eroded in the valve body (usually brass). The water can then flow through this tiny channel into the main tap and will drip out steadily. The only recourse is to grind down the brass seat to a smooth finish. This allows the washer to once again sit neatly on the seat and seal the inlet.

See Project 33 on repairing a dripping tap.

COLD WATER SUPPLY

With a conventional plumbing system the cold water enters the house (usually under the sink unit at the back of the cupboard) through what is called a rising main. This terminates with a mains stopcock inside the building. This stopcock should have a draincock immediately above it, and in the event of a burst pipe or other leak, the cold water system can be drained down quite easily by turning off the stopcock, attaching a hose to the draincock and draining the water to an outside drain.

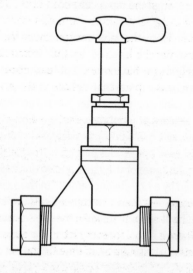

Figure 8.1 A stopcock.

Should your stopcock fail for any reason, there should be another stopcock outside your house, possibly in the pavement or near the road. If you have an emergency you are quite entitled to turn this off and inform the water authorities immediately. Please be aware that some homes, especially older, terraced homes, share an external stopcock and by turning it off you may be cutting off the supply to your neighbours as well.

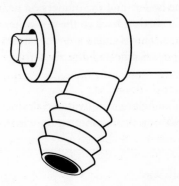

Figure 8.2 A draincock.

When the stopcock is open, water comes into your house and goes straight into the loft where it fills the cold tank. The water for the rest of the house is distributed from this tank. On the way to the roof tank, however, the mains water must feed one tap in the house. This is usually the kitchen tap (and often the cistern to the downstairs toilet, if you have one). You can notice the difference in pressure between this tap and the others in the house.

How do I reach to undo the nut holding my taps on?

You can buy a special spanner called a basin wrench, which reaches up behind the basin or bath and makes this seemingly impossible job easy. There is a tool for every job in the building industry – it's just a question of taking a bit of time to find out about it.

See Project 34 on replacing a tap.

HOT WATER SUPPLY

Direct and indirect water heating systems

In a direct hot water system, the cold water in the tank supplies water to the hot water cylinder (usually in the airing cupboard) and the boiler. The boiler (and the immersion heater, if it is on) heats the water and sends it back to the hot water tank, from where it serves the hot taps. This is called a direct system because the hot water in the tank has been heated directly through the boiler.

....

Insight

Regularly open and close all valves and draincocks in your system. This will stop them jamming up when you really need them.

....

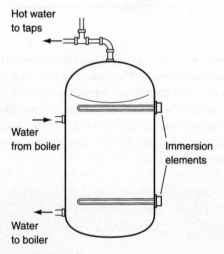

Hot water
to taps

Water
from boiler

Immersion
elements

Water
to boiler

Figure 8.3 Water heater in a direct hot water system.

There is another system, called the indirect boiler system, in which the boiler is used to heat the central heating system as well as the hot water. In this very clever system, the water for the central heating is sent through the boiler and when it is hot it passes through pipes called the primary flow and return pipes. These pipes form a loop, or spring shape, in the hot water tank and as the water passes through the loop it heats the water in the tank.

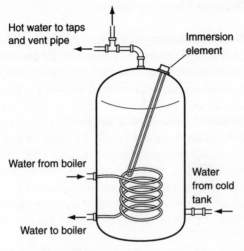

Figure 8.4 Water heater in an indirect hot water system.

Hot water can also be provided by the immersion heater alone. Immersion heaters can be fitted in a horizontal or vertical position and two elements can be fitted. With two elements you have the choice of heating up just the top section of the tank for smaller amounts of hot water. The cylinder, in all cases, should be well insulated and, if placed on a timer, the water can be heated at night (when the electricity is cheaper) for use during the day.

How do I replace the element in my immersion heater?

Again, there is a specific spanner to do this job. The removal of an element is easy, so this can be done before you buy the new one. You can then guarantee that you buy the right one. Full instructions for complete replacement can be found on the web at www.diydoctor.org.uk.

A standard hot water tank holds around 25 gallons, which is enough for two hot baths, but larger tanks are available, with another common size being 30 gallons.

In a hot water tank, the cold water from the tank enters at the bottom. As it is heated it rises to the top and the pressure from the incoming cold (remember the cold tank is situated well above the hot tank) forces it out when a hot tap is opened.

Vented and unvented water heating systems

The hot water system described here is a vented system. This means that there will be a pipe coming out of the top of the hot water tank which, as well as feeding the hot taps, carries on back up to the roof where it terminates just over the top of the cold water tank. This is called a vent pipe and allows for any expansion in the volume of water, as it is being heated, to vent into the cold tank.

Another system, used since 1989 in the UK, is the unvented hot water system. This system supplies all of the taps, both hot and cold, at mains pressure. It does this by sending the mains cold water directly to the cold taps and directly to the hot water tank. The water is heated either directly or indirectly and, as it warms, it is allowed to expand into an expansion vessel incorporated into the system. A pressure-/temperature-release valve operates when the system becomes too hot.

Insight

Type 'water saving devices' into a search engine on the Internet. It is surprising how many ways there are to save money.

The advantages of an unvented system are that the water to all taps is at the same (higher) pressure, as the hot water in the hot tank is forced out at mains pressure by the incoming mains cold. There is no cold tank in the loft, which means more room in the loft and no cold pipes to freeze in the winter. All taps supply mains water for drinking, rather than water which has been hanging around in a tank. The hot water tank can be placed anywhere as it does not rely on being fed from a cold tank placed above it.

Why does my overflow pipe drip constantly?

This could be because the valve, which lets water into the tank (either your toilet cistern, your boiler or other tank, depending on where the problem is), is faulty and is not shutting off the supply as it should do. It could also be that the device used to detect the amount of water in the tank is not set to shut off the water early enough. Neither of these problems is difficult to resolve and detailed advice can be found at www.diydoctor.org.uk.

Insight

Make a habit of checking your overflow pipe regularly. Even a tiny drip can cost a lot of money over a few days.

Combination boilers

Another way of heating water is by using a combination boiler. This boiler simply heats the water as it comes from the mains into the house. To do this it has to slow the flow of water slightly to heat it, and its main disadvantage is that it has a slower hot water flow. However, the advantage of having hot water instantly and not having to house hot water or expansion tanks in the loft means that combination boilers are a great asset.

Condensing boilers

Regulations now state that, if it is reasonable to do so, the only boiler type that can be fitted from new is a condensing boiler. If the circumstances are too difficult (your installer will advise you) you may still replace an existing boiler with the same type.

Insight

Whichever boiler you have, make sure it is serviced at the recommended intervals.

Condensing boilers are far more efficient that ordinary boilers because they use larger heat exchangers to get the absolute maximum amount of heat from the fuel used, and they even reuse some of the heat from the flue gases. Because a lot of the heat is taken from the flue gas, any moisture in the remaining gas will condense and this moisture is drained from the boiler to a condensing drain. The installation of a condensing boiler is therefore more expensive, but with up to 94 per cent efficiency, it is money well spent.

Conventional combination boilers can also be replaced by condensing combination boilers, which are ideal for cutting costs by saving energy. Replacing a ten-year-old boiler with a new, energy-efficient one can reduce your energy consumption by up to a third!

Why does no water/a spluttering supply come out of the hot tap?

If no water, or a spluttering supply, comes out of the hot tap when it is opened, the likely cause is an air lock.

See Project 35 for how to deal with an air lock in your hot water system.

Central heating

There are many ways to heat a house, but this section looks at the most commonly encountered system, the standard 'wet radiator' system (a system which uses heated water to provide the heat). For more detailed advice on undertaking plumbing and central heating maintenance, see *Master Basic Plumbing and Central Heating*.

Most heating systems these days are pumped, allowing water to move more quickly round a circuit, and allowing smaller bore (microbore) pipes to be used. This means that less water is needed, enabling it to be heated more quickly, using less energy and making the whole system more efficient. Timers and thermostatic controls are used on boilers and radiators to make sure the heating is used only when and where it is required, and if your home is insulated well a good heating system can be very efficient indeed.

It pays to know which system you have and these are the basic varieties.

SINGLE-PIPE SYSTEM

This system operates through a single feed pipe, which comes from the boiler and runs along at floor level to each radiator. A pipe is branched off the feed pipe to take hot water to (usually) the top of the radiator, where it passes through the radiator, coming out, a little cooler, to mix with the hot water in the main feed pipe again. This is a very inefficient system which leads to the first radiator being very hot, while the last radiator in the system is usually cold, the hot water having by now mixed with a great deal of cool water.

Insight

We have many customers who take advantage of our 'Draw me a plan' service. Ask your local plumber to map out your heating system for you, identifying its various components. You will have to pay him but if you are an avid DIYer it will save you money in the long term.

DOUBLE-PIPE SYSTEM

Two separate pipes go to each radiator, one feeding the radiator (flow) and one taking water back to the boiler (return). Much more efficient than the single-pipe system, this system can be balanced properly. A pressure-relief valve is fitted between the feed and return pipes allowing the pump simply to circulate the water if the radiators are closed.

MICROBORE

Large pipes (up to 28 mm) are fed with hot water from the boiler. A manifold (a pipe fitting that resembles a small chamber which branches into several openings) is connected to this pipe. There is a separate manifold for each of the feed and return paths. The radiators are serviced from this manifold by (usually) 8 mm flexible copper pipes. The distance the water travels in the smaller pipes is kept to a maximum of 5 m wherever possible, for maximum efficiency. A fairly major drawback to the microbore system is that it is not practical to add another radiator to the system should you plan an extension as, unless there is a spare flow and return port at the manifold, a new manifold is required. If all radiators are closed, the water can still circulate by means of a bypass valve.

Insight

We take extra special care bending microbore pipe as it kinks very easily.

How do I bend copper pipe?

Anyone who has tried this will know that when you try to bend the pipe it simply folds over and kinks. This can be avoided by sliding a special pipe-bending spring inside the pipe. These springs are available from DIY stores and allow you to bend the pipe without it kinking. Once the pipe is bent, you simply pull the spring out.

TROUBLESHOOTING

In its simplest form, a central heating system takes hot water from a boiler, passes it through radiators and reheats it to send it round again. As seen above, there are many other things to consider in this process but, rather than running through every possible scenario, this section of the book serves as a troubleshooting guide for a standard wet system.

Programmers and timers, together with motorized valves and pumps, send the water to the areas that need it, when they need it, and efficiency is the name of the game, but because there are so many moving parts in central heating systems things can, and often do, go wrong.

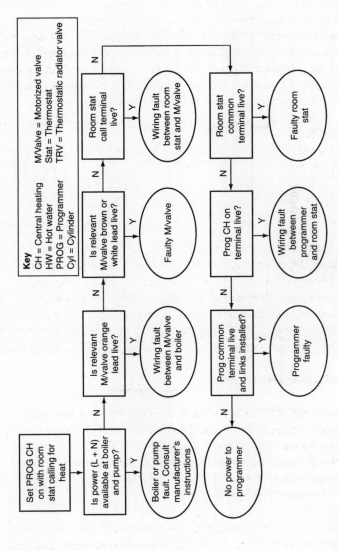

Key

CH = Central heating
HW = Hot water
PROG = Programmer
Cyl = Cylinder

M/Valve = Motorized valve
Stat = Thermostat
TRV = Thermostatic radiator valve

Set PROG CH on with room stat calling for heat

Is power (L + N) available at boiler and pump? — Y → Boiler or pump fault. Consult manufacturer's instructions

↓ N

Is relevant M/valve orange lead live? — Y → Wiring fault between M/valve and boiler

↓ N

Is relevant M/valve brown or white lead live? — Y → Faulty M/valve

↓ N

Room stat call terminal live? — Y → Wiring fault between room stat and M/valve

↓ N

Room stat common terminal live? — Y → Faulty room stat

↓ N

Prog CH on terminal live? — Y → Wiring fault between programmer and room stat

↓ N

Prog common terminal live and links installed? — Y → Programmer faulty

↓ N

No power to programmer

Figure 8.5 No heating.

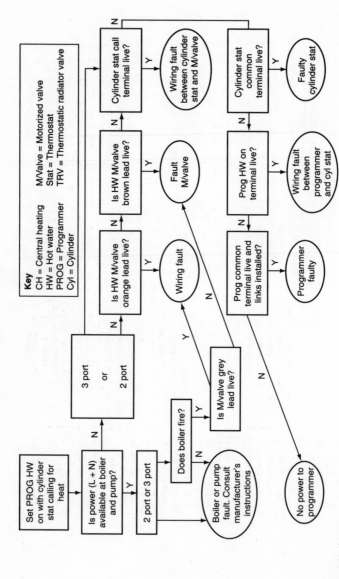

Figure 8.6 No hot water.

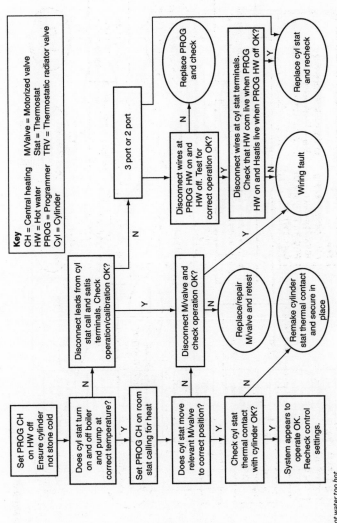

Figure 8.7 Hot water too hot.

Key
CH = Central heating   M/Valve = Motorized valve
HW = Hot water   Stat = Thermostat
PROG = Programmer   TRV = Thermostatic radiator valve
Cyl = Cylinder

Set PROG CH on HW off Ensure cylinder not stone cold

Does cyl stat turn on and off boiler and pump at correct temperature?

Disconnect leads from cyl stat call and satis terminals. Check operation/calibration OK?

3 port or 2 port

Replace PROG and check

Disconnect wires at PROG HW on and HW off. Test for correct operation OK?

Disconnect wires at cyl stat terminals. Check that HW com live when PROG HW on and Hsatis live when PROG HW off OK?

Replace cyl stat and recheck

Set PROG CH on room stat calling for heat

Does cyl stat move relevant M/valve to correct position?

Disconnect M/valve and check operation OK?

Replace/repair M/valve and retest

Wiring fault

Check cyl stat thermal contact with cylinder OK?

Remake cylinder stat thermal contact and secure in place

System appears to operate OK. Recheck control settings.

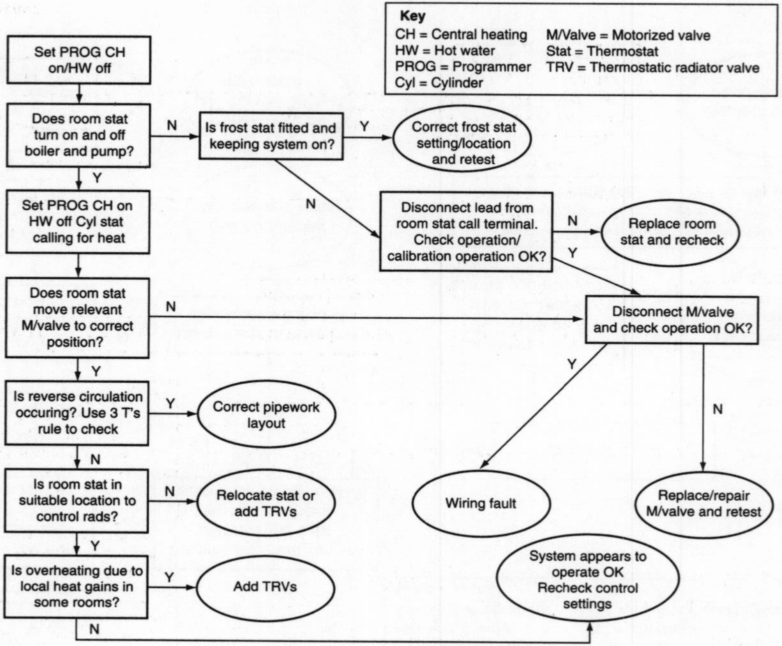

Key
CH = Central heating   M/Valve = Motorized valve
HW = Hot water   Stat = Thermostat
PROG = Programmer   TRV = Thermostatic radiator valve
Cyl = Cylinder

Set PROG CH on/HW off

Does room stat turn on and off boiler and pump?

Is frost stat fitted and keeping system on?

Correct frost stat setting/location and retest

Set PROG CH on HW off Cyl stat calling for heat

Disconnect lead from room stat call terminal. Check operation/ calibration operation OK?

Replace room stat and recheck

Does room stat move relevant M/valve to correct position?

Disconnect M/valve and check operation OK?

Replace/repair M/valve and retest

Wiring fault

Is reverse circulation occuring? Use 3 T's rule to check

Correct pipework layout

Is room stat in suitable location to control rads?

Relocate stat or add TRVs

Is overheating due to local heat gains in some rooms?

Add TRVs

System appears to operate OK Recheck control settings

Figure 8.8 Heating too hot.

140

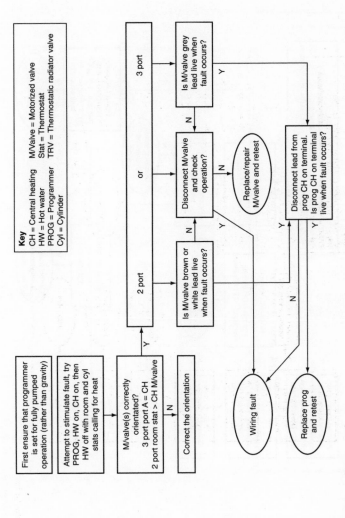

Key
CH = Central heating | M/Valve = Motorized valve
HW = Hot water | Stat = Thermostat
PROG = Programmer | TRV = Thermostatic radiator valve
Cyl = Cylinder

First ensure that programmer is set for fully pumped operation (rather than gravity)

Attempt to stimulate fault, try PROG, HW on, CH on, then HW off with room and cyl stats calling for heat

M/valve(s) correctly orientated?
3 port port A = CH
2 port room stat > CH M/valve

Correct the orientation

2 port — or — 3 port

Is M/valve brown or white lead live when fault occurs?

Is M/valve grey lead live when fault occurs?

Disconnect M/valve and check operation?

Replace/repair M/valve and retest

Disconnect lead from prog CH on terminal. Is prog CH on terminal live when fault occurs?

Wiring fault

Replace prog and retest

Figure 8.9 Hot water on when not wanted.

8. Plumbing, central heating and drainage 141

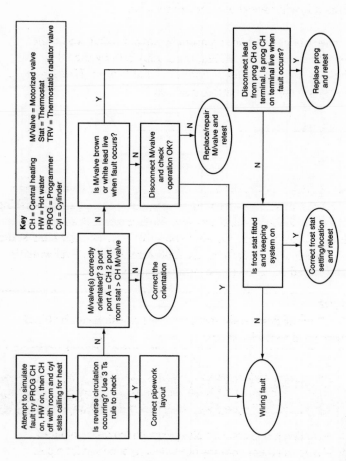

Key

CH = Central heating   M/valve = Motorized valve
HW = Hot water   Stat = Thermostat
PROG = Programmer   TRV = Thermostatic radiator valve
Cyl = Cylinder

Attempt to simulate fault try PROG CH on, HW on, then CH off with room and cyl stats calling for heat

Is reverse circulation occurring? Use 3 Ts rule to check

Correct pipework layout

M/valve(s) correctly orientated? 3 port port A = CH 2 port room stat > CH M/valve

Correct the orientation

Is M/valve brown or white lead live when fault occurs?

Disconnect M/valve and check operation OK?

Replace/repair M/valve and retest

Disconnect lead from prog CH on terminal. Is prog CH on terminal live when fault occurs?

Replace prog and retest

Is frost stat fitted and keeping system on

Correct frost stat setting/location and retest

Wiring fault

Figure 8.10 Heating on when not wanted.

Even though it is possible to track down a fault using the charts on the previous pages, it may not be a good idea to attempt the repairs yourself. However, the diagnosis of a fault is very often the expensive part when calling on heating engineers, so you may well have saved the bulk of the fee. Using professionals for jobs such as this will save you money in the end.

For more in-depth advice regarding central heating and boiler faults which can be diagnosed, if not repaired, by the DIY enthusiast, see *Master Basic Plumbing and Central Heating* or go to www.centralheatingrepair.co.uk.

Drainage

There are two types of drainage in use in the home. Foul drainage removes the waste from the toilet, bidet, bath, basins, sinks, washing machines, dishwashers and showers. Surface water drainage deals with rainfall as it collects around your property. In older houses, the surface water is often fed into the foul-water system. Foul water is never allowed to be fed into a surface-water system.

Insight

A full set of drain rods and protective clothing can be hired from local tool-hire shops.

Tip: underground pipes

All underground drainage pipes must be brown in colour to distinguish them from any other underground service pipes.

When the toilet is flushed, or water is released from basins, etc., it passes first through a 'trap', usually shaped like a P or an S on their sides. This trap is designed to hold water in the bend of the P or S. Under some basins and showers, special traps are placed which do not have these shapes, but whose internal workings are designed to fulfil the same purpose. The objective of these traps is to stop foul gases from the drain runs and manholes entering the home. The water sitting in the U of the trap prevents the gases from getting through.

As you can see in Figure 8.11, when the toilet is flushed, water and waste in the bowl is forced round the bend into the pipe that carries it through the wall of the property, at some point, to the main sewer. This pipe is called a soil and vent pipe (SVP). The 'vent' part of the name indicates that the pipe serves two purposes: as well as removing the waste it also carries the foul gases up to and beyond the roof, thanks to the 'trap' of water. All traps work in this way.

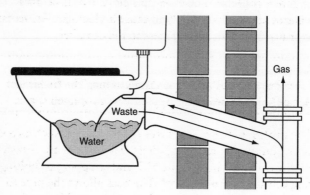

Figure 8.11 Toilet plumbing.

Why does my toilet pipe go up through the roof?

The toilet pipe or pipes in the house carry some really bad smelling stuff away for you! This smell is a gas and if this gas is allowed to build up and become pressurized in any way it is dangerous. The gas therefore needs to be allowed to escape. The main toilet pipe in your house is called a soil and vent pipe. It carries the waste away and allows the gases to escape somewhere above all the windows in your house.

Once the waste has left the property, it is taken to an inspection chamber where more pipes may join. These pipes can come from other outlets in your home, or from other houses in your area. Inspection chambers are placed wherever two or more pipes join, or where a single pipe changes direction. This is because these scenarios are the most likely to cause a blockage. An access chamber or manhole will allow access to the chamber.

Insight

We never inspect manholes and drains alone. The fumes can sometimes be overpowering, especially in a confined space.

The SVP may also 'pick up' pipes from other outlets, such as basins and showers, on its way to the manhole. These pipes are connected to the SVP by drilling a hole in the SVP and strapping or bolting on a fitting called a 'strap-on boss'. The boss allows the pipe to be inserted into a plastic collar, inside which is a rubber seal. A strap-on boss is easily fixed and a very useful fitting for the DIY enthusiast involved in fitting a new bathroom or shower.

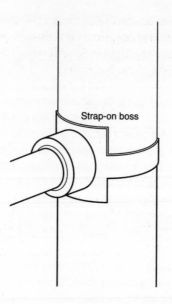

Figure 8.12 A strap-on boss.

Insight

Sometimes connections can be very difficult. In these cases we use a flexible pan connector which gives us many more options.

When fitting a new toilet, the chances of the new outlet pipe matching up with the position of the SVP connection are small. DIY stores, plumbers' merchants and builders' merchants sell a variety of adapters specifically for this problem. These adapters are called pan connectors.

The SVP, or some of it, can sometimes be indoors, usually boxed in. In certain circumstances (you should check this with the Building Control Officer of your local council) it is permissible to place an air admittance valve on top of an internal SVP (see Figure 8.13). This saves the expense of taking the pipe up to roof level to vent it. An air admittance valve allows air from the room to be 'sucked' into the pipe but does not allow the foul air to escape.

There are restrictions on the use of these valves, so please check. If you are allowed to use one, the valve must be positioned at a height which is above the highest flood level of the room. In most cases this is the height of the basin rim.

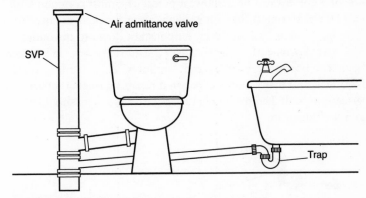

Figure 8.13 Toilet system including an air admittance valve.

SURFACE WATER DRAINAGE AND GUTTERS

Rainwater lands on your roof and runs down into your gutters. From your gutters it is directed to the surface water drainage pipes in your garden. From these, via manholes and access chambers, it is sent to the main 'storm' drain network of the town.

Some properties do not have a surface water drainage system. The rainwater in these cases is taken to a large drainage pit in the garden, called a soakaway (see Chapter 4 and Project 8).

Insight

When digging a soakaway, think about creating a hill or mound feature in your garden with the excavated soil. It is much cheaper than paying for it to be carted away.

The surface water drainage system operates in much the same way as the foul drainage, with manholes at junctions and changes of direction. The guttering system around your house is much more likely to concern you, and the names of the various parts of a gutter are shown in Figure 8.14.

Water will always find the lowest point to drain to, so the outlet pipe of a gutter must be the lowest point. The most common fault with DIY guttering is that not enough gutter brackets are used to keep the slope or 'fall' of the gutter constant down to the outlet pipe. The shortage of brackets causes the gutter to bow in between them. The bow collects water and overflows. This overflow looks like a leak and many hours are wasted repairing joints that are perfectly sound! The spacing between gutter brackets should be no more than 1 m.

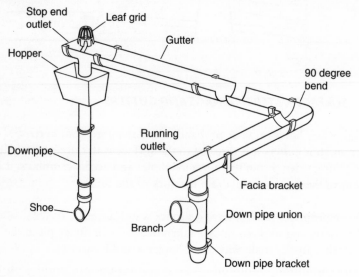

Figure 8.14 The parts of a gutter.

Insight
We always have somebody at the bottom of the ladder when cleaning gutters. If you lean too far, the ladder WILL move!

Gutters should be cleaned regularly, especially if there are trees nearby. Clogged gutters can lead to wet walls, which in turn can lead to damp and mould. A leaf grid in the top of the gutter's downpipe will help keep leaves in the gutter where they are easier to clean out, rather than let them block the downpipes or gulleys.

The surface water not collected by the gutters should drain away harmlessly on your land. If it does not, see Project 7.

For more in-depth advice regarding domestic plumbing and drainage, see *Master Basic Plumbing and Central Heating*.

10 THINGS TO REMEMBER

1 *Research and plan your intended project carefully.*

2 *Keep a supply of tap washers handy.*

3 *Keep clear access to your mains stopcock and turn it on and off periodically to keep it free.*

4 *Insulate your loft tanks and pipes.*

5 *Draw a plan of your water and heating system to understand how it works.*

6 *Check overflows regularly.*

7 *Do not cover access chambers, access pipes or manholes.*

8 *Clean gutters and downpipes regularly.*

9 *All connections to existing drains need building regulation approval.*

10 *Toilet gases can be dangerous, so make sure there is adequate ventilation.*

9

Plastering, plasterboard and partition walls

In this chapter you will learn:
- *about the different types of plaster*
- *how to mix plaster*
- *about the different types of plasterboard*
- *how to use plasterboard to make partition walls.*

Plastering

If you were building an extension, you would now have a waterproof 'shell' and would have completed the first fix and would be ready to plaster. Plastering is a difficult skill to learn and impossible to teach in a book. The basics can be described, but getting the wall level, flat and smooth is done by 'feel', rather than technique. The technique is important, of course, and that is outlined here, but this is another of those jobs where practice is invaluable. Do not expect to do a perfect job the first time you attempt plastering.

Insight

Wear gloves when working with plaster. As with cement, the lime can cause a lot of skin damage.

How can I remove Artex?

Artex is a very common application, especially on ceilings, but should you want a smooth wall or ceiling it is not hard to remove the Artex. Trying to remove it with sanders and scrapers will create a mess. The only safe and relatively non-messy way to remove it is to use a special textured-coating remover. The best of these are NOT solvent-based so there is no horrid smell. Please be mindful that Artex applied pre-1970 may contain asbestos, so only use the method suggested here.

DIFFERENT TYPES OF PLASTER

The plasters described below are all made by British Gypsum and belong to the Thistle range. They are the plasters a plasterer will use and are also suitable for the DIY enthusiast. There is nothing wrong with stores' own-brand plasters, but Thistle plasters are no more expensive and are the best.

Bonding

Bonding is an undercoat plaster. This means it is the first coat to be applied to a new (or to be patched) wall. When it is smoothed over with a trowel, it is scratched with a nail to give a 'key' for the topcoat or finish plaster to adhere to. Bonding plaster has incredible 'stickability' and does not rely on an absorbent surface to bond to. Bonding can be applied to really dense concrete blocks or engineering bricks and even to concrete itself. These surfaces are where you would use bonding plaster as a scratch coat.

Bonding plaster does not need the wall underneath to be scratched or have a mechanical 'key', and bonding agents, such as latex SBR adhesive, are usually applied to the wall before the bonding plaster. In short, bonding plaster will stick to all types of masonry and stone as long as the surface is clean.

Browning

Browning plaster is also an undercoat plaster, for use on more absorbent surfaces. Browning plaster works much better on surfaces with a mechanical key and you will often see bricklayers 'raking out' the joints of block and brick walls which are to have a browning plaster covering.

Hardwall

Hardwall is similar to browning except that it offers a higher impact resistance and quicker drying surface. It is the undercoat plaster used most often these days, and can be applied to most masonry surfaces.

Tough coat

Even tougher than hardwall as an undercoat plaster, this has a greater coverage based on the nominal depth of 11 mm. Again, it is suitable for most masonry walls.

Dri-Coat

Dri-Coat plaster is a cement-based plaster used when resurfacing a wall after installation of a new DPC.

Multifinish

Thistle multifinish is a topcoat plaster which is suitable for a great finish on all the other surfaces. Multifinish is ideal for (indeed, is manufactured for) using as a finishing plaster when there are a variety of backing surfaces to be covered.

Board finish

Board finish plaster is used on surfaces with low–medium suction. Plasterboard and Dri-Coat plaster will accept board finish well.

One-coat

Sometimes called patching plaster, this plaster is a mix of something like bonding plaster and multifinish. It is designed to fill patches in one go and can be 'laid on' to far greater thicknesses than normal undercoat plasters – anything up to 50 mm some manufacturers claim – but it is not advisable to lay on at any more than 25 mm. Once on the wall, this plaster can be trowelled up to a very smooth finish and no further application is required. In our experience it is not possible to get as good a finish with one-coat as with two-coat plaster work.

MIXING PLASTER

Mixing plaster for the first time is a process of trial and error. Plasterers use different consistencies of plaster for different jobs, and being a plasterer's labourer is the hardest job in the world! The important thing to remember is to add the plaster to the water, not the water to the plaster.

Basecoat plaster

> **Insight**
> Wear a hat when plastering! Even us pros make a mess and getting solid plaster out of hair is no fun.

Mixing basecoat plaster is considerably easier than topcoat or finish plaster. To mix basecoat, you need a large container. Nowadays it is not uncommon to see basecoat being mixed in a cement mixer. The plaster should be mixed well and there should be no lumps in it at all. The consistency is up to you – experiment by mixing separate piles to see how you like it. It is worth the additional cost of a bag of plaster to do the job properly. You are looking for a muddy consistency – the kind of mud that is so soft you slide through it as you walk, but when you pick your feet up there is lots of it stuck to your boots!

Finish plaster

Finish plaster is mixed in a bucket (a two-gallon builders' bucket is ideal for novices) with (ideally) a variable-speed electric drill and a 'paddle'. Paddles can be bought at all DIY stores.

Clean cold water should be put in the bucket first, to about one-third of the depth. The finishing plaster is then tipped in gently, until the heap rises above the surface of the water. The paddle, on a low speed, should then be placed in the bucket and moved up and down and side to side, to mix the plaster. You may have to add more plaster to get a consistency of thick porridge.

Always have another bucket of water close by to clean off your tools immediately, including the paddle. If you mix a new batch of plaster and there is still some of the old plaster on any of the tools, it will go hard much quicker. The mixing bucket should be cleaned thoroughly.

Tip: small tools

There is a great variety of small tools to get into various nooks and crannies around the house, and all are available from good tool stores.

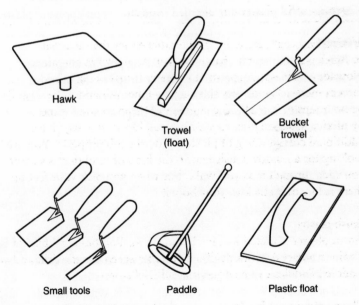

Hawk

Trowel
(float)

Bucket
trowel

Small tools

Paddle

Plastic float

Figure 9.1 Tools needed for mixing and applying plaster.

Read Project 16 on screeding a floor. For novice plasterers, the same technique can be used to divide the wall into manageable sections to plaster. Builders' merchants can supply you with 10 mm plaster stop beads, which you simply fix to the wall. The beads can be fixed by placing a few small dabs of plaster on the wall and pushing the bead into it. After a few minutes the plaster will grip the bead.

If you have any external corners to negotiate, external 'angle beads' can be fixed in position to make these easier for you. Stop beads can also be bought at 3 mm thick for application and division of the finish coat. Ideally the two coats of plaster should measure 13 mm thick in total, and if the wall is the correct, consistent thickness it will dry out uniformly, with no cracks.

See Projects 18 and 19 for detailed instructions on applying plaster.

Insight

We use an inflatable children's paddling pool to keep water in for cleaning tools, etc. The plaster drops to the bottom. As the air is let out the clean water flows over the sides and we can pick the whole thing up and dispose of the waste elsewhere.

How long must I wait before I can paint new plaster?

When a wall or ceiling is plastered, the wall will remain damp for some time. There is no definitive answer to this question as all walls and ceilings will dry out at different speeds. With a normal centrally heated house you can be pretty sure of safely painting after four weeks, but it can take as long as six weeks and with extra heat in the room it may be ready in three.

The reason for not painting before the wall is completely dry is that most paints will simply form an airtight skin over the wall. The moisture from the new plaster is then trapped behind this skin and cannot evaporate off. The damp then retreats back into the wall where it either develops mould growth or reacts with the salts in the wall to become efflorescence. Either way you have a problem on your hands that is incredibly difficult to deal with.

See Project 38 for painting and papering new plaster.

Plasterboard and partition walls

Building a partition or non-load-bearing wall is great way of dividing space. The easiest way to build a partition wall is to make a timber frame and attach plasterboard to it.

WORKING WITH PLASTERBOARD

Insight

Never stand a piece of plasterboard on its corner. It will collapse in an instant.

There are two thicknesses of plasterboard, 9.5 mm and 12.5 mm. If using 12.5 mm, the studs, or main timbers in the frame, must be placed no further apart than 600 mm; if using 9.5 mm, the studs must be placed no further apart than 400 mm. These two distances will allow you to move the studs very slightly, so that a piece of plasterboard (usually 1.22 m wide) can be fitted into the centre of a stud if a join is necessary. The timbers used can be either 100 mm × 50 mm or 75 mm × 50 mm. This is a personal choice and largely based on the space you have. Using 100 mm timbers with 12.5 mm plasterboard and 3 mm of skim plaster, the final thickness of the wall is 131 mm (a little over 5 inches). Sawn timber can be used – there is no need to use prepared timber.

If you are adding a partition wall to divide one room into two, you will need to put in a doorway. Internal timber doorframes, or liners as they are known, are the easiest way to create such an opening and can be bought in kit form from builders' merchants. They are available at 105 mm (4½ inches) or 131 mm (5½ inches) deep. The liners can be assembled to fit standard door widths of 2 ft 3 in and 2 ft 6 in.

See Project 20 for detailed instructions on building a partition wall.

Tips for installing plasterboard:

▶ *Plasterboard should be joined on a stud or the smaller horizontal timbers in the frame (noggins), preferably using drywall screws rather than nails.*
▶ *Use a battery-operated screwdriver to fix the screws at no more than 400 mm centrally in both horizontal and vertical planes.*
▶ *Cables for switches and sockets can be 'built in' to the wall void by drilling the correct sized hole through the studs and noggins. Special plasterboard switch and socket boxes can be used. These clip to the plasterboard and do not need to be fixed to a stud or noggin (see Figure 9.2).*
▶ *Insulation can also be packed into the void to a) keep heat in a room and b) dull any sound. This is particularly useful if you are partitioning off for a bathroom. Insulation must not be placed around cables.*

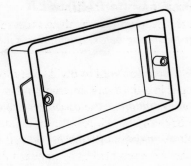

Figure 9.2 Plasterboard switch and socket box.

See Project 21 on repairing plasterboard.

10 THINGS TO REMEMBER

1 Practise your plastering before attempting a job indoors.

2 Wear gloves when handling plaster.

3 Older Artex may contain asbestos. Strip carefully.

4 Use only the recommended plaster for the job in hand.

5 Always add the plaster to the water, not water to the plaster.

6 Basecoat plaster can be mixed in a cement mixer for larger jobs.

7 Divide large areas into sections until you are confident.

8 Do not place insulation around cables in partition walls.

9 Screw plasterboard to timber whenever possible rather than nail it.

10 Allow adequate time for new plaster to dry before painting it.

Part two
Projects

Basics

1 Mixing concrete

INTRODUCTION

Concrete is a mixture of cement, sand (fine aggregate), small stone or gravel (coarse aggregate) and water. It has many applications, from fence posts to motorway bases and, because of this, there are many different ratios to which the constituents can be mixed.

Insight

As with mortar and plaster, wear gloves when mixing concrete. Eye protection is a good idea when mixing as splashes from the mixer can sting a great deal.

This project will concentrate on a general-purpose mix suitable for DIY projects such as garden paths, fence posts and shallow retaining wall foundations. It is a medium-strength mix and is known as a C20 mix. This means it will attain a strength equivalent to withstanding a compression of 20 Newtons per square millimetre after 28 days. This mix is not suitable for house foundations.

AGGREGATE

You can buy bags (usually 40 kg) of ready-mixed aggregate. In most areas of the country, this mix of aggregates (sharp grit sand and small stones or gravel) is called 'ballast'; in the West Country it is most often called '½ inch/10 mm to dust'. This describes the sieved state of the stone as it comes out of the quarry crushers.

Aggregate can also be bought loose (delivered by lorry). This is generally cheaper and, if you have the room to have it delivered, it makes working a little easier as you do not have to open all the bags.

CEMENT

Cement can be bought (usually in 25 kg bags, although some stores still sell 50 kg bags) from all builders' merchants and, more expensively, from DIY stores. It is crushed limestone, blended with other raw materials (sometimes shale and/or sand), ground into a powder and then heated in a kiln. This process produces a cement clinker, which is mixed with gypsum and ground further to produce the cement.

A cement mixer can be hired from all tool-hire shops but if you need to mix a large quantity of cement, it often pays to buy your own. You can always sell it after completion of your project, which is what most self builders do.

WATER

Water is a very important part of the mix and the volume of water used can dictate the strength of the finished mix. On site, or in ready-mixed concrete yards, a 'slump test' is used to test the water content of the concrete. A cone made of steel is used for this test. The cone is 300 mm high, with a top opening of 100 mm diameter and a bottom opening of 200 mm diameter. The mixed concrete is placed into the cone through the top, a bar is used to compact the concrete and remove air pockets within the cone. The cone is then lifted clear. By placing the metal cone next to the newly formed concrete cone, then laying the bar on top of the metal cone, it is possible to measure how far the concrete 'slumps'. A slump of approx 50 mm is acceptable for C20 concrete.

QUANTITIES

The quantities of aggregate, cement and water you need will depend on the total amount of concrete you need for your project, but it is the proportions of the ingredients that is most important.

The proportions of materials for a C20P (P = Portland cement) mix are:

1 *1 × cement, 2 × fine aggregate (sand) and 4 × coarse aggregate*
2 *if you are using a pre-mixed ballast, then 6 of these are mixed with 1 cement*
3 *in an ideal world, where everything is delivered dry, then a water-to-cement ratio of approximately 0.55 should be used, e.g. if you require 25 kg of cement in your mix, then 25 × 0.55 = 13.75 kg (litres) of water. This is the maximum amount of water that should be used. Most of the time, however, the sand etc. is damp, or even wringing wet, and care has to be taken to ensure that your mix does not become too sloppy. It should be able to support itself, almost fully, in a heap on the shovel.*

When mixing a very strong mix, normally labelled C35P, the mix is: 1 × cement, 1 × stone and 2 × sand; or 1 × cement to 3 × ready-mixed aggregate.

Insight

If mixing any more than 3 cubic metres of concrete get a price from your local ready-mix supplier. It may seem expensive but consider the many hours of back-breaking shovel work it will save you.

Tip

When mixing concrete you will find that, while the ballast will heap up nicely on your shovel, the cement will slide off. This will give you incorrect proportions when mixing, so it is better to measure your quantities using a bucket to ensure correct proportions. Mixing by hand is a bad idea unless you only have a tiny amount to do. Only very rarely will you be able to get the cement evenly distributed throughout the mix and this leads to weak concrete.

You will need:

- ▶ *the correct quantity of ready-mixed aggregate (available from most builders' merchants)*
- ▶ *the correct quantity of cement*
- ▶ *the correct volume of water*
- ▶ *a cement mixer*
- ▶ *a shovel*
- ▶ *a bucket.*

To mix the concrete:

1 *To ensure a well-mixed batch, add your ingredients to the mixer in the following order: 75 per cent of the water followed by 50 per cent of the aggregates.*
2 *Add all of the cement and then the rest of the aggregates and the remainder of the water.*
3 *Don't forget to clean all your tools thoroughly, as it will not take long for the concrete to go hard, making cleaning much more difficult.*

2 Laying bricks and blocks

Insight

We always lay out the first course 'dry' before laying any bricks or blocks. This way we can see immediately if our planned construction will fit and bond properly.

It is up to you which bond you choose to build your wall with, but whichever you choose it's a good idea to practise your brickwork before you start a major project.

Many of the frequently used brickwork bonds can be seen in Chapter 5; this project relates to the technique of actually laying bricks. The same technique is employed whatever you are laying.

You will need:

▶ *a wooden batten the length of the proposed height of the wall*
▶ *mortar mix*
▶ *a board for placing a couple of shovels-full of mortar on (commonly called a spotboard)*
▶ *a trowel*
▶ *a spirit level*
▶ *a boat level.*

What to do:

1 *To make sure your wall finishes at the right height, get a timber batten the same length as the proposed height of the wall. Using the measurements of the bricks and blocks you intend to use, mark the proposed courses on to the batten, working from the bottom up. See where the last mark comes to on the batten and measure from there to the end of the batten. Whatever is left over can be 'made up' by slightly increasing the depth of the mortar in each bed joint (although these should be no more than 15 mm) or, if it is easier to add another full course, the bed joints can be made a little shallower (but ideally no less than 6 mm deep).*

2 *To begin laying, place some of your mortar mix on a spotboard close to the wall. Use your trowel to roll some of the mortar from the top of the pile downwards until it forms a sausage at the bottom. Slide the trowel under the sausage and then let it slide off again into position on the foundation for the first course of bricks.*

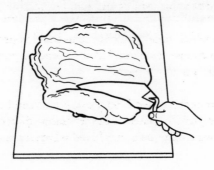

3 Use the point of your trowel to form a V in the mortar bed.
   This V allows for displacement of mortar as you push the
   brick down. (The same principle can be applied to many jobs,
   e.g. ceramic tiling.)

4 Place your bricks carefully but firmly onto the bed. Push down
   with a slight twisting movement, leaving a bed of 10 mm
   under the brick. Place the spirit level at the back (or front) of
   the bricks to check that they are being laid in a straight line.
5 Make sure you fill the joints between the bricks.

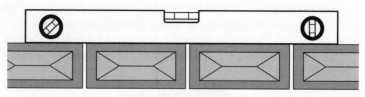

View from above

6 *Lay the bricks to stretcher bond (see Chapter 5) and, once you have built two or three courses, put your spirit level on the brick course to check that it is level and then stand it vertically against the ends of the wall to check that it is perfectly upright.*

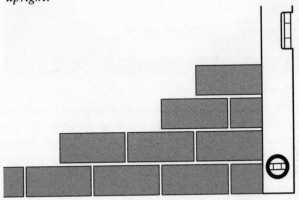

7 *Do this for each subsequent course, at the front and at both ends (see the boat level in the picture below).*

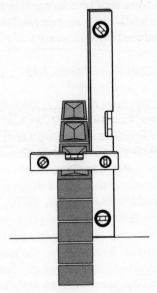

8 Lay the first course throughout the length of the wall, with the ends built up to about five courses (see the diagram below). These ends then become known as corners.

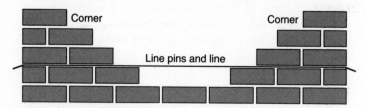

9 When the corners are up, use them as a template for the rest of the wall by stretching a string line between them, using bricklayers' lines and line pins (which can be bought from all DIY stores). Push the pins into the mortar joints and stretch the string between them.

10 Lay the bricks so the top edge of each one is touching the line. If your corners have been built properly, the rest is easy.

Tip

Do not use a line for a wall that is over 6 m long as it will sag in the middle. For walls this long you need to build another 'corner' in the centre of the wall.

OTHER BRICK AND BLOCK LAYING TIPS

▶ If the last brick you have laid is not level, do not bash it with a trowel or hammer, as doing so may knock several others out of position. However robust a brick wall appears to be, while the mortar is wet the bricks or blocks can move all over the place if not handled properly. This is especially true of heavy blocks.

▶ If your bed of mortar is the correct depth and the mix is pliable enough, you should be able to place the bricks down gently and, with a gentle twisting motion, get them into the correct, level position. Now and again a gentle tap is required with the handle of a trowel (making sure you heed the warnings in Chapter 5 regarding trowel tapping!), but after this tap a bricklayer will always stand back to make sure nothing else has moved. If time and care are taken over the first few courses, *the rest become easier. If the first few courses are uneven in any way, it becomes very difficult to achieve a satisfactory finish.*

Insight

Keep your trowel and level spotlessly clean. A dirty trowel will not allow mortar to slide off easily and a dirty level will soon start giving inaccurate readings.

▶ *As you build the wall, check not only the line, level and how upright the wall is, but also check the level across the width of the wall. Bricks and blocks can be level along their length, and can be upright both from the front and from the side, but can still look imperfect when you stand back to check them (see the diagram below). This is always because the wall is not level across its width. The bricks can tilt one way and then the other, but at least one part of the brick is touching the spirit level when it is laid lengthways, so the wall appears to be correct. It takes time and experience to become proficient enough to avoid this problem, but until then using a spirit level, in all directions, is the best way to ensure a good finish to your wall. The result of not doing this may look a little exaggerated in the diagram but, if you try it yourself, you will see it is not!*

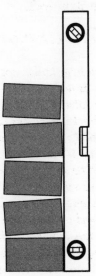

3 Mixing sand and cement mortar

You will need:

▶ *sand*
▶ *cement and/or lime*
▶ *water*
▶ *a shovel or trowel for mixing.*

To mix the mortar:

1 *First, place the required quantity of sand in a heap and hollow the heap out a little.*
2 *Tip in the cement and/or lime required. Mix these together thoroughly.*

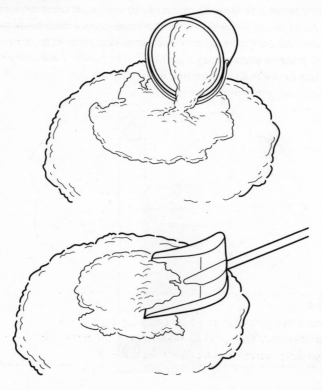

3 *Then hollow the heap out again and add water.*

4 *Start putting the mixed sand and cement into the water from around the edges of the heap and mixing from the middle out to the edges. If you want to use any additives in your mix, e.g. frost protector, they should be mixed with the water first (read the instructions on the tub).*

Insight

Quite often you will see us pros mixing mortar in a wheelbarrow. This gives us sides to keep the place tidy and stops dirty water running down the drive.

4 Matching mortar colours

If you can track down the type of sand used in the mortar you are trying to match (see Chapter 5), all that remains is to match the cement content. You will need to make up several mixes to get this right.

You will need:

▶ *a small cup or other receptacle*
▶ *a way of measuring the sand accurately.*

To mix the mortar:

1 *Start with a mix of 3 sand to 1 cement.*
2 *Then move on to 3½ to 1, 4 to 1, 4½ to 1 and so on.*
3 *Do not go past 6 to 1 or the mix will be too weak for ordinary brickwork.*
4 *Wait until your mini mixes have dried and use the mix closest to the colour of that in your wall.*

Some mortars are artificially coloured with a cement dye. This makes the permutations endless. It is important to mix the dye into the cement before you add the water. Dyes are available in a variety of colours from all builders' merchants.

We suggest you make up a table, similar to the one opposite, to keep track of the different mixes.

Mix number	Sand type	Sand amount	Cement amount	Dye added?
1	Soft yellow	3	3	Y
2				
3				
4				
5				

5 Pointing and jointing brickwork

POINTING

Pointing and repointing brickwork and stonework can be a very time-consuming job and, although it may look easy, it takes a bit of experience to get a professional finish. The basic process is outlined here.

You will need:

▶ *a plugging chisel or small bolster chisel*
▶ *a screwdriver or similar*
▶ *a plasterer's 'hawk'*
▶ *a pointing trowel.*

To point the brickwork:

1 *First, cut out all loose and damaged mortar. If you find that some of the faces of the bricks have been damaged as a result of water getting into the joints, you may want to replace them (see Project 6).*
2 *Use a plugging chisel or small bolster to do the cutting out. Simply rake out very loose stuff with a screwdriver or similar.*
3 *Mix (and match, if necessary) the mortar (see Projects 3 and 4).*
4 *Place a small amount of mortar on a plasterer's 'hawk', as shown on the next page.*

5 *Push the new mortar into the brickwork joints firmly, using a pointing trowel.*

Tip

If the wall is quite dry when you repoint, the moisture will be sucked out of the new mortar quite quickly by the existing, porous mortar. To counteract this you can simply damp down the wall with a bucket of water and a brush. Do not saturate it; watch to see it change colour from light to dark without dripping.

JOINTING

Insight

Quite often there are very awkward places to get mortar into with a pointing trowel. If you look carefully you may see the odd pro pushing mortar in with his fingers. Be sure to wear your gloves if you do this.

Pointing and jointing brickwork have these days come to mean the same thing. It used to be, however, that jointing a wall meant applying the desired finish to the joints of the wall as one built it. Pointing was used to describe the operation of filling joints after they had either fallen out or been 'raked' out to change the texture, colour or mix of a bed joint or 'perp' (perpendicular, or vertical joint). There are four main types of joint, with variations on each one:

1 *The bucket-handle joint is so called because it is the shape of a metal bucket handle. It is formed by running a bricklayer's jointing iron or a piece of hosepipe over the joint when it has just started to go hard.*

2 *The flush or bagged joint is formed by cutting off the mortar flush with the face of the wall. In some cases this is rubbed over with a piece of cement bag or soft brush to close, or fill up, any tiny holes in the surface of the joint.*

3 *The weather-struck joint can be struck once (a pointing trowel is pushed into the face of the joint at an angle) as shown below. A joint which is struck twice is pointed to the shape of a horizontal V.*

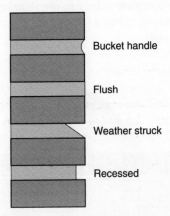

Bucket handle

Flush

Weather struck

Recessed

4 *A recessed joint is used when the builder (or architect) particularly wants to show off the shape of the brick being used.*

6 Replacing a damaged brick or ceramic tile

This project, although it shows a brick being replaced, can also be used to replace a cracked ceramic tile. When applying the principle to tiles, however, it is important to take the drill off the hammer setting.

For a variety of reasons, bricks can be damaged, marked or stained. You may simply have had a hanging basket fixed to a brick with a hook in a wall plug and are now left with a messy hole.

You will need:

▶ *a power drill*
▶ *a 6 mm or 7 mm masonry bit*
▶ *a lump hammer*
▶ *a sharp cold chisel*
▶ *a jointing or plugging chisel*
▶ *a paintbrush or similar*
▶ *a little sand and cement mixed to the required strength and colour (see Projects 3 and 4)*
▶ *a pointing trowel.*

To replace the brick:

1 *First, use the drill and masonry bit to drill holes in the joint surrounding the brick and in the brick itself. The more holes the better.*

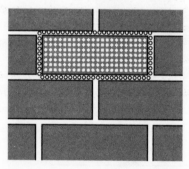

2 *Next, using the cold chisel, even a bolster chisel, chop out the brick. The drilling will have made this considerably easier and if you have drilled all the way into the brick, about 100 mm, you should have no trouble removing all of it.*
3 *For fiddly corners and sections of the mortar bed, which always seem to want to stay there, use a jointing or plugging*

chisel. These are really sharp and the acute angle of the blade allows you to get right to where you need to be.

4 Having removed the brick, sweep out the hole with a paintbrush or similar.

5 Place a bed of your sand and cement mix on the floor of the hole and make sure it is a little thicker than the bed joint you removed.

6 Now, if you can, use the pointing trowel to get some of the mixture to stick to either side of the hole. If not, don't worry – it can be forced in later.

7 Now spread some of the mixture on the top of the new brick and pat it down a little to help it adhere to the surface.

Insight

If there is more than one brick to replace we always ask ourselves (and the customer) if the wall might look better with some different bricks inserted as features or patterns.

8 Push the brick into the opening by sitting it on the pointing trowel and gently lowering it onto the bed of mortar. Some mortar will squash out, so cut this off with the trowel.

9 Wiggle the brick about so it sits level in the opening and the joints line up with the existing joints.

10 Use the pointing trowel to push in more mortar where you can see any voids.

11 Finally, point up the new joints to match the existing shape, using a brick jointer (see Project 5).

10 THINGS TO REMEMBER FROM PROJECTS 1–6

1 Check to see if any permissions are required to complete your project.

2 Allow plenty of time for projects and always have an alternative plan for bad weather.

3 Prepare an area to mix concrete and mortar in including facilities for cleaning mixers and tools.

4 Wash off any mortar and concrete splashes immediately as lime can irritate.

5 Damp existing masonry surfaces down before applying new concrete or mortar.

6 Do not rush pointing or repointing jobs. Done properly they can make old work look brand new.

7 Hire tools you do not have, e.g. cement mixers.

8 Cement dyes can be mixed with each other as well as the mortar to achieve the correct colour.

9 Never bang a brick or block down to level it. This will always affect those around it.

10 Use a string line and a spirit level in combination wherever possible. This will always give you the best job.

Outside

7 Installing land drainage

INTRODUCTION

Perforated plastic drainage pipe (80 mm) can now be bought from many garden centres and all builders' merchants in 25 m rolls. This type of pipe is easily laid in small trenches and surrounded by shingle (small stones), which will allow water through but will filter out silt. The pipe can be joined using a waterproof repair tape also available from builders' merchants.

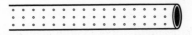

Land drain pipe can also be bought in clay sections, but the introduction of plastic has made their use, for domestic application, virtually obsolete. Pipe can also be bought which only has holes half way round. This, for drainage purposes, is laid with the holes uppermost to allow water in from the surface and then to allow it to be carried away completely. However, the use of this type of pipe is not advised in a British garden as it can dry out the ground too much (see the tip on page 182) – a fully perforated pipe will allow a more even distribution of the water from wetter to drier parts on its journey to the outlet.

It is also possible to wrap the pipe in what is commonly called 'weed fabric', or Geo Textile fabric to give it its proper name, which is a polypropylene mat used to suppress weeds and control soil erosion while allowing the controlled passage of water and air. This should stop any silt getting into the pipe or, if it is used to line the trench itself, will stop any silt getting into the trench. This gives the land drain a much longer life as silt can build up in a matter of weeks and clog all of the voids that are vital to proper drainage. The Geo Textile fabric will also stop, or at least dissuade, any local roots seeking out a greater water source. A root system can clog or even break a land drain system quite easily. Land drains and French drains can also be used to direct water to a part of your garden which needs more water than others. This is particularly useful for gardeners.

> **Tip**
>
> A word of warning is required here. Land drains and French drains are there to remove water from areas of your garden. When laid properly, they will continue to do this in drier spells and can cause parts of the garden, especially in prolonged dry spells, to scorch. You may notice that the lines of the land drain stay greener and more lush for longer, as this is where the water is!

LAYING LAND DRAINS

You will need:

▶ *the appropriate length of plastic drainage pipe*
▶ *a bag of sand*
▶ *weed fabric*
▶ *shingle (small stones) – clean stones with an average diameter of 20 mm.*

> **Tip**
>
> ▶ *To ensure that all applicable parts of your garden are drained, the most effective method of laying land drains is in a herring-bone pattern.*

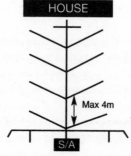

▸ *The pipes should be laid so that no point in the garden is more than 2 m away from a pipe. The maximum distance between pipes is therefore 4 m.*

▸ *The centre line, or spine, of the drain takes the water to the soakaway and all of the other lines, or ribs, feed into the spine.*

Insight

Many people place a pond at the lowest point of the garden to collect all the water. You must remember that, great idea though this is, it does not get rid of any water, only collects it.

To lay the drains:

1 *Measure out the distances between your pipes, then sprinkle sand where you want to insert each line of pipe. This will show clearly the layout of the drainage system before you start excavating the trenches.*

2 *Excavate the trenches, ensuring that any turf is cut carefully and stored to be relaid later.*

3 *Dig the trenches to three times the width of the pipe and to the required gentle fall to get the water to the soakaway or outlet. There is a certain amount of flexibility in so much as the pipe level can be adjusted by some of the bedding.*

4 *Line the trench with weed fabric and then lay the pipe in the centre.*

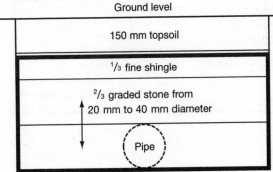

Ground level

150 mm topsoil

$^1/_3$ fine shingle

$^2/_3$ graded stone from
20 mm to 40 mm diameter

Pipe

Weed fabric lining if required

5 Surround the pipe with small stones (shingle), available from builders' merchants and garden centres.

6 When the pipe is surrounded by an equal thickness of stone – i.e. there should be a top covering of stone equal to, or greater than, the side covering – fold the weed fabric over the top.

7 Replace at least 150 mm of topsoil on which to lay your turf.

8 Relay the turf and then roll the area to assist with regrowth.

LAYING FRENCH DRAINS

A French drain is simply a land drain without the pipe, although this terminology is becoming somewhat confused these days, with many people referring to land drains as French drains. It is a cheaper method of achieving land drainage, which is historically used to remove surface water from the perimeter of a house or patio.

A French drain is excavated in the same way as a land drain, filled with stone in the same way and backfilled in the same way. The construction only differs in so much as it is much more important, with a French drain, to excavate the bottom of the trench to the exact slope required all the way to the outlet.

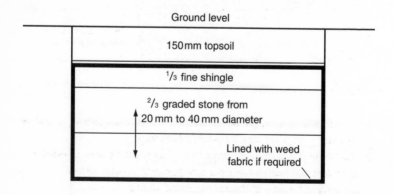

8 Building a soakaway

INTRODUCTION

Land drains and French drains are usually drained to a central point, and this is usually a soakaway. A soakaway is simply a hole in the ground filled with rubble and coarse stone with a drainage pipe laid to it removing surface (rain) water from other areas. The soil in which the soakaway is placed must be granular, with good drainage properties. It is pointless sinking a soakaway in clay unless there is a more porous layer underneath. The pipes flowing into it for land and French drains will usually be 100 mm in diameter, but for surface water (roof, gutter and driveway or patio water) the pipes are usually of a smaller diameter.

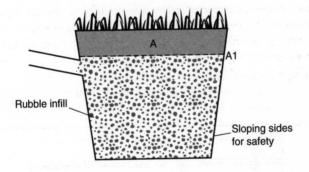

Soakaway requirements:

1 *Local authority regulations stipulate that a soakaway must be at least 5 m from any habitable building.*
2 *The pipe flowing to it should be of at least 75 mm diameter, which is the minimum pipe size for any surface water drainage; 80 mm is the recommended size.*
3 *This pipe should be laid to a fall of 1 in 100, which means for every 1 m of pipe length the slope should fall about 10 mm (1 cm). However gradual the slope, water will find its way down it.*

4 *The size of the soakaway should be a minimum of 1 m², with a depth of 1 m below the bottom of the incoming pipe.*

5 *The stone infill should surround the pipe and finish approximately 100 mm above it.*

Tip

As the soakaway needs to be 1 m deep below the bottom of the incoming land drain, it makes sense to measure the distance of the land drain you intend to lay (if you are building your soakaway first) and work out, using the fall of 1:100, how deep the bottom of the pipe will be when it gets to the soakaway.

For example, if your soakaway is to be placed at the bottom of the garden and your garden is 30 m long, the pipe will be 300 mm deeper when it gets to the soakaway. If the pipe starts in a trench 300 mm deep, the bottom of the pipe will be 600 mm below the ground when it gets to the soakaway. This means, in total, your soakaway is 1,600 mm or 1.6 m deep.

You will need:

▶ *rubble and/or stone infill (it is important that the stones are large enough to allow the free passage of water filtering through them)*
▶ *impervious material (such as thick polythene, tarpaulin or even a bed of concrete) to go over the infill*
▶ *ideally some weed fabric.*

To build the soakaway:

1 *Dig the hole for the soakaway in the required spot, to the required dimensions (see above) and with sloping sides for safety. Store the best topsoil and any turf for covering the soakaway when it is complete.*

Insight

Wherever possible, and always with customer approval, we double the size of the soakaway. If you have the room, we suggest you do the same.

2 *If you can afford it, line the soakaway with weed fabric.*
3 *Fill in the hole with the rubble to the level of the incoming pipe.*
4 *Cover the incoming pipe with stones, preferably pea shingle from your local builders' merchant, to approximately 100 mm above it.*
5 *Place an impervious layer over the stone (see A1 in the diagram on page 185).*
6 *Replace the topsoil over this layer to restore the garden level (see A in the diagram).*
7 *Replace the turf over the topsoil.*
8 *Waste soil can be used to make a flowerbed somewhere else in the garden.*

9 Brick and block paving

You will need:

▶ *an electric breaker if you need to remove old concrete (available to hire from a tool-hire shop)*

- ▶ scalping stone (crushed stone aggregate) or hardcore (the former is preferable)
- ▶ a vibrating plate, which can be hired from a tool-hire shop
- ▶ a supply of sharp sand (enough to cover the area to a depth of 50 mm)
- ▶ a wooden flooring float or a piece of batten
- ▶ paving bricks or blocks
- ▶ either a disk cutter (for smaller areas) or a splitter (a proprietary cutter) for a larger area, both of which can be hired from a tool-hire shop
- ▶ silver (play pit) sand
- ▶ a brush or broom for brushing the sand into the joints.

To lay the paving:

1 Set out the area to be paved and make sure the levels you are laying to will drain water away from the house (note any paving near the house should be at least 150 mm below the DPC).
2 Remove any surplus soil or concrete, which could affect the levels. Concrete can be removed using an electric breaker.
3 Construct sub-base using scalping stone or very well-compacted hardcore. Scalping stone can be bought from builders' merchants and is ideal for bases of this kind. It is very much easier to work with than hardcore and should be laid to a bed of between 100 mm and 150 mm.
4 Compact the scalping stone using a vibrating plate.
5 Then place a layer of sharp sand over the scalpings. This layer should be 50 mm deep.

Tip

If you have an instance where a section of the existing path or area is not square, you can avoid cutting the bricks or blocks by matching some concrete to the brick or block colour (see Project 4). The concrete can be dyed and placed in a way which will allow the bricks or blocks to start off square to the sides.

6 *Once the sand is in, vibrate it before laying the paving bricks. Lumps can form in the sand and these can go unnoticed until you compact the pathway. Then the lumps may burst and a brick or two may immediately drop into the void created.*

7 *Once compacted, level out the sand using a wooden flooring float or a piece of batten. Make sure you have a completely flat sand base.*

8 *Once the sand is laid, the bricks can be laid across it. Make sure you press them up together as closely as possible and bed them down gently in the sand.*

9 *As with a brick wall, the bricks should be laid so that the joints overlap. This will leave gaps at the ends of each row. Bricks can then be cut and placed into the gaps. The best way to make the cuts, if there is only a small number to do, is with a disk cutter. Larger areas require more cuts and it is easier to cut these with a proprietary cutter, or splitter as it is called.*

10 *Do not attempt to rush this job – each brick has a small spacing burr or two on each side to give a little joint between them, so make sure you lay them square and check if any brick feels like it hasn't gone down properly. On soft sand, it may be that there is a lump of gravel or something in the way, so take the brick out and check. You will be vibrating these bricks down soon so it is important they all sit on the bed properly.*

11 When the path is laid and cuts complete, cover it with silver (play pit) sand and brush the sand into all the joints. Again, don't rush this job as it is this sand that binds the whole lot together and will stop bricks moving once traffic starts to use the path or driveway.

Insight

It is better to make 100 too many passes with the compaction plate than one too few.

12 When you have brushed in as much sand as possible, run the vibrating plate over the path for ten minutes. Make sure you have covered every square inch and do not dwell in one place for too long. Do not clean all surplus sand off path before vibrating.

13 After ten minutes, tip some more silver sand over the surface and start brushing in again, then vibrate again. Continue with this until you are sure every single joint is full.

Block paving needs to be surrounded by something to give it a firm edge. The edges of any paving are the most vulnerable and you should either lay edging stones (see Project 10) or lay an edge of the paving blocks you are using. If using the same paving bricks or blocks to form the edges, they should be laid on a small foundation (see Projects 1 and 2 and Chapter 5).

10 Laying edging stones

A concrete edging stone is a mini kerb. Whereas kerbs are used for roads, edgings are used for driveways and paths. Edging stones come in all shapes and sizes for driveways, paths, garden borders and even roads. They are a good way of separating parts of your garden in a permanent way and providing a good solid edge to work to. Some just sit in soil, some on a mortar bed and some need concreting. The principle is always the same: they are used to stop the base spreading as weight is applied to it and, as such, must be laid in a strong mix of concrete.

Usually, the stone has one rounded 'bull-nosed' edge, which softens the look of the stone and also protects car tyres when used on a driveway. This project deals with straight, concrete edging stones. The image below shows edging stones used for a path.

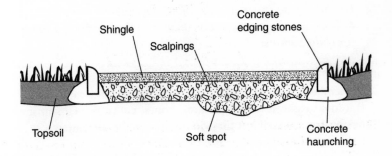

You will need:

▶ *a shovel*
▶ *some scalping stone*

▶ some concrete mixed at 6 to 1 (see Project 1)
▶ a paving mallet or a lump (or club) hammer
▶ a piece of string slightly longer than the length of the path/drive
▶ a long piece of timber to level across if using edgings on both sides
▶ pegs and a spirit level for widths too great to use a piece of timber
▶ edging stones
▶ a disk cutter, with stone-cutting disks (this can be hired from a tool-hire shop)
▶ a wooden or plastic plastering float.

To lay the edging stones:

1 First, excavate the path and dig out any soft spots and spongy areas. Fill these with scalping stone. Once the edgings are down, the finish of the path can be anything you choose – edging stones are ideal for holding in shingle or other loose coverings such as bark.
2 Lay a couple of inches (50–75 mm) of concrete along the line you would like the edgings to follow.
3 Lay an edging stone at each end of the concrete line and tap it to level, usually with a paving mallet or the handle of a lump (or club) hammer.

Insight

Remember there are no real rules to aesthetic landscaping. If it looks right, it is right. Edging stones, pathways, etc. must be constructed well but they do not have to be absolutely level and straight.

4 Attach a string line to the back edge of the stone, then run it out to the other end of the drive or path and attach it to the edging stone at that end. This second stone will probably be temporary, as it may have to be replaced by a cut stone, depending on the length of the path or drive.

5   *Remember to take into account the slope of the drive and, if using edgings on both sides, use a long piece of timber to level across. If the distance is too great, transfer the level using pegs banged into the ground and levelling across them with a spirit level.*

6   *Once the two end stones are in and the string line is in position, lay the rest of the edgings. Tap each one down into the concrete, butting one up against the next one. There is no need for a joint.*

7   *You may need to cut one or two edgings to fit the length of the drive or path, and this can be done with a disk cutter. Make sure you hire or buy stone-cutting disks as metal-cutting disks will not get through stone or concrete.*

8   *When all the edging stones are in position, place concrete at the back and front of them. Almost always the main pressure against the edging stone is from the front, so most of the concrete needs to be at the back as you will probably have a sub-base of some kind at the front.*

9   *Remember to leave enough depth for a little soil if you are reinstating turf behind the stones, and compact the concrete well using a flat piece of timber or preferably a wooden or plastic plastering float.*

10 *Angle the concrete away from the stone so water does not sit on top of the concrete.*

11 Repointing a patio

The ground moves and, in turn, patios move. The first casualty of this movement is usually the cement joints in between the patio or paving slabs.

Repointing need not be the huge dilemma a great many people have found it to be. For example, there is no need to point it as you would do a brick wall. Brickwork pointing is designed to go hard quickly and is not at all flexible, as you can see from cracks in many new houses. If you have a patio which has been pointed this way then follow Project 5 pointing brickwork, as the principle is the same. You may need to match the sand and cement for the right consistency and colour, in which case see Project 3.

You will need:

▶ *a hammer*
▶ *a bolster chisel*
▶ *a plugging chisel*
▶ *sand and cement mixture (see 2 and 3 below)*
▶ *a brush or broom for brushing the mixture into the joints.*

To cover the stain:

1 *If you are working on a patio or paving where there is not a lot of the existing pointing left, it is better to cut out all of the old stuff and start again. A hammer and a bolster chisel are the best tools for this, along with a plugging chisel for tight joints. Do not attempt to use an angle grinder unless you are used to handling one as they can quite easily skid across the surface of your slabs, marking them badly.*

Tip

Pointing of all kinds should be carried out on a dry day and when your patio itself is dry.

2 *Prepare your sand and cement mixture. The type of sand you use will depend on the width of your joints. For joints that are less than ½ inch (13 mm) you should use silver sand. This is more commonly called play pit sand. Mix the sand with cement at a ratio of 1 to 1 and spread out to dry thoroughly. Do not mix on the patio.*

Insight

We always get the family kids to run about on the patio after pointing. If there are any joints not properly filled, this will locate them!

3 *If the joints are wider than ½ inch, use sharp sand. Make sure this is dry and that all the lumps are squashed. This should be mixed at 3 parts sand to 1 part cement. This makes it slightly leaner and even more flexible. It should be left to dry as above.*

4 *Using a bucket, sprinkle this mix along a couple of joints. Then, using a soft brush, brush carefully into the joint. Make sure the joint is absolutely full, even to the point of having to tamp the mix down with a piece of timber.*

5 *When the joints are full, brush any surplus off the surface and leave. The moisture in the air, plus the moisture from the ground underneath, will eventually make the jointing hard. This slow hardening process keeps the joint flexible and, providing you have filled the joints up, they will not crack.*

Tip

The most common cause of patio pointing failure is when voids are present either within the joint or under it. These are easily formed when a lump of sand clogs up the joint – it may look as though this joint is full when in fact it is not. Water soon gets into these voids and, with a freeze-thaw action, soon destroys the rest of the joint.

Patios can be pointed quite quickly using this method and providing everything is dry there need be no staining of the slabs associated with ordinary pointing.

12 Concreting fence posts

A fence post should be chosen to allow 25 per cent of its length to be in the ground. A 6-foot fence should have an 8-foot post, with 2 foot in the ground. A 5-foot fence should have a 6-foot 6-inch post with 1 foot 6 inches in the ground, and so on.

For fences of 6 feet and over, 4 × 4 inch posts are recommended; for anything under 6 feet, 3 × 3 inch posts are recommended.

Insight

It is always worth remembering that farmers rarely concrete their fence posts. They simply drive them into the ground. If a strong wind blows the fence over at an angle at least it doesn't break as the earth is much more likely to give way than concrete. The choice is yours.

You will need:

▶ *the correct number and size of timbers for your fence*
▶ *a shovel*
▶ *a general concrete mixture (see Project 1)*
▶ *a stick or broom handle*
▶ *pieces of timber to use as temporary struts to hold the post steady while the concrete dries.*

To concrete the posts:

1 *Dig a hole three times as wide as the post and as deep as is necessary for the height of the fence (see page 195). For a 4-inch post the hole should be at least 12 inches wide.*
2 *Place the concrete mix in the hole and settle it into place by poking it with a stick or broom handle to make sure no air voids are present.*
3 *The top of the concrete should be sloped away from the posts to allow water to run away from the timber.*
4 *Leave 150 mm between the top of the concrete and the top of the hole for backfilling with soil, and turf if required.*
5 *Level the post vertically with a spirit level.*
6 *Add temporary struts to hold it in position for at least four hours to stop any wind or accidental bumping moving it from its vertical position.*

13 Basic timber decking

Note: This project should not be attempted by anyone who does not have at least a basic knowledge of carpentry. It is a big undertaking and is too complicated to work through in the kind of detail needed for someone who has never done any DIY. However, for those confident in their ability to measure and cut the timber correctly it provides useful guidance and suggestions.

Insight

You can easily cut a piece of timber but it's not so easy to add some on. Measure twice – cut once.

Decking has risen dramatically in popularity, probably due to a large extent to its versatility. A raised deck does not create half as many problems, or half as much work, as a raised patio. Decks can curve with ease, and blend in beautifully with other wooden features in the garden such as trees and fences. Decking is still, however, carpentry and some skill is required to get it right.

This project deals with a straightforward raised deck. The same principles apply whatever height you want to raise your decking by. If you have a patio you wish to turn into a deck, the frame shown on page 198 can simply be built directly onto the patio. In this situation it's a good idea to lay the frame in line with the fall of the patio so water cannot lie up against the timbers.

You will need:

▶ *your decking plan (see 1 and 2 on page 198)*
▶ *timbers for the frame and posts*
▶ *proprietary decking timbers*
▶ *a Jack saw*
▶ *a shovel*
▶ *screws and screwdriver*
▶ *timber preservative.*

To build your deck:

1 *It is vital that you draw out your decking plan first. This will enable you to work out exactly where you need to put posts for support and how much timber you need. The bigger the timber, the greater the distance you can allow between the posts. If you are using frame and joist timbers of 225 mm × 50 mm, there should be no more than 2 m between the posts holding up the frame, but 4 m can be allowed between ends of the frame, provided that the joists are no more than 450 mm apart. This means that using 225 mm × 50 mm timbers, a frame 4 m × 4 m (12 ft × 12 ft) can be built using eight posts – 100 mm square posts are recommended. The diagram shows a deck 4 m long by 1.8 m wide (not to scale).*

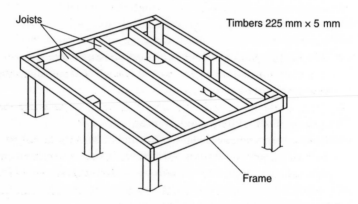

Joists

Timbers 225 mm × 5 mm

Frame

2 *The easiest way to work out the exact position for posts is to build the frame first. Lay this on the ground and mark the positions of the posts.*
3 *Spend some time thinking about where to site your deck. If you plan it as a shaded area, remember that this may lead to damp in the timbers and the growth of lichen and algae if it will not see any sunshine for months on end.*
4 *There is no reason why the decking timbers cannot overshoot the frame by a sensible amount. You can work this out by standing on the boards. Using this feature enables you to cut the decking boards to a shape which blends into your garden and, if you plan this shape first, you can make your frame to suit.*

5   Position the posts in the ground (see Project 12). Take care when digging holes for posts as you may be near drains, etc. in your garden.

6   Screw in rather than nail all the decking frames and timbers. Timber moves a great deal with expansion and contraction and this movement can work nails loose in no time.

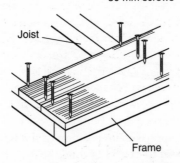

50 mm screws

Joist

Frame

7   The timbers forming the deck are proprietary timbers with grooves cut into them. Lay these to a slight fall to help water run off the deck.

8   Treat all the timber with a timber preservative, including the bare ends left when you make a cut.

9   Take all leftover cut timbers to the tip – they should not be burned. Timber which has been treated with preservative can split and spit in a fire, throwing ashes and splinters many feet.

Tips

Decks over 300 mm from the ground may require a handrail. The posts for the rail can be bolted to the side of the frame.

Very large decks and decks raised more than 600 mm may need planning permission as they may affect your neighbours. Check the situation with the Building Control Department of your local council.

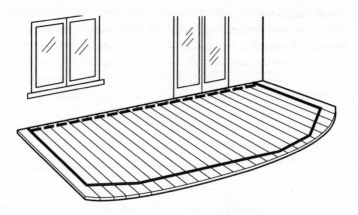

The image above shows a deck built to be cut to a curve. The lines represent the approximate position of the frame. The deck timbers were allowed to extend beyond the deck by about 400 mm, allowing plenty of room for a curve to be cut.

Insight

Timber decking can get very slippery after rain. Be careful!

14 Building a shed base

A shed base is constructed in exactly the same way as a ground floor slab. If done properly (as all of your projects should be), it will last for years. How to build a shed base is a very popular question put to DIY Doctor and there are, in fact, a number of ways to do it. A standard construction method is described here which allows for a damp proof membrane under the slab to stop damp rising up through it. The slab is designed to be above ground and is 6 inches thick.

Tip

For small sheds the base could be dug into the ground, removing the need for brickwork to the edges.

Simply dig the hole 300 mm wider and longer than your shed floor, 100 mm deep (providing the ground underneath is solid) and pour the concrete on to a damp proof membrane you have laid inside.

You will need:

▶ *a shovel*
▶ *scalping stone (crushed stone aggregate) if necessary (see 2 below)*
▶ *a 'whacker plate' or vibrating plate if necessary (see 3 on page 202)*
▶ *damp proof membrane, which should be at least 1,000 gauge polythene (available from builders' merchants)*
▶ *150 mm × 25 mm sawn and treated timber*
▶ *a lump hammer*
▶ *50 mm × 50 mm posts*
▶ *a spirit level*
▶ *small nails (40 mm)*
▶ *a sharp saw*
▶ *a tape measure*
▶ *soft building sand (enough to cover the base to a depth of 25 mm)*
▶ *concrete mix (see Project 1)*
▶ *a straight piece of timber the length of your base*
▶ *a claw hammer*
▶ *bricks to face the slab.*

To construct your shed base:

1 *First, check that the ground where you wish to build your shed is firm enough to lay a slab without a hardcore sub-base. To do this, take a 50 mm × 50 mm post and, without sharpening the end, try and drive it into the ground. It should be difficult to get it any deeper than 150 mm.*
2 *If the ground is firm enough, then carry on with the instructions below. If the post goes in too easily, remove 4 inches of soil from an area of ground which is 500 mm*

wider and longer than the floor of your shed. Fill this with scalping stone. Scalpings are a little more expensive than broken brick hardcore but much easier to lay and compact.

3 If it is necessary to compact scalpings for your base, then a machine called a 'whacker plate' or 'vibrating plate' can be hired from your local tool-hire shop.

4 In all cases your base area should be 300 mm longer and wider than your shed floor and as level as possible. Check that this is the case if you have not had to carry out 2 and 3 above.

5 Now, using the diagram below, follow the instructions for an above-ground base.

6 Cut the four sides of the formwork (frame) for your base from your timber. This timber should be 300 mm longer than your base and 300 mm wider.

7 Lay the timber out where you want the base and, using a heavy lump hammer, bang in some 50 mm × 50 mm posts along the line of the timber. These will hold the timber on its edge, but more importantly they will stop the timber bowing out as you place the concrete. The posts should be no more than 900 mm apart.

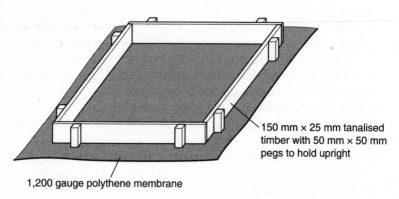

150 mm × 25 mm tanalised timber with 50 mm × 50 mm pegs to hold upright

1,200 gauge polythene membrane

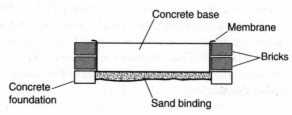

Concrete base

Membrane

Bricks

Concrete foundation

Sand binding

8 *When the posts are banged in, use a spirit level to make sure the top of the formwork is level. When it is, fix the boards to the posts using small nails (40 mm). There is no need to use large nails or screws as the concrete will hold the boards in place.*

9 *If any of the posts stick up above the boards, cut them off using a sharp saw. You will realize the benefit of this when you come to level and 'tamp' the concrete.*

10 *To make sure the corners of your formwork are square at 90 degrees, measure from corner to corner across both diagonals. The measurements should be identical.*

Insight

We have learned the hard way that if your shed base is even a tiny bit out of level it can lead to the door not opening or closing properly as the frame will be slightly twisted.

11 *With a level, square frame in place you can now lay soft building sand in the bottom to a depth of 25 mm. This is to stop the polythene damp proof membrane getting punctured.*

12 *Next, lay your damp proof membrane. In the diagram, this is shown going under the formwork (frame) of the base. This is only done so that you can see where it goes in relation to the construction – its actual position is inside the frame, and it should be lapped up inside the frame and folded as tightly as possible into the corners.*

13 *Now mix and lay the concrete.*

14 *Enlist a friend to help you level out the concrete. Lay another piece of timber across the top of the frame and concrete, holding an end each. Stand the timber on its edge and push and pull it across the frame while dragging it from one end to the other. This will level it roughly.*

15 *Then lift the board at both ends, about 4 inches above the frame, and tap it back down on the frame, moving up and down the frame as you do so. Try and tap together, so both ends of the board hit the frame at the same time. This vibrates the concrete into place and it will find its own level. This is called tamping.*

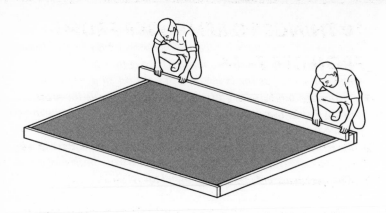

16 *Finally, wander around the frame tapping gently on the outside, all the way round, with a claw hammer. This will vibrate out any air bubbles trapped between the frame and the concrete.*

17 *Leave the base for a couple of days, after which you will be able to pull up the posts and remove the formwork.*

18 *To finish the job really well, you can now dig a small trench around the base, put 150 mm of concrete in the bottom and build a brick wall around the base to hide the face of the concrete. Remember to fold up the damp proof membrane between the bricks and the face of the slab.*

10 THINGS TO REMEMBER FROM PROJECTS 7–14

1 Too much land drainage can cause dry and scorched areas of garden in the summer.

2 Make sure your soil is not clay before deciding on a soakaway.

3 Keep excavations safe by digging sides at an angle.

4 Check level frequently. It is very difficult to rectify a mistake once things get out of level.

5 Always wear protective equipment such as gloves and goggles.

6 Always keep moving when using compaction equipment. Staying still will cause hollows.

7 Driveways, drainage and pathways must always be laid to a slope. Work out your slope before you start.

8 Learn the difference between different types of sand and aggregates and where/when to use them.

9 Any posts or poles used in your garden should have at least 25 per cent of their length concreted in the ground.

10 Sink all fixings in timber below the surface level where possible.

Inside

15 Fixing to masonry

TOOLS

Fixing brackets for shelves, curtain poles, picture rails, dado rails, anything in the home that requires drilling into masonry or concrete, requires special tools and fixing techniques.

▶ *To get through most masonry surfaces you will need to own or hire a powerful electric drill with a hammer action of no less than 500 W.*

Insight

When buying your hammer drill, buy the lightest one you can find, as long as it is at least 500 W (we suggest 650 W). After drilling a few holes drills can feel very heavy!

▶ *You will also need a masonry drill. You can tell if a drill bit is for drilling masonry or concrete by the shape of the end. A masonry bit has a flat cutting section at the end, which is slightly wider than the shaft of the drill bit. This allows the drill bit to cut its way through the masonry or concrete, and the cut material can escape through the grooves back to the opening of the hole. It is a false economy to buy cheap masonry bits, as they will blunt quickly and, to compensate for this, you will have to push the drill harder, which makes the drill bit wobble and enlarges the hole beyond the size you want. All sorts of complications then develop which are a major source of questions to DIY Doctor.*

▶ *If you need to drill a large hole, say 10 mm, through a very hard surface, it is asking a lot of the drill bit (and drill) to do this in one go, especially if you do not have the powerful tools the professionals use. It is easier to drill a smaller hole first and then increase it with a larger drill bit. You will then end up with a hole the correct size in the exact position you want it.*

▶ *When you have drilled the correct size hole you will need to insert a wall plug. Wall plugs essentially come in four sizes and colours. You will see various grey and other coloured plugs on the market and each has a job to do, but for the purposes of this project and to assist you in getting a good fixing to a brick, block or concrete wall or ceiling, we will just deal with the four major players:*

  ▷ *yellow plugs fit into holes made by a 5 mm drill bit and are for screw sizes 4–8*
  ▷ *red plugs fit into a hole made by a 6 mm drill bit and are for screw sizes 6–10*
  ▷ *brown plugs fit into a hole made by a 7 mm drill bit and are for screw sizes 10–14*
  ▷ *blue plugs fit into a hole made by a 10 mm drill bit and are for screw sizes 14–18.*

▶ *Screws come in all shapes and sizes. The larger the number of the screw, the larger the diameter. For example, a number 8 screw is smaller than a number 10. This is the gauge number of a screw and is measured using the head of the screw rather than the diameter of the shaft. Numbers 8 and 10 are the most popular screw sizes and suitable for most fixings at home.*

TACKLING THE JOBS

Now you have all of the equipment you can start fixing. The two jobs covered in this project are fixing a simple external candleholder and fixing timber battens to hold basic shelves.

Fixing a candleholder to an external wall
You will need:

▶ *some tape (e.g. gaffer tape)*
▶ *an electric hammer-action drill*
▶ *a masonry drill bit of the correct size*
▶ *wall plugs of the correct size*
▶ *screws of an appropriate size*
▶ *your candleholder*
▶ *a screwdriver, preferably electric.*

To fix the candleholder:

1 *First, lay out everything you need.*
2 *Use a little tape of some kind to wrap round your drill bit to mark the depth of the hole you wish to drill. This will be determined by the length of the screw you use to attach the bracket – in this example the attachment point of the candleholder is 7 mm thick and the screw is 50 mm long.*

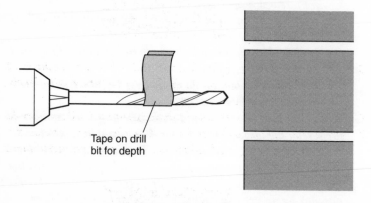

Tape on drill
bit for depth

3 *As the screw does not go right to the very end of the wall plug, and there is always a little drilling dust left at the end of the hole, it is a good idea to add 10 mm to the depth of the hole. In this example, 43 mm of screw will be in the wall (the other 7 mm will be in the bracket), so adding a 10 mm allowance means you need to drill a hole 53 mm deep.*
4 *Next, hold the candleholder up to the wall to mark the position of the screws. If this is not possible, measuring accurately will do the same job. Mark this with a V shape, as shown opposite. The point of the V is where you want to drill. Using just a dot or a line can result (after an interruptive phone call or a sudden rush to the toilet) in forgetting just where the dot is or which end of the line you were going to drill to. There is no doubt with a V and most professionals will use this method. Make sure that whichever mark you make will be covered by the work.*

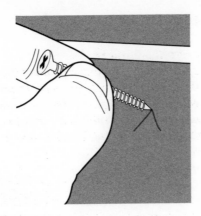

5 Next, drill the hole! Make sure the drill is level and going in at right angles to the wall. Some drills even have tiny spirit levels incorporated into the body for this.
6 Push in the plug you are using, making sure it is all in the hole.
7 Screw your candleholder to the wall. In the picture an electric screwdriver is being used, which is a powerful and useful piece of equipment.

Fixing timber battens to masonry

You will need:

▶ *a pencil*
▶ *a spirit level*
▶ *some tape (e.g. gaffer tape)*
▶ *an electric hammer-action drill*
▶ *your timber batten*
▶ *a 6 mm masonry drill bit*
▶ *wall plugs of the correct size*
▶ *screws of an appropriate size*
▶ *a screwdriver, preferably electric.*

To fix timber battens:

1 *Again, lay out everything you need.*
2 *Hold the batten in position against the wall, making sure it is level.*
3 *Mark the position of the batten on the wall with a pencil.*
4 *Take down the batten and drill a 5 mm hole in the centre of it, through which to push the screw.*
5 *Put the batten back against the wall in line with your pencil mark.*
6 *Push a screw through the pre-drilled hole and wiggle it on the wall to mark it. Then mark it with a V as shown on page 209.*
7 *As shown on page 208, use a little tape of some kind to wrap round your drill bit to mark the depth of the hole you wish to drill.*
8 *Using a 6 mm masonry bit, drill a hole to the correct depth.*
9 *Push in the wall plug and screw the timber up tight to the line.*
10 *You can now use the masonry bit to drill right through the timber and the wall for the other screws. There is no need to keep taking off the batten. Don't forget to alter your depth marker now that you are drilling through the timber as well.*
11 *Push the wall plug into the timber, turn the screw in a couple of turns and tap it through with a hammer. You will feel the plug slip through the timber into the wall, at which point you screw the screw in.*

This method saves you marking each hole individually, which can lead to mistakes. It does eventually blunt the masonry bit slightly, but it takes about 650 holes through timber to do this and the time saved, together with the accuracy involved, makes it worth it.

Battens fixed in this way can be used for shelves and once you have become confident with fixing to masonry you can use exactly the same technique to fix to concrete.

---

16 Screeding a floor

Laying a level floor screed over a large area is difficult, and to do so 'by eye' requires years of experience. However, there is an easier way to do it and this is where the word screed comes from – it actually means an accurately levelled 'strip' of material (e.g. wood or metal) laid on a wall or floor as a guide for the even application of a covering. Screed now also refers to the covering itself. For this project we will use the correct terms, but will differentiate between them by referring to them as the timber screed, mixed screed (the mixture and a line of the mixture once it is laid) and the finished product, the floor screed.

For the purposes of this project we will work with a 50 mm covering and we will use some 100 mm × 50 mm timber of a suitable length for our timber screed. This is a standard size of timber, commonly called 4 × 2 (these are the measurements in inches). Make sure you examine the timber before you buy it as you need a straight piece, not a piece that bows as this will make the job harder and will not guarantee a level finish.

To cover approximately 15 square metres of floor when laid at a thickness of 50 mm you will need:

▶ *1 tonne of flooring grit or sharp sand mixed 4:1 with cement*
▶ *100 mm × 50 mm timber (length will vary depending on the size of room)*
▶ *a shovel*

▶ a plasterer's polyurethane float (available from DIY stores or builders' merchants).

To screed the floor:

1 Mix your floor screed at 4 parts sand to 1 part cement, and use the water content testing method described in Chapter 4 to get it to the required consistency.
2 Lay the timber screed on to the floor and place a spirit level on it. If it is not level the timber can be packed up in the appropriate places using some of your screed mixture.
3 The side of the timber is used as a 'former' against which to place the screed mixture, so you can be sure that each mixed screed is of the correct thickness. Use the timber screed repeatedly to form mixed screeds at regular intervals across and along the floor, as shown in the plan below (the mixed screeds should be placed at no more than 1 m apart).

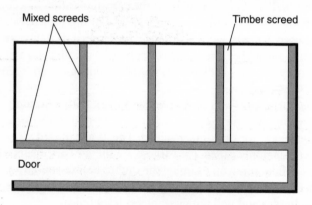

Mixed screeds   Timber screed

Door

4 Always wet the timber before laying the mixed screed against it, so that the wood does not suck moisture from the mixture. This can be done quite simply with a paintbrush and a container of water.
5 When the timber is in position, place a shovel-full of the mixture every 300 mm along it and flatten this out with a plasterer's polyurethane float. The mixed screed should be about 75 mm wide and will naturally fall away at an angle at the side. When you have finished each mixed screed, cut

it back square to the timber screed as shown by the white cut-line in the diagram below.

6 *When you have finished a mixed screed, remove the timber and place it in the next position. This needs to be done carefully to avoid damaging the edge of the mixed screed.*

7 *Leave the newly cast screeds for a day and then check that they are level using your spirit level or a straight-edged piece of timber.*

8 *Fill in the gaps between the mixed screeds with the same mixture. Move the mixture around until it is absolutely level between each parallel pair of mixed screeds.*

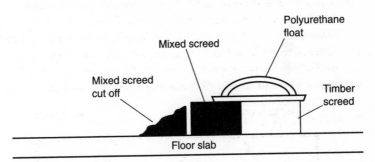

9 *Fill in any voids.*

10 *Rub the covering with the float to a void-free finish.*

Insight

If there has been any cold weather, especially frost in the lead time to doing your floor, make sure you allow extra time in the mixer to break up any frozen lumps of sand which may have formed.

Tip

Floor screeds should be dried out slowly (cured) – they need to retain their moisture for as long as possible. Rapid drying could lead to cracks because of the high cement content.

11 *To cure, place a polythene sheet over the screed and allow several days before walking on the surface.*

17 Laying floor tiles

Note: The fixing of any permanent or semi-permanent floor covering will affect access to pipes and cables running under the floor. Please check that access to these cables and pipes is not required under building regulations and, if it is, make alternative arrangements for access.

The principles of laying floor tiles are the same whether they are quarry tiles or vinyl.

▶ *Measure up and set out the room, as described in 'Using chalk lines' on page 216.*
▶ *Apply the adhesive and lay the tiles, cutting around anything that stands in the way.*

This project can be used for all floor tiles, but the preparation for differing floor surfaces will need attention. Please check the manufacturer's instructions on the tiles and adhesive.

PREPARATION

Removing existing quarry tiles
▶ *To remove existing quarry tiles there is little option but to get stuck in with a hammer and bolster chisel.*

Tip

An electric chisel, which will make the job easier, can be hired from tool-hire centres. However, please do not expect to have a perfectly flat floor when you have finished with one of these!

▶ *Wear good gloves and goggles, as splintered quarry tiles can be very sharp indeed.*

Removing old vinyl tiles

▶ *A good floor scraper is a must for this job, but even these do take a lot of muscle.*

▶ *If you use a hammer and bolster, some tiles will 'chip' up if you hit them close to the edge with the hammer.*

▶ *A hot air gun, applied gently to the adhesive, will loosen it and allow it to be scraped up as well.*

Skirting boards

....

Insight
If you plan to use a breaker for more than 1 minute, wear ear defenders also.

....

With all floor tiling, you will achieve a much better finish if you can remove the skirting boards, lay the floor and then reinstate the boards. For one thing, the skirting will then hide any less-than-perfect cuts you have made, and for another, the difference in height of your new floor, especially with quarry tiles or vinyl bedded onto new plywood, will not hide any of the skirting board.

Tiling over timber

When tiling over existing floorboards, it is strongly suggested that you first cover these boards with plywood which is at least 12 mm thick. This will stop your floor moving (expanding and contracting) and cracking or splitting the tiles.

The ply should be laid in large sheets, with long joints running at 90 degrees to the long joints of your existing boards or sheets, carefully marking out for obstructions and cutting around them. It should then be fixed to the existing boards at no less than 200 mm centres in both directions. Use number 8 screws long enough to go through the plywood and the floorboards underneath, making sure each screw head is countersunk (see Project 23 on pilot holes and countersinking) to finish flush with the surface of the ply.

Having raised the floor level in one room, it is obvious that there will be a step between that room and the room it abuts. This step will be the thickness of the ply sub-floor plus the tiles you have used. Proprietary hardwood mouldings can be bought at DIY stores to make this step into a gentle 'ramp', making a nice tidy finish to your work.

Concrete or screeded floors

Concrete and screeded floors should be entirely free from dust and any flaking or loose material. If quarry tiles are being laid onto concrete or screed, the adhesive will make up any depressions and bumps in the floor, as long as they are no more than about 5 mm deep. Damp the floor down slightly when laying quarry tiles on concrete or screed.

Insight

Never use screed powder or cement products that have been lying about in the garage or shed for any length of time. If any moisture has permeated the container the product will have lost its integrity and will break down. Buy new.

If you are laying vinyl or other soft tiles, you will need to apply a self-levelling floor screed if the surface is not absolutely flat and has bumps and depressions. This is bought in bags from builders' merchants and some of the larger DIY stores. It comes with a drum of latex liquid with which the powder is mixed to an easy flowing creamy consistency, in a bucket. The liquid is then poured onto the floor and pushed around with a plasterers' trowel until it self-levels, filling small depressions and leaving a perfectly flat, smooth surface. It is not necessary to seal this surface and it gives excellent adhesion to all flooring adhesives.

TOOLS, EQUIPMENT AND TECHNIQUES

Using chalk lines

Most tiles are square, or at least rectangular, with corners at 90 degrees. Most rooms, however, are far from square: the majority of rooms have slight bows in the walls, and some have pronounced bows; internal corners are very rarely 90 degrees. This does not mean your house has been built badly – this is fairly standard!

To lay tiles properly it is necessary to mark out the room so that the tiles are at least laid square to each other. They are therefore laid completely independently of any walls in the room. The easiest way to mark a line the full length of the room is with a chalk line (a line wound in a container full of chalk). These are inexpensive, available from DIY stores and make marking out work very easy. (See pages 219–23.)

Using trowels

Notched trowels are used to spread both quarry tile and vinyl tile adhesives for two reasons. With the end of the notches touching the existing wall or floor, moving the trowel around guarantees a uniform depth of adhesive. The void left by the notches gives the adhesive room to move when pressing down on a tile to bed it in well.

Using adhesive

Most vinyl floor tile manufacturers will recommend a certain floor-laying adhesive and it's always best to use this wherever possible. Should any fault develop with the adhesion of the tiles and you have used an alternative adhesive, you may not have any comeback on the manufacturers. However, all proprietary vinyl floor-laying adhesives have common properties with high adhesive qualities and are now available in solvent-free form.

Only spread the amount of adhesive for the number of tiles you will easily lay in ten minutes. When you have cuts to make, do not spread the adhesive in these areas – marking and cutting is much easier on 'dry' floors.

Using grout

Grout for quarry tiles comes in ready-mixed and powder form. The advantage of the powder is that it is easily mixed, in a bucket, in quantities that you can work with.

Apply a liberal amount of grout to the tiles, then spread it about, pushing into the gaps in a regimental way. Make sure each tile gap is filled, as it will sink later if not. A grout trowel can be used for this and in tight corners a sponge can be very useful.

When an area of approximately 3 m × 3 m has been covered, wipe off the excess grout with the sponge. Rinse out the sponge well in a separate bucket full of water (do not be tempted to use the sink; this will clog up in no time). Wring out to damp and wipe the sponge over the tiles again. You will need to do this several times to remove all the excess grout from the surface of the tiles. Using newspaper can achieve the same result, but you will use quite a lot of it!

The grout will dry quite quickly, and you will (probably) find a very thin dust residue on the surface of your tiles. This can be polished off easily with a dry cloth.

CUTTING TILES

Vinyl tiles

You will sometimes see a tiler using a small blowlamp to warm up vinyl tiles before cutting them. This makes the tiles easier to cut and stops the knife skidding across the surface. The same effect can be achieved with a hot-air gun and you are much less likely to set fire to the tile!

A sharp utility knife is essential, with lots of spare blades. Make straight cuts against a metal ruler, and curved cuts in a series of short lines. Always cut away from your body.

Quarry tiles

Quarry tiles are cut using a proprietary tile cutter, either handheld or mechanical. Most quarry tiles these days are quite thin and a normal ceramic tile cutter will do the job. For thicker tiles, a quarry tile cutter can be hired from tool-hire stores. It is the same as a mechanical ceramic tile cutter, but far more robust.

LAYING THE TILES

Once you have prepared your floor, as described in the preparation section on pages 214–16, you are ready to lay your tiles.

You will need:

▶ *a chalk line*
▶ *your tiles*
▶ *the appropriate cutting equipment for the type of tile you are using*
▶ *the appropriate adhesive or grout for the type of tile you are using*
▶ *the adhesive or grout mixture*
▶ *a notched trowel*
▶ *a sponge and a bucket of water (if you are using grout)*
▶ *tile spacers (if desired).*

To lay the tiles:

1 *First, using the diagram on page 220 as a guide (the dotted lines show the possible shape of a room), lay the horizontal row of tiles 1 to 35, without using any grout or adhesive yet. Space the row out so that tiles 12 and 39 will be roughly the same size.*

130	129	128	127	116	110	103	95	51	52
126	125	124	123	115	109	102	94	45	50
122	121	120	114	108	101	93	86	44	49
119	118	113	107	100	92	85	78	43	48
117	112	106	99	91	84	77	70	42	47
111	105	98	90	83	76	69	63	41	46
104	97	89	82	75	68	62	57	6	22
96	88	81	74	67	61	56	32	5	21
87	80	73	66	60	55	31	30	4	20
79	72	65	59	54	29	28	27	3	19
71	64	58	53	26	25	24	23	2	18
39	35	34	33	10	9	8	7	1	12
40	38	37	36	17	16	15	14	11	13

2 *Now dry-lay the vertical row of tiles 2 to 45, making sure that the spaces for tiles 11 and 51 are equal.*

3 *Next, mark on the floor, with a pencil or felt-tipped pen, the corner of tile 1 where it meets tiles 11, 12 and 13. This is the starting point of your square.*

4 *Now remove the tiles and mark the line A–A down the room. This is best achieved using a chalk line (a job for two people). Once it is unwound, each take one end of the line and hold it close to the surface you are going to tile. Lift the line (much like drawing a bow string) and release it. The 'ping' of the line leaves a perfect chalk mark across the wall or floor.*

5 *When you have marked line A–A, dry-lay tiles 1 to 6 again.
Then, using the diagram below, mark the cuts you will need
for tiles 12 to 22. (Some people like to produce and lay the cut
tiles as they go; others like to finish the main area of the floor,
allow it to dry and then come back and do the cuts.) Tile A
is dry-laid, with tile B placed on top of it against the skirting
board (or wall if the boards have been removed). A line is then
drawn on tile A against the edge of tile B. This is the cut-line.
When cut, tile B replaces tile A and the cut from tile A will
drop neatly into the gap. The same process is repeated all the
way down the wall.*

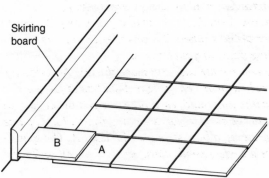

Skirting
board

B   A

6 *Pay particular attention to the tiles along line A. This is your setting-out point. The effectiveness and quality of the whole floor depends on keeping to this line. Some tilers apply this line in the centre of the floor and lay tiles from that point, but this can be irritating – laid tiles have to be stepped over to lay other tiles, and all of the tiles have to be stepped on to make the cuts. Once you have made a start on your floor, it's good to get it finished as quickly as possible, and the method outlined here allows you to make the cuts as you go. Work towards the door where you can escape without treading on newly-laid tiles and stack tiles in plenty of space, near to where you want them, without them getting in your way.*

Insight

Grout comes in different colours. Try experimenting with one that contrasts the colour of the tiles rather than just blending in.

7 *If the walls have a pronounced bow, as shown below, then a 'scribing' method can be used to mark the tile.*
  ▷ *Cut a batten (say 1½ inch by 1 inch) and drill a hole in the end of it to accommodate a tight fit for a pencil or felt-tipped pen.*
  ▷ *Measure the width of a tile from this hole and cut the batten to this length.*
  ▷ *Dry-lay the tiles as shown on page 221.*

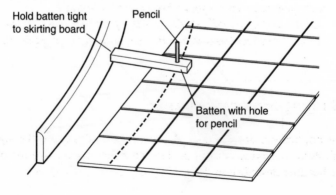

Hold batten tight to skirting board

Pencil

Batten with hole for pencil

▷ Holding the end of the batten tightly against the skirting board or wall and, keeping the batten at 90 degrees to the wall, pull back along the tiles and wall. This will transfer the shape of the wall to the tiles.

▷ When the marked tiles are cut, they lay against the wall and a full tile will fit into the space previously occupied by the marked tile.

Tip

Awkward cuts around doorframes/architraves can be accomplished by cutting out a cardboard template first and transferring the shape to a tile. You can also buy what is called a profile gauge. This is a bar housing hundreds of plastic or metal needles. As the needles are pushed against the profile, they move back, leaving the shape of the profile, which can then be transferred to the tile.

8 Follow the numbering on the diagram on page 220 to lay your tiles. Keep an eye on every joint, making sure it lays square against the tile next to it. If one of the tiles gets out of square, they are very difficult to get back.

9 Use tile spacers if you are not sure that you can lay the tiles evenly.

10 When laying quarry tiles, do not be afraid to leave a good joint in between the tiles. Although you will use more grout, it is easier to apply and you will at least have a little room to manoeuvre when trying to keep the tiles square.

11 Grout and apply adhesive as per the guidance given in the tools, equipment and techniques section on pages 216–18.

18 Laying on undercoat plaster

The application of undercoat plaster to the wall is called 'laying on'. Before carrying out this project, complete the application of the beading described in 'Preparing to plaster' in Chapter 9.

You will need:

- ► *a bucket of water*
- ► *a large emulsion brush*
- ► *undercoat plaster mix (see Chapter 9 for details on mixing the plaster)*
- ► *a hawk*
- ► *a bucket trowel*
- ► *a steel trowel/float*
- ► *a straight-edged length of metal 1.5 m long*
- ► *a plastic float*
- ► *a small tool for filling narrow gaps (see Figure 9.1)*
- ► *a nail or a small screwdriver to scratch the plaster.*

Before you start to apply plaster, damp the wall down with a large emulsion brush and water. Don't let the water run down the wall – use just enough to make it damp.

To apply the undercoat plaster:

1 *Place the mixed plaster on your hawk (see Figure 9.1), about two trowels full at a time.*
2 *Then scoop it from the hawk to the steel trowel (sometimes called a steel float) onto the wall. Spread it about so it is slightly proud of the beads on the wall.*

Plaster stop beads

3 *Then take a straight edge (metal is better than timber) and lay it over the two beads at the bottom of the section you have filled. Push the straight edge against the beads and pull upwards, sliding side-to-side as you go. Do not worry if some chunks come out as you drag upwards.*

The gap between the beads is filled with plaster and then the straight edge is pulled up the wall, over the beads, to drag off any surplus plaster

4 *Scrape the plaster off the straight edge back into the bucket and go back to your hawk and trowel. Fill the holes and any areas that may be a little low. There should be some surface fissures, but not too many and none too deep.*
5 *Repeat the process a couple of times until the section is full, flat and relatively smooth, then move to the next section.*
6 *The metal beads are galvanized (so they don't rust) and will stay in the wall. There is no need to remove them. When you have done two or three sections, the plaster should be beginning to go hard.*
7 *When you can put your finger lightly on the surface without leaving a mark, it is time to 'rub in'. This means getting the plastic float and rubbing in a circular motion over the wall to close any fissures still remaining.*
8 *You will feel the surface go smooth under your touch and after a while you should be able to sense any depressions or high spots in the wall. You can add, or remove, a little plaster to correct these.*

9 *When you have finished you will have a smooth-looking wall. Any narrow areas such as the gap between a doorframe and an adjoining wall can be filled with one of the 'small tools' shown in Figure 9.1.*

10 *If you have fixed angle beads to any external corners, the undercoat plaster should finish just below the tip of the angle. This will allow you to use the same bead to plaster your topcoat to.*

Insight

We push the wall with a flat hand using the same pressure as one would to open a door. If it does not leave an impression your wall is ready for skimming.

11 *After a couple of hours, the undercoat plaster will be hard enough to scratch. Take a nail, or a small screwdriver, and drag it lightly, in a coil shape, over the surface of the plaster. The scratch should be no more than 1 mm deep and all of the wall should be covered, with no more than 150 mm between each of the scratches.*

Tip

There are special metal 'combs' for this, but these are not really necessary for the area that you are likely to be scratching – the novice should aim for a maximum of 4 m_2 in one go.

12 *Rub over the wall lightly once more with your plastic float, just to flatten out the burrs caused by the scratching.*

Your wall is now ready to apply the topcoat.

19 Applying a plaster topcoat (skimming)

Once you have 'scratched' your undercoat and placed your topcoat beads (see Chapter 9) it is time to apply the topcoat, or skim.

Tip

It is important to get your finish right first time. The average mix of finish/topcoat plaster will start to go hard after approximately ten minutes on a medium-suction surface such as plasterboard. When it starts to go hard, it does so very quickly, and once it is hard and bumpy there is absolutely nothing you can do with it except chop it off or plaster over it. Getting it right can only be achieved with practice, so it is worth investing, say, £15.00 on a sheet of plasterboard and a bag of finish plaster to practise with before tackling the real thing.

You will need:

- ▶ *a bucket of water*
- ▶ *a large emulsion brush*
- ▶ *topcoat plaster mix (see Chapter 9 for details on mixing the plaster)*
- ▶ *a hawk*
- ▶ *a bucket trowel*
- ▶ *a steel trowel/float*
- ▶ *a plastic float*
- ▶ *a small tool for filling narrow gaps (see Figure 9.1).*

If three or more hours have passed since you finished the undercoat, it's a good idea to dampen the wall again. This will give you a little longer to work with your topcoat (finish).

To apply the topcoat:

1 *Position yourself so you can see the thickness of plaster you are applying.*
2 *Ideally you will apply the plaster in two layers: a very quick 'flash' coat of 1 mm, then a more deliberate coat of 2 mm. Lay it on as you did the undercoat.*
3 *Try to get the plaster to an approximately even thickness, but do not spend time trying to get it perfectly flat at this stage as this is impossible.*

4 *Cover the area as quickly as you can, then go back to the starting point and trowel over the plaster again, gradually achieving a flatter and smoother finish.*

5 *Repeat this as many times as necessary. Each time you revisit it, the plaster will have gone a little harder. It is the timing that is really important in topcoat plastering or 'skimming', as it is known. Each pass on the hardening plaster should see more and more trowel marks and bumps disappearing.*

6 *When the plaster is almost fully hard, your final pass will trowel it to a lovely flat finish.*

Insight

We use a water spray, such as the type used for spraying flowers for greenfly, to damp down the walls.

7 *To assist with the last couple of passes it is perfectly acceptable to 'flick' water on the wall using the emulsion brush you used to damp the wall down. This will assist in getting rid of trowel marks.*

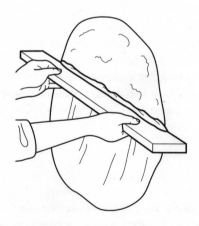

Don't worry if the wall still has one or two marks on it; when it's dry, it can be sanded down lightly.

Tip

Almost exactly the same method is used to fill patches of wall that need plastering, but instead of using metal beads as a guide to depth, use the side of the hole you are patching. Simply run a straight-edged piece of timber over the wall.

20 Building a partition wall

Before attempting this project, read the section on plasterboard and partition walls in Chapter 9.

Take care to measure your room and plan the partition wall before you start work. You will then be able to work out how much timber and board you need, as well as knowing where your studs and noggins are going to fit.

You will need:

▶ *the correct amount of plasterboard*
▶ *the correct amount of timber*
▶ *a pad saw*
▶ *the number of studs required*
▶ *the number of noggins required*
▶ *number 8 (3-inch) screws to attach it to a wooden floor, or 4-inch screws to attach it to a concrete floor*
▶ *scrim (plasterboard tape).*

To build the wall:

1 *Cut your timber to the correct dimensions for your project.*
2 *Position the first timber. This will be the head timber, or the head plate as it is also known. It can be fixed up through the ceiling into the ceiling joists if the joists are running the right way, that is, at 90 degrees to the wall. If the joists are running in the same direction as the new stud wall, then it is a good idea to mark the position of the head timber on the*

ceiling and then cut the plasterboard out between the lines to insert timber noggins at 400 mm intervals along the joists to fix the head timber to.

3 Once the head timber is in position, a plumb line can be clipped to the side of it. Mark the position of the sole plate (the timber which sits on the floor directly beneath the head plate) in three places along its proposed length on the floor.

4 Fix the sole plate, using number 8 (3-inch) screws to attach it to a wooden floor, or 4-inch screws to attach it to a concrete floor. (See Project 15 on fixing to masonry for more instructions on this.) The screws should be no more than 600 mm apart.

5 Now fix the two end studs to existing walls using the same methods.

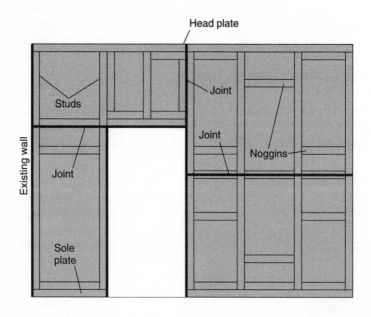

6 *Cut the vertical studs to length and fit them tightly in between the head and sole plates. They can either be screwed into the two plates with the screws at an angle (side fixing) or (as shown opposite) a noggin can be inserted between the studs. The bottom noggin serves two purposes: it keeps the studs secure and allows a larger area for skirting boards. When screwing studs and noggins to each other, use 100 mm number 8 screws.*

7 *Cut the plasterboard to size, cutting it in as few places as possible (joints shown on the diagram opposite).*

8 *Screw the plasterboard onto the studs and noggins.*

9 *Cover the joints of the board using special plasterboard tape, which is a very fine mesh, called 'scrim'. It comes in self-adhesive rolls for ease of use. Tape the scrim over the joints, as shown in the figure below, allowing the joints to be plastered over without fear of cracking.*

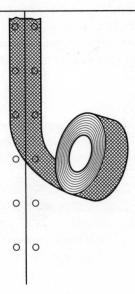

10 *If a door is required, put in a timber liner (see Chapter 9) in the appropriate place.*

11 *Hang your door as described in Project 26.*

---

21 Repairing a hole in plasterboard

You will need:

▶ *a heavy-duty hobby knife or plasterboard saw*
▶ *timber or plasterboard*
▶ *a carpenter's Jack saw*
▶ *heavy-duty, construction adhesive, such as Gripfil (available from all builders' merchants)*
▶ *a suitable filler.*

To repair a hole in a hollow door, wall, or ceiling:

1 *Trim the edge of the hole.*
2 *Prepare a piece of timber or plasterboard. Cut the new piece the same width as the widest part of the hole and 1 inch longer than the height.*
3 *Turn in a screw just a couple of threads, in the middle of the piece, to enable you to pick up the timber or plasterboard and manoeuvre it.*

Insight

Instead of adhesive, plaster can be used to stick the new piece of board to the back of the plasterboard. This is what the pros use as it goes hard much quicker and allows us to get on with the job.

4 *Go around the edge with some heavy-duty, construction adhesive, such as Gripfil.*
5 *Using the screw, push the piece into the hole.*
6 *Once you have it all the way in, pull back on the screw so the adhesive touches the back of the hole surround. Use gentle*

pulling pressure, while moving around slightly to ensure good contact between the adhesive and the back of the surface, until you are sure the adhesive will hold the piece in place, at which time you can remove the screw.

7 *Leave for 24 hours and the hole can then be filled with a filler suitable for the surface you are repairing.*

Wall

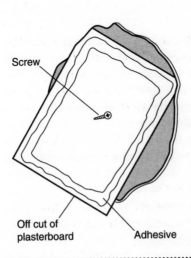

Screw

Off cut of
plasterboard

Adhesive

There is another way to fill a hole in plasterboard.

You will need:

▶ *a heavy-duty hobby knife or plasterboard saw*
▶ *timber or plasterboard*
▶ *a carpenter's Jack saw*
▶ *two timber battens*
▶ *drywall screws and screwdriver.*

To repair the hole:

1 *Enlarge the hole first to make a square of a suitable size.*
2 *Then cut two battens (19 mm × 38 mm timber will suffice) and make sure they are 100 mm longer than the size of the square you have cut.*

Insight

If the hole is not too big, one batten is enough.

3 *Feed a batten into the hole and twist it so it is either upright or horizontal and one-third of the distance either up or down or across the hole. Make sure you have a 50 mm overhang either side of the hole.*
4 *Then screw the batten in place through the front of the plasterboard, making sure the screw heads go below the skim of plaster on the board. Do this with both battens.*
5 *Cut a square of plasterboard to fit in the hole.*
6 *Screw this to the battens with drywall screws.*
7 *Then plaster the square and fill the holes made by fixing the battens either side.*

22 Sawing timber

Like all building work, it takes practice and a little know-how to get a straight line when sawing timber.

Look at the teeth on a saw. They are 'set' at an angle to each other. This allows the saw to cut easily through the wood leaving a cut wide enough for the saw to get through without sticking. This only works if the saw is going in a straight line. If the cut you are making veers from the straight in any way, by even a few millimetres, the saw will stick.

New saws cost very little these days, so make sure you have a new, sharp one for your project. Old, blunt saws have to be forced through the wood and that can lead to problems.

To saw your timber:

1 *First, make sure you have created a solid platform to work on. If it is possible to clamp the project, even better, but make sure you get some weight on it to stop it moving. It is imperative that the work and workbench are solid and secure. One little rock and the saw will move off line.*

Insight

The smaller the teeth the saw has, the neater the cut will be. If you are making something which will be seen, a fine-toothed saw will leave you with less sanding to do.

2 *Second, get right over your work. Ideally you should have an eye either side of the saw blade. This should ensure that your cut is at 90 degrees to the timber. If you are over to one side of the work, your saw will be at an angle.*
3 *Stroke the saw gently; let it do the work. You are only there as a guide.*

Tip

Using power tools to make your cut certainly makes life easier but, unlike a hand saw, one tiny slip can ruin a job. A slip with a hand saw can cause a little cut in a piece of work which, most of the time, can be sanded out. A slip with a circular saw is a huge cut halfway across a door! Stick with hand saws until you are used to them, before moving on to a power saw.

23 Pilot holes and countersinking

Countersinking is a way to enlarge and/or bevel the side of a hole to allow any given fixing to be sunk below the surface of that hole. When the fixing has been put in, the countersink can then be filled and sanded to allow the surface to be completely flat with no visible signs of fixing.

A pilot hole is a preparatory hole drilled to allow easier passage of
a larger object. In the diagram below a pilot hole is drilled to allow
a screw to be driven in, making its passage through the timber
easier. Because the pilot hole has a diameter of less than the screw
itself, the thread of the screw can still bite into the surrounding
timber making a perfectly secure fixing. Pilot holes are used almost
all the time through metal as it is impossible for most screws, even
run-of-the-mill self-tapping screws, to force their way through.

Some timbers, especially when cut into narrow or thin strips, are
prone to splitting when nailed or screwed. Countersinking and
drilling a pilot hole prevent this happening. If the fixing, even a nail,
has less timber to displace as you force it through, it is much less
likely to split the timber. And if, because of a countersink, it can
slip down below the surface of the timber, there is little chance of
it splitting as the conical shape of the underside of the screw head
touches the top of the timber.

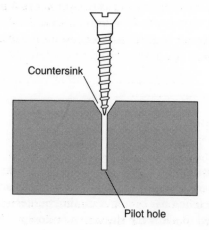

To drill a pilot hole:

1 *Measure the diameter of the screw, for example a number
 8 screw has a diameter of 3 mm, from outside of thread to
 outside of thread. A sensible size for the pilot hole is therefore
 1 or 1.5 mm. This will still allow the thread to cut its way
 through the timber without splitting it, while getting great grip
 on the timber.*
2 *Drill your hole using a timber drill bit of the appropriate size.*

Tip

It is an excellent idea, when fixing to a concrete lintel, for
example, to drill a series of pilot holes, one through the other,
getting slightly larger every time, until the required hole size
is reached. Trying to drill a very large hole through concrete,
hard masonry and metal will quickly blunt the drill as cutting
(drilling) with a large surface area drill bit is very much
harder than with a small one.

To countersink:

1 *Place the countersink bit in your drill and push down lightly
 on the pilot hole.*
2 *For those who prefer a hands-on approach, a handheld
 countersink tool can be bought from most DIY stores. This is
 a countersink bit in a handle that you push and twist on the
 surface of the wood.*

24 Boxing in pipes

The picture on page 238 shows a simple pipe boxing. A and B
represent, in this case, two walls, with the pipes fixed to or running
up wall B. This could just as easily be a box fixed between the
wall and the floor if your pipes are running horizontally, with
A representing the floor and B the wall or skirting. The principle is
the same in both cases.

The materials you will use will vary depending on the size of your box but for most applications either ½-inch plywood or plasterboard is good. Plywood can be bought at DIY stores and in many of them you can (for a small charge) get it cut to size.

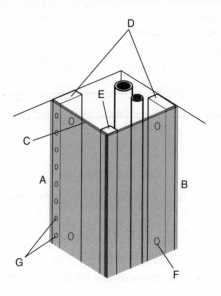

Tip

With all carpentry-related projects, remember: measure twice, cut once. You can always take more off a piece of timber, but it is very hard to add some on.

When the two sides of your boxing meet, there will be a join. Ideally this joint will be as discreet as possible. If you use the diagram above and the instructions below, the joint will always be seen on the same face as the board you have fixed the batten to. Read this entire project before starting work.

You will need:

▶ *enough ½-inch plywood or plasterboard for your project*
▶ *a Jack saw*

- ▶ *three battens (50 mm × 25 mm is usually a good size, although in most applications 38 mm × 19 mm is also fine)*
- ▶ *a tape measure*
- ▶ *a hammer-action power drill*
- ▶ *a 5.5 mm or 6 mm masonry drill bit*
- ▶ *red wall plugs*
- ▶ *2-inch number 8 screws*
- ▶ *screws or panel pins*
- ▶ *wood glue.*

(The drill bit, wall plugs and screws listed above are for masonry walls. Different walls will need different types of fixing, so make sure you know which type of wall you have.)

To box your pipes:

1 *Fix the two battens (D on the diagram opposite) to the surfaces (A and B), as close to the pipes as possible. The screws (F) should be about 400 mm apart.*
2 *Next, measure the required width of board C.*
3 *Then measure the length of the piece of board you need from floor to ceiling or whatever two surfaces this box is between.*
4 *Cut board C.*
5 *Cut batten E to the same length as your boxing and maybe just a millimetre or so longer. This will give it enough length to fit tightly between the two surfaces and give the boxing greater strength. Be careful not to cut it too long and damage the ceiling or walls as you push it into position.*

Insight

Do not skimp on nails and screws. The more you use the less gaps in the joints and the easier it will be to fill and decorate.

6 *Fix batten E to board C. The batten can be fixed with either screws or panel pins, but whatever you use for any of the surface fixings, remember you may need to decorate, so get the heads of the fixings slightly below the surface of your*

box. The holes can be filled later. You can use a little wood glue on these joints as well.

7 Having fixed board C to batten E, place them in position against the batten on wall A. A little glue and some panel pins or screws (as shown by G) will hold the board in position, together with the tightness of batten E 'wedged' into position.

8 Now cut the other side of the board and glue, pin or screw into position.

Tip

If you are using plasterboard for your boxing then it's best to use drywall screws as they are guaranteed not to rust and bleed through either your plaster or your paint.

---

9 Fill all the screw holes and pin holes and then run around the edges with some decorator's caulk (flexible filler in a tube, applied using a sealant gun) to hide the joints between box and walls/ceiling.

10 The box can then be decorated to match the rest of the room.

---

25 Working with skirting, architraves, coving and dado rails

There are many occasions when doing work at home, when angles need to be measured and cut. These angles, when fitting materials together in two or more sections, are called mitres. The most common uses of mitres are for putting up coving, cutting and fixing skirting or architraves, fitting dado and picture rails, stud walls and roofing. In all cases it is first necessary to establish if your room is square.

ESTABLISHING IF YOUR ROOM IS SQUARE

To use the 3, 4, 5 method (based on Pythagoras' theorem, for the technically minded):

1 Measure 3 feet (or metres or any other unit) along one wall.
2 Measure 4 of the same unit along the other wall.

3 *Measure the diagonal line between the two points. If it measures 5 units then your walls are square. If not, you will need to mark some points that are square to start your work.*

··
Insight
If you do have a gap in your mitred joint it is best to fill it with a flexible filler applied from a tube, using a sealant gun.
··

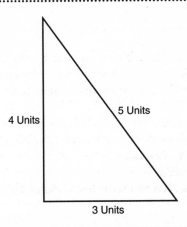

4 Units

5 Units

3 Units

USING MITRE JOINTS BETWEEN SKIRTING BOARDS

DIY Doctor receives hundreds of questions from people about how they can fill big gaps between skirting boards, caused because the walls of the room are not exactly at right angles. Rather than having gaps at skirting joints and having to fill them, it is better to fit them snugly in the first place, using a mitre joint.

To cut mitre joints in skirting boards:

1 *Use the 3, 4, 5 method to check the angle of the walls. You can then divide this by two to get the angle at which the work needs to be cut. A square 90 degree angle requires two cuts at 45 degrees.*
2 *If your wall, doorway or ceiling is not square, you will need to buy an angle finder from Screwfix.com to measure the exact angle before you can cut the angles or 'mitres'.*
3 *The image on page 242 shows the walls along which you can imagine placing skirting. On the top wall, if you had to join*

the skirting on the indicated line, you would need to make
two cuts at 90 degrees to get a tidy joint. On the middle piece,
make two mitre cuts of 72.5 degrees and on the last piece,
two mitre cuts of 45 degrees.

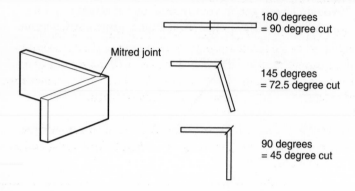

4 *The angle should be cut using either a mitre saw or an ordinary*
   saw placed in a mitre block. Both are readily available from
   DIY stores.

USING MITRE JOINTS IN DADO RAILS

The same principle can be applied to a dado rail going up the stairs.

1 *Draw lines on the wall (using a spirit level as a straight edge)*
   at the height you want the dado to go.
2 *Where the lines meet at the top of the stairs, measure the*
   angle. An ordinary protractor can be used to do this.
3 *Then continue as for skirting boards.*

---

26 Hanging a door

DOOR SIZES

Standard door sizes are available to fit most existing frames, but
houses move. Some older houses will have moved dramatically and

some of the first things that twist and bend are the doorframes. Almost all doors have to be trimmed to fit the opening they are to go into and sometimes the opening has been specially made for a feature door. In this situation it is fairly easy to adapt or 'build out' the frame to suit the new door.

If you are ever in the position of adapting a frame, do not be tempted to fit the frame to suit the door or the existing opening. If the existing frame is leaning over or twisted, insert your new timbers upright and square. You should always endeavour to start with a square frame and cut the door down to suit.

Carpentry is not easy. It takes time to learn and you should try to get some basic techniques under your belt before trying major projects like this.

Tip

The first mistake some people make when hanging a door is to start fitting furniture (handles, hinges, etc.) before the door is cut to size. The very first thing you should do is ensure that your door is the correct size for the opening.

The table below shows standard internal door sizes.

525 mm × 2,040 mm	Metric sized door for metric frame
626 mm × 2,040 mm	Metric sized door for metric frame
726 mm × 2,040 mm	Metric sized door for metric frame
826 mm × 2,040 mm	Metric sized door for metric frame
926 mm × 2,040 mm	Metric sized door for metric frame
610 mm × 1,981 mm	**2 ft × 6 ft 6 ins**
686 mm × 1,981 mm	**2 ft 3 ins × 6 ft 6 ins**
762 mm × 1,981 mm	**2 ft 6 ins × 6 ft 6 ins**
838 mm × 1,981 mm	2 ft 9 ins × 6 ft 6 ins

It is possible to get other door sizes 'off the shelf' so always enquire, but generally speaking these are the most common door sizes. You are unlikely to get anything other than the three highlighted sizes in DIY stores. You may need to go to builders' merchants for other sizes. For extreme sizes or sizes which cannot be matched or made up, it is possible to buy 'door blanks'. These are oversize, solid, flush doors that can be cut down to any size.

Doors come in thicknesses of 1⅜ inch, 1¾ inch and 2 inches. Check the measurement between the front of your frame and your doorstop before you start work.

DOOR STYLES

Doors are either 'flush' or 'panelled'. Panelled means that the door is divided into panels with two side rails, a top and bottom rail and a middle rail. A flush door is simply flat on both sides.

Internal doors are available as 'hollow' lightweight doors or fire-check doors. Fire-check doors should always be fitted to the kitchen and internal garage door, and if you have a loft conversion they will be stipulated throughout. Their construction means that, when closed, the fire will take either half or three-quarters of an hour to burn through, depending on the door used. Intumescent strips can also be fitted into doors and frames. These are strips that swell up at the first sign of heat and prevent smoke from getting through any gaps. You will also, on the construction of a loft conversion, need to install automatic door closers to arrest the spread of any fire.

HANGING YOUR DOOR

You will need:

- ▶ *your door*
- ▶ *a pencil*
- ▶ *a Jack saw*
- ▶ *filler*
- ▶ *a wood plane (preferably a power plane)*
- ▶ *two hinges (standard butt hinges will suffice)*
- ▶ *a sharp chisel*
- ▶ *a hammer or mallet*

► *screws for attaching hinges to door and frame*
► *screwdriver.*

To hang your door:

1 *The first step is to make sure you have the door the right way round. At the top of a new flush or hollow-panelled lightweight door the word 'lock' will be printed over to one side (see the picture below). This indicates that there is a section of timber fixed inside the frame of the door to allow the door lock or latch to be fitted (see Project 27 on fitting a mortise latch). Obviously the hinges are hung on the opposite edge to the lock block. The lock block usually extends approximately 200 mm up and down from the centre of the door.*

2 *Now place the door in position up against the new frame and mark the inside of the frame on the door with a pencil. You will probably need a hand with this, as someone will have to hold the door against the frame while someone else is the other side of the door to mark the frame on it.*

3 *If you hang your new door on the opposite side to the old one you will need to fill the old hinge recesses. You can either do this by applying filler in a couple of layers, or you can try your carpentry skills and cut down a timber block, gluing and pinning it in place (punching the heads of the pins down with a nail punch) and sanding it down to finish flush with the frame. This is called 'scarfing'.*

4 *Once you have the door marked to the internal size of the frame you can cut it to size. Remember that the saw is about 3 mm thick including the set of the teeth, so if you cut along the line, the door will be 3 mm smaller than you intended. As the line you have drawn is the exact size you want the wood to be you must cut along the side of the line, leaving the line in place. With the line still visible you cannot be wrong. You can always plane a little more off, but you can't stick it back on!*

5 *You may find, with older frames, that you have twists and kinks and it will not be possible to use a saw to cut the door to size. Using a plane is the correct option here – preferably a power plane. Take some time to practise using the plane on some off-cuts of timber before you use it on a proper job.*

6 *Having cut the door to the correct size you can now attach the hinges. A variety of hinges can be used, but for most doors the standard butt hinge is used. There is no regulation regarding where these hinges should be positioned on the door or frame, but one way to do it is to have the top of the top hinge 7 inches below the top of the door and the bottom of the bottom hinge 11 inches above the bottom of the door. Mark the position of the hinge by opening it at right angles and laying it on the side of the door to be hung. A lot of DIY websites will tell you to mark round the hinge with a hobby knife. Do not do this as it is dangerous and almost impossible to cut along the grain neatly. Mark it with a pencil and then scribe the long edges with a mortise gauge if you need to.*

7 *Using a sharp chisel, cut as shown opposite, tapping firmly with your hammer or mallet. Remember that the pencil line is outside the hinge so you need to cut inside this line. Chisel out the surplus and make sure your hinge fits neatly and is not 'proud' of the timber. Neither should it be set too far in as this will cause the door to bind. The hinge should be set*

*in just enough to be flush with the edge of the door. If you
have a number of doors to hang practising this cut on an
off-cut of wood first will benefit you greatly.*

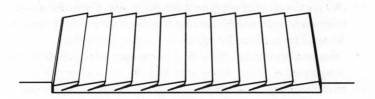

8   Drill pilot holes for your hinge screws and make sure they
    are in the centre of the hinge holes. A screw which is
    against the edge of the hole will push the hinge over and
    out of line.
9   When the hinges are cut and screwed in, stand the door in the
    opening. Check that the gap is uniform all the way round.
    Make sure you have enough depth under the door if you are
    going to lay carpets or other flooring later.
10 Wedge the door in place. You can cut some timber wedges for
    this, or you can use chisels (see below).

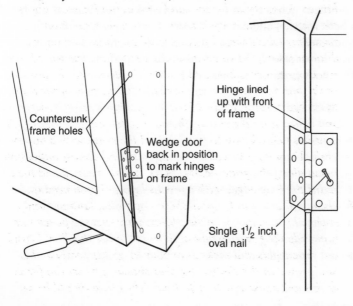

Countersunk frame holes

Wedge door back in position to mark hinges on frame

Hinge lined up with front of frame

Single 1½ inch oval nail

11   *With the door in the correct place, you can mark the position of the hinges on the frame.*

12   *Take the door away again and chisel out the rebates (recesses) for the hinges on the frame.*

13   *Wedge the door in position once again and, if you are on your own, you may find it easier to keep the top of the door in place by pinning the top hinge temporarily in place. This ensures that the door does not move as you screw the hinges in.*

14   *Once you have screwed your hinges to the frame your door should swing easily back and forth. You can now fit the door furniture you have chosen.*

Insight

If you are hanging a front door it is much easier to fit the letter box on a work bench than when it is hanging. Do it first.

27 Fitting a mortise latch

A mortise latch is the most common of door furniture, being fitted to both internal and external doors. It is simply a catch with a handle either side. Flush doors and lightweight hollow-panelled doors have lock blocks fitted inside them to allow for the lock or other door furniture to be fitted in.

You will need:

▶ *a pencil*
▶ *a carpenter's square*
▶ *a suitable drill*
▶ *a drill bit of the right size for your latch*
▶ *the latch*
▶ *a pencil*
▶ *some tape (e.g. gaffer tape)*
▶ *a 3 mm drill bit*

▶ *screws*
▶ *a chisel.*

To fix the latch:

1 *First, mark on the door the position where you want your handle. Using a carpenter's square, draw a line around the edge and both sides of the door, extending about 3 inches into the centre of the door. This serves as a marker for every operation while fitting a mortise latch. Draw the line lightly so it can be rubbed off later before painting. On the edge of the door, mark the centre of the line.*

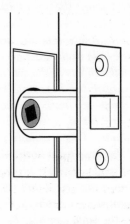

2 *Using a suitable drill with either a flat wood bit or an auger bit, drill into the door. The diameter of door latches varies, so either measure yours or see the fitting instructions on the packet. Common sizes are 18 mm and 22 mm. Keep the drill absolutely level while you drill and if you are using a panelled door, as shown on page 247, mark your drill bit with a piece of tape to make sure you do not drill too deeply (see Project 15 on fixing to masonry). Measure the length of the barrel of the latch, including the latch plate itself.*
3 *Once the hole is drilled, push the latch into the door and draw round the latch plate. Remove the latch and chisel out the rebate for the latch plate.*

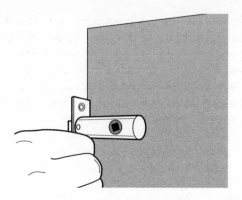

4 *Now hold the latch against the door with the face of the latch plate flush with the edge of the door. Make sure you hold it horizontally, using the line you made earlier to check this.*

5 *Put a pencil into the hole in the latch to mark the position. Make sure the pencil mark is in the centre of the hole.*

6 *Drill a 3 mm hole absolutely horizontally, right through the door, starting on the pencil mark you have just made.*

7 *Change the 3 mm drill bit for a wood bit of the correct size for the door handle spindle. This is usually 16 mm, but check your instructions. Drill this hole from both sides of the door using the 3 mm hole as a guide. If you try to go right through the door with a drill bit of this size it will split the face of the door.*

8 *Push the latch in and slide the spindle through. If all is well and moving freely, the latch can now be screwed in position.*

9 *Try the handles on the latch. Sometimes the spindle is too long for the thickness of the door. If this is the case you can see how much needs cutting off by pushing one handle flat against the face of the door and, with the other handle on, measure the gap between the handle's back plate and the door face. Use a hacksaw to cut the spindle down.*

10 *Fix the handles, using a pilot hole for the screws to ensure they go in square to the faceplate of the handle.*

Insight

If you own a mortise gauge, it is the ideal tool for measuring the frame to place the keep for the latch or any other locks.

11 *Push the new latch up against the frame and mark the position of the catch on the frame. Measure the distance from the leading edge (the edge that first hits the doorstop inside the frame when you close the door) to the flat face of the door catch. This is the measurement for fixing the keep. When the door closes the back of the catch should fit tightly to the keep edge to stop the door rattling.*

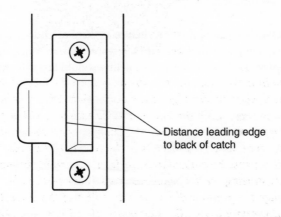

Distance leading edge
to back of catch

12 *Holding the keep against the frame in a position which lines up with the catch and the measurement to the back of the catch, mark round it with a pencil and then chisel out for the keep.*
13 *Screw the keep in place. You can then chisel out the rebate for the keep.*

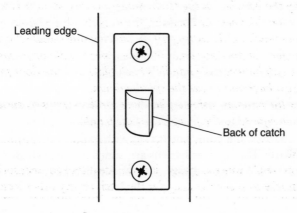

Leading edge

Back of catch

28 Making shelves

The project below outlines how to fit shelves into a chimney recess. You can adapt these instructions to suit your own ideas. The principle of fitting shelves can be applied to any type of shelf and, along with Project 15 on fixing to masonry, the basics are there for all fitments.

These shelves are called floating shelves as there are no visible means of support. They cost the earth at DIY stores and, in most cases, are a little flimsy. The shelves described below should last a lifetime!

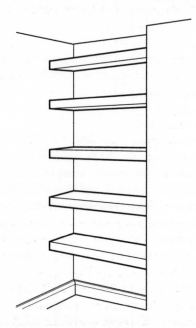

The tops of these shelves were made of redwood (pine), so they could be stained later to match the floor and doors. To hide the support battens the underside is clad with tongue and grooved matchboard. The support battens are 2 inch × 1 inch treated softwood, fixed using red wall plugs and 3-inch number 8 screws.

You will need:

▶ *a pencil*
▶ *a spirit level*
▶ *some tape (e.g. gaffer tape)*
▶ *an electric hammer-action drill*
▶ *timber battens*
▶ *a 6 mm masonry drill bit*
▶ *wall plugs of the correct size*
▶ *screws of an appropriate size*
▶ *an electric screwdriver*
▶ *a Jack saw*
▶ *timber cut to the correct size for the tops and fronts of your shelves*
▶ *wood adhesive*
▶ *2-inch (50 mm) number 8 screws (four for each shelf)*
▶ *matchboard cut to the size of your shelves (readily available in packs from all DIY stores)*
▶ *panel pins*
▶ *50 mm 'lost-head' nails*
▶ *some neutral two-part wood filler.*

To make your shelves:

1 *First, mark out the spacing for your shelves on the wall. Think about what you are going to place on the shelves and make sure there is enough clearance from the shelf above. If the shelves are for books, then be sure to measure the tallest books and designate at least one shelf for them.*
2 *Attach the first batten to the back wall. Refer to Project 15 to see how to fix these battens to the wall.*
3 *With the batten on the back wall fixed solidly in position, mark a level line for the side battens. The mark nearest the front of the batten should also be checked for level from the opposite corner of the batten at the back. If you do not have a spirit level long enough to do this then use a piece of the shelving timber (after checking that it is straight) on its edge to sit across the gap, with the spirit level on top.*

4 When measuring and fixing the side battens, don't forget that in this design there is a face timber which is 25 mm thick, so if you want the shelf to finish flush with the front of an alcove you must leave the battens 25 mm back from the face.

5 Repeat this process for the rest of the shelf battens.

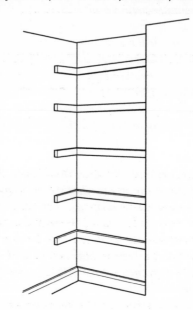

6 The top timbers can now be fixed. Always start multiple shelving from the top shelf and work downwards. You will not have any obstructions if you work this way. In this example the shelf timbers are 150 mm wide and a full width timber should be used at the front. Any cut timbers should go at the back where they are less likely to be seen – the chances are you will need to cut up against the back wall anyway. In an alcove especially, walls are unlikely to be square.

7 Apply wood adhesive to the top of the battens and then screw the timbers down, with two screws in each end of each timber. Use 2-inch (50 mm) number 8 screws. Countersink the heads of the screws into the shelf (see Project 23).

8 Now fix a centre batten from above, using the same countersinking method. This batten, in this instance, is *purely to help support the matchboard that is going to be fixed to the underside of the shelf. It does not support the top planks.*

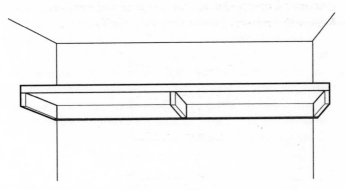

9 *The 25 mm 'planks' used for the top will stay rigid to a span of about 1 m. For distances greater than 1 m, fix the centre batten to the rear batten (before the rear batten is fixed) by drilling a pilot hole and screwing through the back of the rear batten. The complete assembly can then be fixed to the wall. When the front of the shelf is fixed across the battens it will give extra support in the centre, allowing a total rigid span of about 1.8 m.*

10 *Place some wood adhesive on the top of the cross batten and push up to the centre of the planks. Fix from above.*

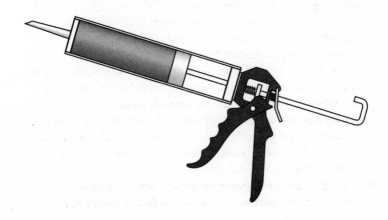

11 *Now repeat the same process, using 10 mm matchboard, to the underside of the shelf. Use adhesive and panel fins to secure this timber. Do not use nails on shelves like this as repeated hammering on struts fixed to old masonry can loosen the fixings. As with the planks above, place the full width timbers at the front and cut the final timber to shape at the back of the shelf, against the wall.*

12 *The last job is to cut the front of the shelves. This is made from the same planks as the top. Carefully measure the width required and cut the timber down. Because of the variation in all timbers it is not safe to assume each front will be the same, so measure each one individually.*

Insight

To save a lot of time with screwing each plank and then filling each screwhead, you can hire a nail gun. The nails are fired in neatly and the heads are so small they disappear beneath the timber. No filling required!

13 *Once they are cut down, nail each front into the end of the battens. The front of the shelves will be highly visible, so keep*

the holes as small as possible – 50 mm 'lost-head' nails can be bought for this purpose. These have a small head, which is banged in flush with the top of the timber, then a nail punch is used to bang them in another millimetre or so, allowing them to disappear under the surface of the timber. If done carefully, the timber all but closes up over the head of the nail.

14 Now sand down the edges of the face timbers and any filling. Always use a neutral two-part wood filler for this kind of joinery work. It is more expensive than ordinary filler, but is much stronger and will accept wood stain more easily. It will not stain to exactly the same colour as the rest of the wood as its composition is obviously different, but using a neutral filler will get it as close as is possible.

15 Now wax or stain your timber to the required finish and stand back to admire your work.

29 Building a cupboard

This project contains basic principles for building a frame for a simple cupboard. It can be expanded to suit different designs: the struts can be moved to accommodate shelves or simply left open plan. It will give you an idea of how to build storage space into your home and can even be adapted to make a corner cupboard. The timber sizes can be changed and more struts can be put in to ensure greater strength if you feel you need it. The structure can be fixed to any wall, ceiling or floor.

Tip

Check the wall, floor and ceiling area for pipes and cables before you drill anything.

For this simple cupboard you should use 50 mm × 50 mm PSE (planed, squared-edge) timber, which simply means it is prepared for joinery, as opposed to the sawn state timber is in when it leaves the timber mill. It is also called, in its prepared state, PAR – planed all round.

With the number of different door designs available from kitchen and DIY stores these days, it may be a good idea to find the doors (if you intend to have them) first. The frame can easily be built around the door size and you can guarantee that they match your existing decor.

No dimensions are given in the project. Even when planed, timber can vary by a millimetre or so and ceiling heights can vary considerably. Measure your own timber and other dimensions carefully and remember: measure twice – cut once.

Tip

The shelves and cladding material are your choice, but the usual suspects for this kind of work are MDF (medium-density fibreboard) or tongue-and-groove timber matchboards. Both can be bought in various thicknesses from DIY stores.

Use a carpenter's square to make all cuts. Neat joints are impossible without a completely square face to begin with. Also, if the timber is not square at the end, a measurement to the other end will vary, depending on which side you measure from. This can make it impossible to get a decent finish.

Tip

Please remember, it takes many years to become a skilled carpenter or joiner. If this is your first project, or you have not done much carpentry, buy an additional length of timber and practise your joints before embarking on a project which will become a feature in your home. An 8-foot length of sawn timber to practise on will cost pennies compared with the waste of materials if you mess up with the real thing.

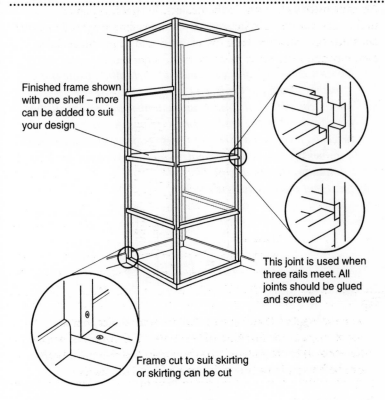

Finished frame shown with one shelf – more can be added to suit your design

This joint is used when three rails meet. All joints should be glued and screwed

Frame cut to suit skirting or skirting can be cut

You will need:

▶ *a tape measure*
▶ *a pencil*
▶ *a carpenter's square*
▶ *a Jack saw*
▶ *enough 50 mm × 50 mm PSE timber to build the frame of your cupboard*

- *material for shelves and cladding (e.g. MDF or tongue-and-groove timber matchboards)*
- *your chosen cupboard doors*
- *wood glue*
- *suitable screws*
- *a screwdriver.*

To build your cupboard:

1 *Check that your walls are square to each other, using the 3, 4 5 method shown in Project 25.*
2 *Make (cut out) all the joints in the timber before any of the frame is fixed to the wall, floor or ceiling. As with other projects, it is a good idea to practise making these joints with a timber off-cut. Basic carpentry skills are required for a good job and practise makes perfect.*
3 *Next, cut the two uprights to size.*

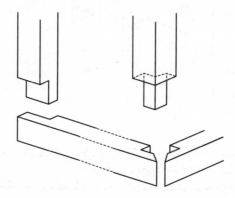

4 *Fix the uprights absolutely vertically on the walls using the struts, or cross-members, as spacers to get them in the right position.*
5 *Fix the struts and the centre upright together using glue and screws. Make sure the screw heads are countersunk into the timber or they will push the cladding, or frame covering, out (see Project 23).*
6 *Use a tenon saw to cut the skirting back if you prefer that to cutting the frame around the skirting.*

7 Fix the frame to the wall using a 7 mm masonry bit with red wall plugs and (for 50 mm timber) 3-inch number 8 screws. If you are fixing the cupboard to a plasterboard wall you will need to buy proprietary plasterboard fixings.

8 Mark the position of any cross-members lightly on the walls when your frame is in place. This will allow you to see where they are when you are fixing the covering to the frame. The pencil marks can be rubbed out later.

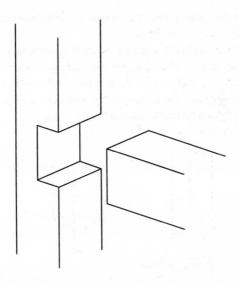

9 Next, cut and fix the shelf or shelves. This can be done more easily when you can get to all sides.

10 The side rails, which support the cladding, should be fixed at no less than 600 mm centres for 12.5 mm cladding at 450 mm centres for thinner cladding.

Insight

If you want to fit doors to your cupboards, the same process is used for hanging a door as shown in Project 28.

10 THINGS TO REMEMBER FROM PROJECTS 15–29

1 *Learn the difference between different types of drill bit and where/when to use them.*

2 *Ditto with types of screw, wall plug and nail.*

3 *Never force power tools – you will burn them out.*

4 *If you have to drill a large diameter hole in masonry or concrete, start with a small one and work up.*

5 *When laying any kind of wet covering such as plaster, concrete, screed, adhesive, paint, etc., ensure the coverage is even.*

6 *When working with any of the above, keep all tools spotlessly clean.*

7 *When working with any of the above, never tackle huge areas in one go. Break down into manageable-sized chunks.*

8 *Practise working with wet coverings – 99 per cent of the time you only get one chance to get it right.*

9 *Measure EVERYTHING twice. Cut it once!*

10 *Keep all woodworking tools sharp and clean. Protect sharp edges with a cloth or similar.*

Electrical

---

30 Stripping cables and wires

Stripping wires can be very easy, but a great deal of care needs to be taken. As with most jobs, it is much easier and safer with the right tools. Electricians will use side cutters for all of the jobs outlined below, but these are not advised for the amateur as using them correctly requires experience – a tiny little nick out of a cable, flex or wire insulation can be lethal as it will allow current to arc across wires.

You will need:

- ▶ *either a pair of side cutters, if you are experienced enough to use these OR*
- ▶ *a set of cable strippers, available from all good DIY stores*
- ▶ *a good pair of scissors/knife to cut through the cable*
- ▶ *a pair of pliers.*

To strip a cable for wiring into a socket or switch:

1 *The cable shown is a 2.5 mm two-core and earth cable. Nick the cable through the sheath at the end, in the centre.*

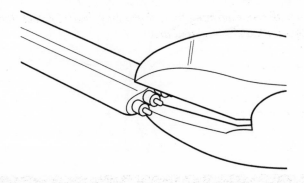

2 *Pull the sheath apart a little and you will see the bare earth wire in the centre.*

3 *Clamp the wire gently with the side cutters or pliers and, holding the end of the cable in your other hand, pull the wire through the insulation. This will tear quite easily.*

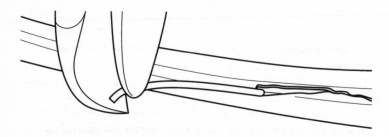

4 *Measure the connections you wish to make and then add on enough extra to turn the wires over at the end (see opposite). Do not skimp on the length – 'stretching' cable to meet connections can mean they will pull out over time. It is better to have a little more than you need folded into a socket than too little.*

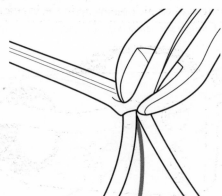

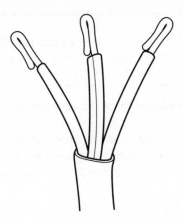

5 *Place an earth sleeve (see Chapter 7) onto any bare earth wires.*

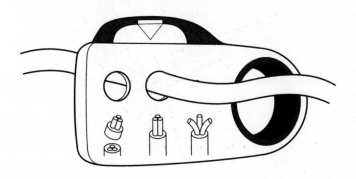

31 Wiring a plug

Care must be taken when changing a plug.

Plugs are bought with an instruction card (see below) over the three pins, which is often taken straight off and thrown away. However, if you read this instruction card you will see that it actually gives some useful information, such as the exact length the wire should be trimmed enabling an easy, safe connection to the plug terminal.

You will find the following wires in a plug.

▶ *The live wire – this is coloured brown and goes to the live terminal on the plug. The connection is made at the end of the fuse in the plug. The live electricity has to pass through the fuse before it gets into the cable leading to your appliance. If anything is wrong, the fuse blows.*
▶ *The neutral wire – this is on the left of the plug and coloured blue.*
▶ *The earth wire – this is at the top of the plug and is coloured green and yellow.*

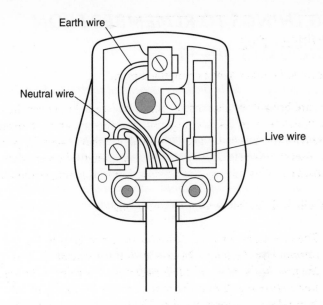

Earth wire

Neutral wire

Live wire

To change a plug:

1 *Strip the wires back to expose the appropriate length (see Project 30 on stripping wires for guidance on this).*
2 *Most plug terminals have small holes in them into which you place the stripped end of the appropriate wire. Some plug terminals have small brass ring clamps under which you position each wire and then screw the clamp down to fix it.*
3 *Make sure all connections are tight, including the clamp which holds the main body of the flex tight to the plug. If this is allowed to move around it will not be long before it loosens the wires in their terminals and a short circuit could occur.*

Insight

Always ensure it is the outer sleeve that is trapped in the plug clamp. If the clamp is tightened onto the conductor wires they may split to cause a short circuit.

10 THINGS TO REMEMBER FROM PROJECTS 30–31

1   *Always keep within the laws associated with Part P of the building regulations.*

2   *Only use approved tools and fittings. Check you have the correct cables and fuses for your installations.*

3   *Never turn power off without warning other occupants. Place warning signs on main switches when you have turned them off.*

4   *You are legally obliged to ensure all those in and on your property are kept as safe as possible.*

5   *Do not just reset trip switches without finding out why they have tripped.*

6   *The earth wire in a plug should be cut a little longer than required. This kink will ensure it is the last wire to be pulled out in the case of an accident with the plug.*

7   *Draw a map of your electrical supply to learn where each socket and light is fed from.*

8   *Never work on live circuits.*

9   *Cheap bulbs will blow more often.*

10 *Electricity kills – do not take chances.*

Plumbing

---

32 Repairing a burst pipe

This method of repairing a pipe can also be used when you have accidentally punctured a pipe, for example with a nail.

You will need:

- *a hacksaw*
- *some emery paper, glass paper or a file*
- *a slip coupler of the right size for the pipe*
- *an adjustable spanner or one of the right size to tighten the nuts on the coupler.*

Proprietary slip couplers, available for all sizes of pipe, can be bought from plumbers' merchants and, ideally, all DIY enthusiasts will have one of these in their toolbox. It is a sheath with an internal diameter slightly larger than the copper pipe it will cover.

To mend the pipe:

1 *First, turn the water off at the mains as soon as you realize there is a problem. A small amount of water will dry out reasonably quickly; a large amount of water can cause a great deal of damage. If you do not know where your mains stopcock is, go and find it now!*
2 *Locate the damaged area of the pipe. Remember, this may not be directly behind the visible signs of water. The ceiling may slope, or the pressure may have forced a spray of water away from the actual split, so search thoroughly.*
3 *The hole, burst or split in the pipe will only be small, so cut the pipe either side of it with a hacksaw. The saw will*

leave burrs around the edges of the cuts and these need to be smoothed off with some emery paper, glass paper or a file.

Insight

Even when the water is turned off and all is drained down, there will be water in the pipes. As you cut be prepared for this with some cloths and a small bowl.

---

4 *Undo the slip coupling into its various component parts. Take the nuts from each end, releasing the two olives, as shown in the diagram. The olives are brass rings that are squeezed between the fitting and the pipe by the action of tightening the end nuts up against them. This fills the joint between slip coupling and pipe, preventing water seeping through.*

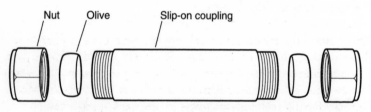

Nut   Olive   Slip-on coupling

5 *Place a nut over each end of the cut pipe, then slide on the two olives. Then slide the slip coupling on to one of the cut ends of the pipe and push it back over the other end of the cut pipe. Position the slip coupling so that the cut-out section of the pipe is roughly in the middle, and then slide the two olives up to it. Then tightened the nuts at each end of the slip coupling.*

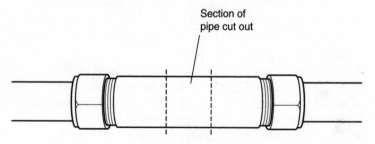

Section of
pipe cut out

Tighten both nuts ensuring
centering of slip-on coupling

6 *Turn on the water and check that there are no leaks.*

Tip

Tightening should not be overdone and, if done carefully, you
should be able to feel the olive squeezing closed. Overtightening
will cause leaks as it can squash the copper pipe, so it is better
to tighten to a point where you can feel good resistance on the
nuts. If you have not tightened the fitting enough, you will only
get a small drip when you turn the water on, which you can
stop by tightening a little more. This is a tiny job compared with
overtightening and having to start again.

33 Repairing a dripping tap

The principles of tap operation are the same with most taps, and the
illustration below can be referred to for the names of the various parts
of a tap. Essentially, turning the handle of a tap turns a spindle, which
in turn lifts a valve (called a jumper), together with a rubber washer,
from the tap inlet. This allows water to flow through the spout.

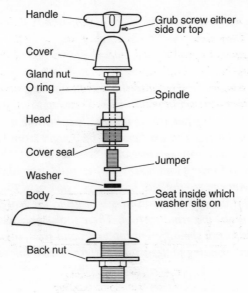

You will need:

▶ *a good adjustable spanner or a plumber's wrench*
▶ *a grinding tool, usually called a tap reseating tool.*

To repair the tap:

1 *First, turn off the water and, if you are working on an upstairs tap, open one of the taps downstairs to drain the pipes.*
2 *Prise up the cover of the tap or remove the screw at the side of the handle to allow access to the gland nut which holds the spindle and jumper in place.*
3 *Once this nut is undone you will be able to lift out the tap mechanism to get to the seat.*

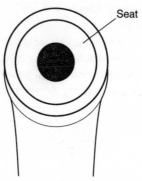

Seat

4 *The washer will be fixed to the bottom of the jumper, so first check that it is still in good order. Your repair may well be one of the lucky few where it actually is just the washer that needs replacing. Tap washers can be bought from DIY stores and these days you can buy plumbers' repair kits that contain numerous O rings and washers often used around the home.*
5 *Once you can see the seat (even if you just need to replace the washer it will not hurt to smooth or grind the seat down a little), insert the grinding tool. These tools come with various threads to suit the different tap types and sizes, together with different grinding plates to suit different sized tap seats.*

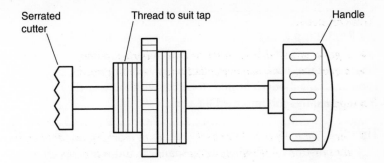

Serrated cutter | Thread to suit tap | Handle

Insight

Do not be afraid to push down hard. It takes quite a lot of effort to grind down a valve seat.

6 *Place the correct thread in the tap body and tighten it. Press down on the handle and twist. Some people prefer to twist in the same direction and keep turning clockwise, while others prefer to twist backwards and forwards to grind the seat down. It doesn't matter which way you do it as long as you end up with a smooth seat for the washer to sit on.*

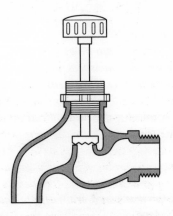

7 *When you have finished grinding (you will be able to feel a really smooth seat with your fingers), tip a cup of water down the tap body to rinse away any ground brass which could otherwise get trapped between seat and washer.*

34 Replacing a tap

Changing taps in a bathroom can give a whole new look to the room, and the modern fittings, together with the way they are fitted, bring this job into the DIY zone.

> **Tip**
> Care must be taken when using spanners and wrenches on taps and other fittings as these can easily slip and damage the fitting, or you!

The trickiest part of this job is removing the old taps. Very old taps may be held in with putty or Plumber's Mait (a waterproof plumbing putty) which will bind very hard over time. The back nuts and tap connectors which hold a tap in place and provide the connection for the water are almost impossible to manipulate with anything other than the correct basin spanner which, at the time of writing, costs less than £10 and will save you many hours.

You will need:

- ▶ *a basin spanner/wrench*
- ▶ *a cloth to clean around tap holes*
- ▶ *the new tap, with all its washers and nuts*
- ▶ *replacement fibre washer if you reuse the existing tap connectors*
- ▶ *a flexible tap connector if your connections do not reach the new taps or are too long.*

To replace the tap:

1 *First, turn off the water and drain off any water in the pipes by opening the taps.*
2 *Then undo the tap connector nut which holds the copper pipe onto the thread of the tap. If this is stiff, get someone to hold the tap for you while you apply extra elbow grease. If the entire tap starts to turn, you will again need some help or you*

can wedge the tap still with a piece of wood pushed between the taps.

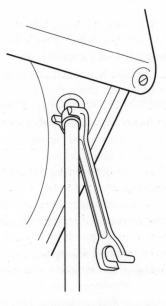

Tip

Before removing the taps, make a note of which side was hot and which cold. The hot tap is usually on the left, but not always!

3 *Once the tap connector is removed, undo the back nut. This is the nut which actually clamps the tap to the bath and it could be a bit stiff.*

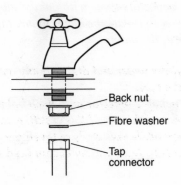

Back nut

Fibre washer

Tap connector

4 *Once the taps are off, clean the area round the tap holes. This should be done above and below the bath, basin or sink.*

Insight

Do not attempt this job without the correct tools as described here. If you cannot get the tap nuts done up properly, your tap will leak. Much damage could then be done.

---

5 *Check the instructions that come with the tap to make sure you have all of the required washers, then insert the tap through the hole. When working on a bath it is usually easier to remove the overflow connection from the bath, but remember to put it back!*

6 *Tighten the back nut of the new tap with all washers and spacers (sometimes called top hats because of their shape).*

7 *If the existing feed pipes are the right length for the new tap then these can be used; if not, you will need to alter them. If you do reuse the existing tap connectors, replace the fibre washer which you will find in the nut. This washer seals the joint between pipe and tap and without it your connection will leak.*

8 *If your connections do not reach the new taps or are too long (even a few millimetres can make a watertight joint impossible), the easiest way to connect them is to cut the pipes back from the tap connector and clean the pipe ends thoroughly and then push on a flexible tap connector. Some flexible tap connectors come with on/off valves attached and these allow you to isolate the water to any tap without turning off the water at the mains.*

Push-on fitting with valve

Tap connector

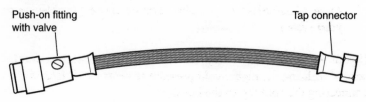

35 Curing an air lock in the hot water system

If you have an automatic washing machine, and have both the hot and cold supplies connected, an effective remedy to this problem can be implemented quite easily.

The cold water to at least one of the downstairs taps will be connected directly to the mains (this is generally the kitchen sink tap). The washing machine will be connected to this run of cold pipe as it needs mains pressure to work properly. The mains pressure of the cold water is much greater than that of the hot water and we can use this greater pressure to push any air locks back to the hot water storage tank.

To remove the air lock using your washing machine:

1 *Disconnect the cold water hose from the back of the washing machine. (Turn the valve off first.)*
2 *Disconnect the hot water hose from the valve on the hot water pipe. (Turn this valve off first also.)*
3 *Now connect the free end of the cold hose to the free hot valve.*
4 *Turn on the hot water valve and then the cold water valve. This will allow the greater pressure of the cold water to push any air back up the hot water pipe.*
5 *Leave both valves open for approximately 30 seconds and then close them, cold first.*
6 *Now check the flow from the hot tap at the kitchen sink – the air should have been dispelled. If not, repeat the procedure outlined above. If, after three attempts, the problem is still there, please contact a plumber. There may be a problem with your system.*

If your washing machine only has a cold water connection, another way of utilizing the higher cold pressure to clear an air lock is by connecting the cold tap to the hot tap.

You will need:

▶ *a piece of hosepipe*
▶ *a couple of jubilee clips.*

To remove the air block using the kitchen taps:

1 *Attach the hosepipe between the pipes using the jubilee clips.*
2 *Make absolutely sure the connections are sound and do not leave the taps unattended.*
3 *Turn on the cold water tap. Then follow the instructions as for the washing machine method on page 277.*

To remove the air block using mixer taps:

▶ *If you have a mixer tap in the kitchen, the same method can be used, but you will need a longer piece of hose to connect the kitchen tap (where the cold water comes from the mains) to another hot tap.*

OR

▶ *Another method for a mixer tap is to squeeze the single mixer tap outlet so that the palm of your hand covers it firmly. Turn on the hot, then the cold (this order is important to prevent confined mains pressure from forcing your hand away from the tap outlet). The cold supply, now unable to exit from the hand-blocked tap outlet, will instead flow across to the hot water pipe, causing a backflow in the hot water system, clearing the air lock.*

36 Unblocking toilets and drains

Unblocking toilets and drains can be relatively easy, but is a dirty job. The key here, as with most DIY jobs, is to have the right tools. It is also necessary to wear a very good pair of rubber gloves.

SINKS, BATHS, BASINS AND SHOWER TRAYS

A sink, bath, basin and shower tray can be unblocked in a few ways.

▶ *An ordinary plunger can be used by placing it over the plughole and pushing up and down on the handle. This creates a force in both directions, compression as you push down and suction as you release. The idea here is that the blockage is dislodged and breaks up, allowing it to flow down the drain.*

▶ *Another option is to use what is known as a power plunger. This tool is simply 'pumped up', by pumping the handle at the end, then placed over the plughole. When you press the trigger, all the compressed air is released, forcing the blockage down the pipe or breaking it up.*

Pump

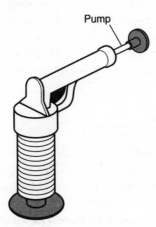

▶ *A favourite at DIY Doctor is the water injector. Put some water in the sink, basin, bath or shower tray and stand the pump in it. Pull up on the handle to fill the injector with water. Next, place it over the plughole and push down hard, then pull up again. The water is pushed at great force through the blockage and then sucked up again, using the same principles as in the plunger method on page 279. Repeat this action several times. If your blockage is within a couple of metres of the plughole it will soon clear.*

▶ *Finally, for sinks, basins, baths and showers there is the corkscrew cable. The flexible wire is pushed into the drainpipe, wiggled about to break up the blockage, and wound back in – very simple, very effective and available from all DIY stores.*

TOILETS

A toilet can also be unblocked using the first method on page 279, if you think your blockage is in the U bend at the back of the toilet. The action is exactly the same, push and pull to break up the blockage.

For blockages that appear to be further down it may be necessary to open the manhole to inspect and clear any blockages.

1   *First you will need to locate the relevant manhole. You may have a visible soil and vent pipe (SVP) coming out of your bathroom, which you can follow down to the ground and look around for the nearest manhole to it. If it is not the right one, you will need to check further afield.*

    ▷ *There are two types of manhole for the purposes of this project: surface water manholes, which collect water from your rain gutters, and the foul water manholes, which collect the waste water from the sinks, basins, baths, showers and toilets. These will smell, so identification should not be too much of a problem.*

    ▷ *Although your toilet may be blocked, there is a chance that some seepage is occurring through the blockage and you may need to identify this to see which manhole it is running into. This can be done by adding a little dye into the water and watching at the various manholes to trace the flow. Tracing dye can be bought at builders' and plumbers' merchants.*

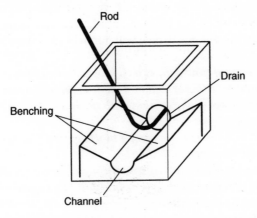

Insight

All of the equipment required for unblocking drains and toilets can be hired from a tool-hire shop. They will be able to supply you with the safety equipment (goggles, gloves, masks) also.

2   Once you have traced the manhole or manholes, you may
    well be able to rod back up towards the house. The diagram
    on page 281 represents the basics of what you will find in a
    manhole. Usually a brick-built structure (modern manholes are
    sometimes formed with pre-cast concrete or plastic rings), with
    a sloping floor called benching. The benching slopes down into a
    half-pipe shape called a channel.

3   After carefully removing the manhole cover, which can
    sometimes be very heavy, the rods should be screwed together
    one at a time and pushed into the drainpipe. Drain rods come
    in lengths of 1 metre and are screwed together to make a long
    length. They are very flexible and are simply inserted into the
    opening and pushed down the drainpipe.

> **Tip**
>
> Drain rods screw together in a normal clockwise direction.
> When you are rodding a drain, the rods will turn in your
> hand – it's impossible to stop them. In order to prevent the
> rods from unscrewing, make sure you deliberately turn the
> rods clockwise as you push and prod. Leaving a length of
> drain rod in your waste pipe will not help your drainage!

4   Sometimes, if your pipe is well blocked, the channel and
    benching may be covered in water making the drain hole
    difficult to see. Poke around with the rod until you find the
    entrance.

5   You will feel when you meet a blockage and you should then
    prod the blockage with the rod.

6   Drain rods come with various fittings to screw on the end
    which, in theory, make the removal of blockages easier.
    It is best to start with nothing except the rod, prodding and
    poking until the obstacle (usually loads of toilet paper or
    nappies) clears.

7   Occasionally it may be necessary to use a worm screw (this
    comes with the set of rods).

8   Sometimes you may not feel a blockage because it is either too
    far to reach or too soft to register. At this point, screw on the
    rubber plunger. Use the rods then as a giant plunger, pushing

and pulling up and down the pipe. This will create the same
pressures as mentioned above and should release the blockage.

Tip

A word of warning: some manholes can be quite deep. These
manholes are normally fitted with iron steps built into the
sides of the brickwork or concrete. This is obviously for
climbing down, BUT manholes are very dangerous places as
the gases they contain can be overpowering. Do not go down
into a manhole without someone at the top to make sure you
are okay.

Very occasionally you will meet a blockage which cannot be reached
from the toilet end or from the manhole end. This means it may be
in the soil and vent pipe itself. Most of these will have access plates,
which should be undone very carefully for obvious reasons. A lot
of SVPs will be boxed in and this can cause real disruption. If you
cannot unblock the drain/pipes by yourself and you feel you have
established that the blockage is in your SVP then it may be time to
call a plumber. The mess that can be created by this kind of blockage
is something you really do not want to deal with if you are not sure
of what you are doing.

37 Repairing a toilet that won't flush

A toilet that won't flush properly is a frequent problem in homes.
If the toilet was working properly and has now stopped flushing,
and there is water in the cistern, there are two probable causes:

▶ *the handle is not connected to the flushing mechanism in*
  the cistern
▶ *the flush diaphragm is split.*

A cistern allows water in through a valve. There are two main
types of valve. The most common is the ball valve; the second, ever
more widely used, is the quieter Torbeck valve. Both operate on

the same principle: the water inlet is controlled by a valve, which is opened and closed by a lever. The lever, or 'float arm', is raised and lowered by the water in the cistern (this is exactly the same system as that used in cold water tanks in most lofts).

Once the water is in the cistern, a flushing mechanism lets it out again. The most popular flushing mechanism is the toilet siphon. The handle is attached, via a wire, to the top of the flush siphon. When the lever is depressed, or the chain pulled, the flush diaphragm is pulled upwards on the diaphragm frame. Because of the frame underneath the flush diaphragm, the water cannot escape and is drawn up and over into the flush pipe where it runs straight into the toilet bowl.

If the toilet is not flushing properly:

1 *Check first that the flushing mechanism is connected together properly. If the lever or chain is not attached to the top of the siphon, it will not pull up the diaphragm and the water will not be released.*

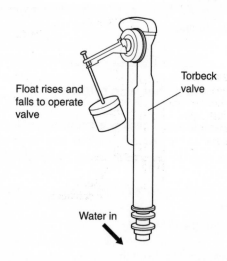

Float rises and falls to operate valve

Torbeck valve

Water in

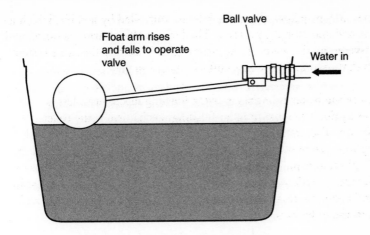

Float arm rises
and falls to operate
valve

Ball valve

Water in

2 *If this is not the problem, move on to check the diaphragm itself. If the flush diaphragm is split, the pressure of the water as the diaphragm is drawn up the chamber simply pushes through the split and does not allow any resistance. The more you flush, the bigger the split becomes. In this case it is time to change the diaphragm.*

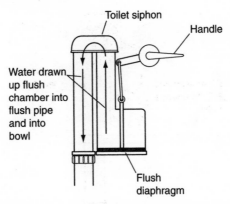

Toilet siphon

Handle

Water drawn
up flush
chamber into
flush pipe
and into
bowl

Flush
diaphragm

You will need:

▶ *a sponge*
▶ *a good adjustable spanner or a plumber's wrench*
▶ *a replacement diaphragm (available from plumbers' merchants).*

To replace a split diaphragm:

Insight

Tiny pumps and hoses can be bought in DIY stores which attach to an electric drill. The drill turns and the pump pumps the remaining water out of the cistern. It's a little easier than using a sponge, but much more expensive!

1 *Turn off the water to the cistern, flush the toilet and soak up any remaining water with a sponge.*

2 *Once the cistern is empty, unclip the connection between the handle arm and the flush unit.*

3 *Release the back nut under the cistern and pull the flush unit clear.*

4 *Unclip the bottom half of the connection clip and pull out the frame, which holds the diaphragm. (There may be a spring over the central dowel – don't forget to return this when reassembling.)*

5 *Unclip and slide off the diaphragm, replace and reassemble (diaphragm is shown below).*

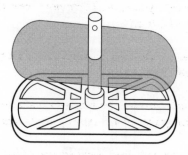

Flush diaphragm.

10 THINGS TO REMEMBER FROM PROJECTS 32–37

1 *Keep a supply of repair fittings handy. Speed fit are more expensive fittings but very easy and quick to use in an emergency.*

2 *Maintain easy access to mains and other stopcocks.*

3 *Give all water valves a turn once in a while to keep them free from jamming.*

4 *Turn water off and drain system when a repair is required.*

5 *Keep all plumbing tools clean, dry and oiled to prevent rusting.*

6 *Never overtighten fittings.*

7 *Research the taps you have. There are many different types and repair methods differ.*

8 *Always clip new pipework at the suggested intervals to prevent knocking pipes.*

9 *Check manholes around the house to make sure you know which manhole takes which type of waste and from where.*

10 *Plumbers' merchants are a good source of help and information. They will usually take the time to explain what you need for any given job.*

Decorating

38 Painting or papering new plaster

PAINTING

New plaster and new Artex are very porous indeed. If you apply any kind of ordinary paint directly onto either of these surfaces, moisture will immediately be sucked out of the paint, which will dry too quickly and will not stick properly. The paint may soon start to blister and flake off.

1 *In a normal centrally heated house, allow four weeks for the plaster to dry before painting.*
2 *Prime or seal the surface first, i.e. apply a coating which is diluted enough to enter the pores of the material with the emulsion or liquid with which it is mixed. So, if you intend to use water-based paint, e.g. emulsion, then mix some of that emulsion paint with water at a ratio of 4 parts paint to 1 part water and stir thoroughly.*
3 *Apply this to the surface – sometimes you can actually hear the plaster or Artex sucking up the liquid. It is rarely necessary to apply two coats of sealer, but it will not harm the surface either.*
4 *When the surface is sealed and dry, you can continue to paint as normal.*

Tip

The humidity in kitchens and bathrooms allows water-based paints, like normal emulsion, to soak up the water vapour, which can make them unstable and likely to peel or harbour mould spores. To avoid these problems, it is advisable to use oil-based paint in kitchens and bathrooms. Some companies make special kitchen and bathroom paint in a great range of colours.

Insight

Mould prevention chemicals can be mixed with normal emulsions to prevent bathroom mould.

If you are in a real hurry to paint your wall, use microporous paint, which allows the surface of the plaster to carry on breathing and evaporating moisture while it is drying out. These paints should not be painted onto wet plaster – at least two weeks' drying time should be allowed in a normally heated house. The paints can be found in many DIY stores and decorators' merchants. They are generally a lot thinner than ordinary water- or solvent-based paints and in many cases, once the wall is dry, it is recommended that you paint over them with emulsion. Please read the instructions on the container for information regarding thinning down and applying the first coat onto new plaster.

WALLPAPERING

To hang wallpaper to new walls:

1 *In a normal centrally heated house, allow four weeks for the plaster to dry before papering.*
2 *Once they are dry, 'size' the walls. Size is a proprietary product for sealing the walls but a dilution of the wallpaper paste you are going to use can also be used as a form of size to seal the wall. Most pastes will have a sizing solution on the packet, but a rough guide is to use 25 per cent more water in a sizing solution.*

Tip

If you intend to apply a vinyl paper to the surface, it is best to prepare the walls by sizing with a dilution of a paste with fungicide in it. Vinyl papers are airproof and, as a result, any dampness trapped behind the paper will not be allowed to evaporate out. This could turn to mould.

3 *Apply the size or diluted paste with a large emulsion brush.*

39 Blocking stains before decoration

If you have a water stain on the ceiling or wall, the first thing to do is to make absolutely sure the leak or other source of water causing the stain has been dealt with. Disguising water leaks in any way will only lead to further problems, as the water will find its way into the room somewhere else. Once you are sure you have dealt with the source of the water you can undertake the following project.

If you have had a leak coming through a painted ceiling, or damp coming through an old wall, it does not matter how many coats of emulsion, or how many layers of wallpaper you put on, the stain will still come through. The only way to stop this happening is to cover the stain with a stain blocker, solvent or an oil-based paint first. You can then emulsion or paper over on top of this.

You will need:

▶ *sugar soap for fire damage, grease problems in the kitchen, soot or nicotine stains*
▶ *a stain blocker, solvent or an oil-based paint.*

To cover the stain:

1 *Ensure the cause of the stain has been dealt with.*
2 *In the event of fire damage, grease problems in the kitchen, soot or nicotine stains, the areas concerned must be washed down thoroughly with a solution of sugar soap. Sugar soap is a crystallized alkaline (which looks like sugar in its powdered form), which can be bought in DIY stores in powder or liquid forms.*
3 *Apply a stain blocker, solvent or an oil-based paint. The stain blockers you can buy in DIY stores are usually solvent-based and require a lot of ventilation when they are applied, so keep the windows open.*
4 *Once this has dried completely you can decorate over it as you choose, with emulsion or with wallpaper.*

40 Ceramic tiling

Ceramic wall tiles are made in an enormous variety of colours, designs and sizes. You will need to spend some time looking at displays to find the tiles that appeal most to you. Keep an eye open for combination tiles. These are basically tiles with the same background colour as the majority being used but with decorated tiles in singles, or sets of two or three. These are used almost like pictures on a wall, being interspaced with the plain tiles. Many of these decorative tiles are hand-painted before being glazed and can bring a tiled wall to life. Look out also for tiles that are a colour match for modern sanitary ware.

Wall tiles sizes are most commonly 150 mm × 150 mm (6 inches × 6 inches), 200 mm × 200 mm (8 inches × 8 inches), 200 mm × 250 mm (8 inches × 10 inches) and 200 mm × 300 mm (8 inches × 12 inches). As a general rule, aim for large tiles in a large room and small tiles in a small room. This is partly for aesthetic reasons and partly for practical reasons. The larger the tile, the quicker it is to finish!

WORKING OUT WALL TILE QUANTITIES

1 *The easiest method of working out how many tiles you need is to measure the height of the wall and calculate how many of your chosen tile size will be needed to fit from floor to ceiling.*
2 *Count any halves or parts of a tile as a whole one.*
3 *Do the same for the wall width.*
4 *Multiply the number required for the height by the number for the width and this will give you the total number of tiles needed for the wall.*
5 *Repeat the process for the other walls.*

6   Use the same process to deduct for doors and windows
    where you will not be tiling, but do not forget the 'reveals' or
    window returns and any sills you intend to tile.

7   When you have a total for the whole room, add 10 per cent,
    i.e. add a further 10 tiles for every 100 that your calculations
    say you need. This is to allow for mistakes and breakages and
    to make sure you have some tiles of the same colour should
    any get broken later on.

Example: A wall 2.7 m long by 2.2 m high is to be tiled using 150 mm ×
150 mm tiles. Divide the wall height by the tile height: 2200 ÷ 150 =
14.67 (15 tiles). Then divide wall length by tile width: 2700 ÷ 150 = 18.
Tiles required are 15 × 18 = 270. Add 10 per cent (27) means you need
to buy 297 tiles. Check the boxes for the number of tiles in each and
get enough to match the number you need.

Tip

You should buy all of your tiles in one go, from the same
place. Colour variations do occur with different batches and
sometimes this is not noticeable until the tiles are on the wall.

ADHESIVES AND GROUT

▶ The long-term success of your tiling depends to a large extent on
  the adhesives you use to bond the tiles to the wall and you should
  always select the correct adhesive for any particular situation.
  For wall tiling work in bathrooms you need a water-resistant tile
  adhesive. Water-resistant adhesive is slightly more expensive than
  standard adhesive but do not be tempted to cut corners.

▶ All ceramic tile adhesives have full instructions printed on the
  containers and these should be followed to the letter.

▶ The spaces between the tiles are filled with a grouting
  compound and again, in a bathroom, this must be a water-
  resistant grout. The grout can be purchased already mixed
  or in powder form to mix by hand. It is very easy to mix.

▶ Adhesive and grout containers state the coverage on the
  containers, so check this out before buying.

PREPARATION

▶ *Remove any and all wallpaper. The adhesion to the wall is only good if the tiles are actually fixed to the wall. Fixing to paper means that if the paper is not fixed well, or the tile adhesive dissolves the wallpaper paste, the whole lot could be on the floor by the time you go to bed.*

▶ *Old tiling does not necessarily have to be removed, but the complications involved in tiling over existing tiles make it rarely worth the effort.*

▶ *Clean down the walls with sugar soap to remove any grease.*

▶ *New plaster should be allowed to dry completely and then sealed with a mist coat of emulsion. Absorbent surfaces can also be sealed with PVA building adhesive diluted 1 part adhesive to 5 parts water. Sealer must be completely dry before tiling is started.*

TILING

You will need:

▶ *a spirit level or plumb bob*

▶ *a good-quality tile cutter, either hand operated or electrical (get the best you can afford as it makes the job so much easier and more pleasurable when you are not struggling with inferior equipment)*

▶ *pincers, pliers or a tile saw*

▶ *tiles*

▶ *plastic spacers to keep a uniform gap that is wide enough (usually 2 mm) to allow you to force grout in*

▶ *a measuring gauge made from a piece of timber (18 mm × 44 mm wide and about 1.8 mm or 2.4 mm long) marked out in exact tile widths, including the spaces in between*

▶ *a timber batten the length of the wall to be tiled*

▶ *a pencil*

▶ *adhesive*

▶ *grout*

▶ *adhesive comb or notched trowel.*

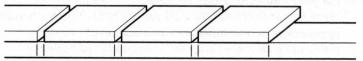

Timber marked out in tile widths and grout gaps

1 *Open all the boxes of tiles and shuffle them around. This distributes any colour variations and makes them unnoticeable over the wall.*

2 *Determine a starting point for your tiling by fixing a perfectly straight length of timber horizontally to the wall, with the top edge just over one tile height above the highest floor or skirting board level.*

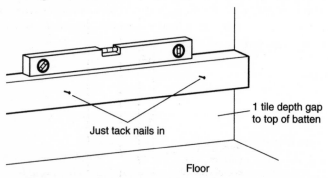

Just tack nails in

1 tile depth gap to top of batten

Floor

3 *Use a spirit level to check that the batten is truly horizontal. This batten, going the full width of the wall, will provide the level at which tiling commences, and will ensure that tiling lines are straight even though the floor may be uneven. Don't drive the nails fully home – they have to be removed later.*

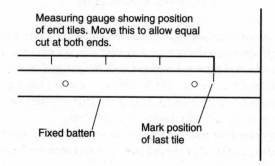

Measuring gauge showing position of end tiles. Move this to allow equal cut at both ends.

Fixed batten

Mark position of last tile

4 Use your measuring gauge vertically from the fixed batten to check that at the top of the wall you are not left with a narrow strip to be tiled. Narrow tile strips are difficult to cut.

5 If this situation arises, drop the horizontal fixed batten to leave roughly equal spacing at the top and bottom of the wall for cut tiles.

6 Measure to find the centre point of the fixed batten (the centre point along the width of the wall). Mark this point on the batten.

7 Use your measuring gauge horizontally along the batten to determine where the last whole tile will be fixed close to the end of the wall. Mark this point on the fixed batten.

8 Use a spirit level to fix a batten vertically up the wall, starting from your mark representing the end of the last full tile in the row.

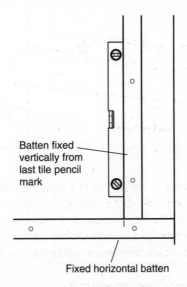

Batten fixed vertically from last tile pencil mark

Fixed horizontal batten

9 When the vertical batten is fixed (remember, this too has to come off again, so don't fix it too well) lay six or eight tiles loose in the right-angled corner you have formed to make sure they sit straight. You should be able to see at a glance if the joints seem to be closing up, indicating that the two battens are not meeting at right angles to each other.

10 It is very rare that walls in a property are absolutely square with each other, so fix all of the full tiles first and then make any cuts

*into the abutting walls, floor or ceiling. Start tiling in the corner.
Follow the instructions supplied with the adhesive, spreading
an area of about 1 square metre at a time, then comb it out.*

11 *Place the tiles firmly onto the ribbed adhesive, with spacers set
in between.*

12 *Working sideways and upwards, complete the fixing of all
whole tiles, then leave for about 24 hours to dry.*

13 *Remove the battens carefully.*

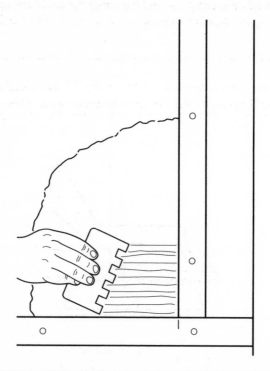

Insight

DIY Doctor uses a tiling (carborundum) stone made of silicone
carbide, to rub down the edge of a cut tile. This makes the
joints much neater.

14 *Cut tiles to fit around the perimeter. Where space is limited, the
adhesive can be applied to the back of the cut tiles instead of*

onto the wall. The simplest method of cutting the wall tiles is to mark the glazed tile surface where it is to be cut then, with the help of a straight edge, score the surface with the tile cutter to break the glaze. Place the scored tile over a couple of matchsticks or spacers, then press down either side to snap the tile.

15 *Pincers, pliers or a tile saw can be used to cut corners or curves out of tiles, to fit around projections. Again, the surface should be scored before the waste area is nibbled away.*

16 *When tiling is complete and has dried for 24 hours, all tile spacers should be removed and all joints filled well with grout.*

Tip

A ceramic tiling video is available on the Wickes website, www.wickes.co.uk, which demonstrates ceramic tiling well.

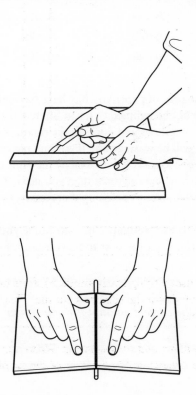

41 Wallpapering

Most wallpapers come is a standard size of 530 mm wide by
10.5 m long. Woodchip paper and lining paper, along with a few
other 'specials' come in longer or differing width rolls. You can
measure round the room for the number of rolls you need using the
chart below.

Perimeter of room	Height of wall		
	2.3–2.4 m	2.4–2.6 m	2.6–2.7 m
10 m	5 rolls	5 rolls	6 rolls
12 m	6 rolls	6 rolls	7 rolls
14 m	7 rolls	7 rolls	8 rolls
16 m	8 rolls	8 rolls	9 rolls
18 m	9 rolls	9 rolls	10 rolls
20 m	10 rolls	10 rolls	11 rolls

Make sure all the rolls of paper you buy have the same batch number
on them, and do not be tempted to try to 'stretch' the quantity you
need. If there are windows and doors in the room, do not deduct rolls
for them – there will be wastage and if you run out of paper it may be
very hard to get one extra roll with exactly the same colour match. It
is much better to buy one roll more than you need. You will always
have some paper left over to patch up if necessary.

If you are going to use wallpaper in your home you will need the
right tools. As usual, get the best tools you can afford.

You will need:

▶ *wallpaper (the correct amount for your room – see the table
  above)*
▶ *a tape measure*
▶ *a pencil*

- ▶ *a spirit level*
- ▶ *paperhanging scissors*
- ▶ *a pasting table*
- ▶ *a paste bucket*
- ▶ *a pasting brush*
- ▶ *a paper-hanging brush*
- ▶ *a seam roller*
- ▶ *a sharp hobby knife or proprietary wallpaper trimming knife*
- ▶ *overlap adhesive if you are using washable or vinyl paper.*

To hang your wallpaper:

1 *Make sure the surface of your wall is free from flaking paint or grease and never paper over existing wallpaper. The paste on the new wallpaper can soak through to any existing wallpaper, dissolving it.*

Tip

If the wall you are papering is already painted, it's a great idea to paint a line with a 25 mm brush on the wall where it meets the ceiling or skirting. The line should be as close to the colour of the paper as possible so that if your cuts are not 100 per cent neat the backing wall does not stick out like a sore thumb.

2 *Check the pattern on the paper (the label will help here). Some papers have a random pattern so it does not matter where you join the lengths. Some have a pattern that only matches at specific distances; there may be a little more wastage with this type of match. Generally, even a staggered match is repeated within 100 mm.*

3 *Decide where you are going to start papering. If the room has a focal point, e.g. a fireplace, then begin there, especially with large-patterned paper, by centring the pattern over the focal point. If there is no obvious focal point, start at a corner, ideally on a wall where there are no windows or doors (if this is not possible, see 'Papering round windows and door openings' on page 303). Wallpaper round the room in a clockwise direction.*

4 *Mark a vertical plumb line on which to start your papering. (It is important to remember that the corners of your room are extremely unlikely to be absolutely vertical or square, so you need to make sure the very first strip of paper you put up is plumb.)*

5 *Then measure along the wall, from one corner of the room, the width of your wallpaper less 25 mm, and mark a vertical line from ceiling to skirting board, using a spirit level. This line is the leading edge of your paper and when the first strip is hung it will go round the corner by about 25 mm.*

6 *Measure the height of your room in a number of places. It will probably vary by a few millimetres.*

7 *Now cut some lengths of wallpaper to length, adding 100 mm (more if the pattern requires it) to the longest measurement to allow for trimming. Remember to allow for pattern repetitions.*

8 *Lay your lengths of paper face down on the pasting table. Prevent the ends from curling back up into a roll by tying a piece of string across the table to the legs.*

9 *Mix the paste in the bucket as per the instructions on the packet. Tie another piece of string across the paste bucket at the point where the handle joins the top of the bucket. This will give you something to rest the brush bristles on to avoid getting the handle covered in paste.*

10 *Paste the paper by working from the middle of each length to the outside. Fold the wet sides together as shown and move*

to one side to store. *If you are careful and line up the lengths*
you have cut with the top edge of the table you should be
able to paste three or four lengths before hanging them. Some
papers need to soak for a while before hanging, so check the
instructions on the label.

Tip

When your paste is mixed well into the bucket, tip it into a
roller tray and paste the paper with a long-haired roller.

11 *Take the first length and place the edge against the line on*
the wall. Unfold the paper gently onto the wall, using your
hanging brush to brush down the middle and out towards
both edges. This brushing makes sure that the paper makes
contact with the wall and at the same time brushes out any
air bubbles that may have been trapped under the paper.

25 mm overlap

Pencil line and
edge of paper

12 *Brush the paper up to the crease between ceiling and wall and also the crease between skirting board and wall.*

13 *Double-check that the edge of the paper is in your pencil plumb line and then press the paper into both the creases with the back edge of your paperhanging scissors. This should give you a line to cut along.*

14 *Pull the paper off the wall far enough to cut it and then brush it back into place.*

15 *Brush the paper tightly into the corner of the room and you should have about 25 mm overlap on the adjoining wall. This can be trimmed back to about 5 mm or 10 mm – this will be covered later by another length of wallpaper.*

Tip

To hang paper round an external corner the same method is applied. The first length should turn round the corner by about 25 mm (turnover) and the next length, on the second wall, should be laid to a vertical line so it overlaps the turnover by as little as possible. Extra care must be taken here when working to a pattern, and sometimes a large overlap will be required on the turnover as it will need to be cut back until it matches the pattern.

16 *The next length of paper to be hung goes on the line also, so you are guaranteed to be hanging vertical lengths around the room.*

CUTTING ROUND SWITCHES AND SOCKETS

When you get to a switch or socket:

1 *First, turn off the power supply to that unit.*

2 *Mark the four corners as shown in the diagram opposite and cut diagonally across to leave an opening slightly smaller than the faceplate of the socket or switch.*

3 *Cut off most of the four flaps as shown by the dotted line. Leave enough to tuck behind the socket or switch.*

4 *Unscrew the faceplate from the wall a little and wiggle it through the cut paper, pushing the paper against the wall as you do.*

5 Tighten the faceplate back to the wall and turn the power back on when the adhesive is dry.

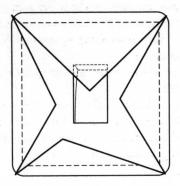

PAPERING ROUND WINDOWS AND DOOR OPENINGS

1 Cut the first overlap on a window as shown by *1* in the diagram on page 304.
2 Fold the flaps round into the window reveal, and smooth the rest of the paper above and below the window, cutting it out around the windowsill.

Insight
Make sure any steps, hop-ups or ladders you are using are placed correctly. Never try and lean or overreach when working off the ground.

----

3 Next, cut and paste the two top lengths above the window (see *2* in the diagram), folding them down and under the head of the window opening.
4 Now cut and paste the two corresponding strips under the window.
5 Note that the cut widths may not work out evenly at either side of the window. Measure to see if the joint between the strips of paper marked *2* in the diagram comes close to the centre of the window. If it does not, then it is fine to start hanging paper at point *2*, either side of the centre of the window, and work out in both directions to the corner of the room. This way you should avoid silly strips of paper running down the window frame.

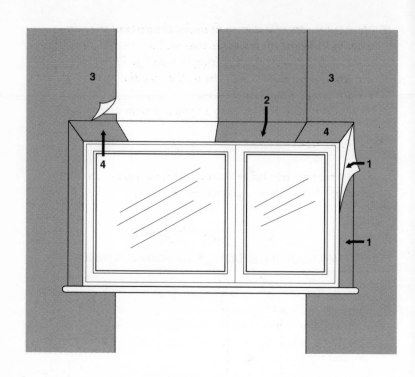

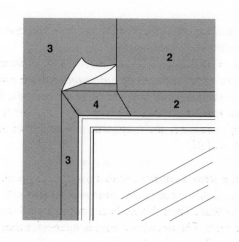

6   Now cut pieces of paper to fit under the head of the window
    opening (4 in the diagram). It is as well to cut and paste these
    pieces before finally pasting lengths 1 and 3. These pieces (4)
    can then be turned up onto the wall above the window where
    lengths 1 and 3 will cover them.
7   Hang strip 3 in the same way as you did strip 1.

WALLPAPERING ARCHES

1   Start papering around an arch in the same way as around a
    window. Paper up to and over the arch (C).

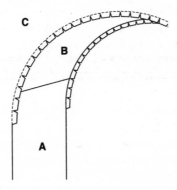

2   Then trim round the shape of the arch allowing a 25–40 mm
    overhang.
3   Cut out small triangles from the overhang, forming a series
    of wedges, or tabs, to allow you to fold it back under the arch.
    If you just cut slits the paper will crease and possibly tear.
4   When all tabs are folded in a strip of paper, just less than the
    width of the arch is stuck up under the arch and down the
    sides (A and B).

Sometimes the strip is cut first, with 25 mm overlap on either side
of the arch, and this is cut in the same way to allow it to be folded
back onto the wall. Then the walls are papered and cut round the
shape of the arch. The drawback to this method is that it involves
a very neat circular cut for the arch.

PAPERING BEHIND RADIATORS

Wherever possible, take the radiator off the wall (after draining down the system if necessary). This makes for a much better job. If this is not possible, cut the paper to the required shape to drop down over the radiator brackets, then smooth it out using a radiator paint roller.

---

42 Stripping paint

WHY STRIP PAINT?

Repainting a surface, especially timber, can only be done so many times before the paint starts to show signs of being tired. When this happens you really need to strip the paint off back to the wood and start again.

There are also times when a natural wood grain finish may look better than the existing paint, or when some amazing mouldings or furniture have been covered by a paint-happy person who simply wanted to hide the real beauty of the wood.

STRIPPING PAINT FROM TIMBER

The three ways of stripping paint from timber are:

▶ *using heat to lift the paint off the surface – nowadays the heat is usually applied by proprietary heat guns, but blowlamps were used for many years*
▶ *using liquid paste or gel paint stripper, either applying it to the surface or dipping the painted object into a vat of stripper (chemical methods)*
▶ *scraping it off using blades and chisels and then sanding it down, or just sanding it down (mechanical methods).*

Until fairly recently, many paints contained lead. If you are at all unsure whether the paint you are going to strip contains lead, then only use the chemical method, preferably with a solvent-free paint-stripping chemical.

You will need a variety of scrapers with all three stripping technique and, as always, if you have the right tools the job is so much easier.

Heat application

Novices are recommended to use a heat gun rather than a blowlamp. With both heat guns and blowlamps, different nozzles can be attached to direct the flow to a smaller or larger area.

Try to ensure that you have the right scraping implement for the job in hand – trying to remove hot paint from a delicate architrave moulding with a blunt screwdriver may damage the timber you are trying to save; a shaped shave hook or putty knife is useful for more intricate areas.

Tip

As with many DIY skills, you may find that a practice session on a piece of painted scrap timber will give you a better idea of the speed at which you should be working.

1 *When applying heat to painted timber, always keep the heat source moving or you can scorch the timber right through the paint. Heat guns are usually set to work best at about 150 mm from the surface.*
2 *Heat the surface until the paint begins to bubble, then move the heat while you scrape the area. It usually takes two or three passes to strip an area using heat.*
3 *When you have finished the stripping, let the area cool down. Heat can bring timber resins to the surface of the timber and cause any existing wood filler to 'pop' out of the hole it is filling. Allow 24 hours for the timber to return to its natural state before sanding down ready for painting. Painting on top of timber that has been heat stripped without sanding down the grain will produce a poor finish.*

Chemical stripping

Many consider this to be the best way of stripping paint from timber, especially when there are any mouldings involved. The timber is not damaged in any way and after stripping the timber is neutralized with warm water, white spirit or a proprietary neutralizer depending on the manufacturer's instructions.

There are several chemical strippers on the market, all of which involve painting a liquid, gel or paste onto the surface, waiting a while for the chemical reaction to take place (it melts the paint), then scraping the paint and chemical off.

> **Tip**
>
> The chemicals used are extremely toxic and, as with all DIY work, you must take care to protect yourself and others. Masks, goggles and gloves should be worn with all stripping techniques. Chemical strippers can also affect the glue used in timber joints.

> **Insight**
>
> Be careful when using a professional dipping tank to clean paint from something like a door. It takes a long while for the timber to dry out properly.

One very efficient type of chemical striper is a paste stripper that is applied to the surface, however intricate, with a special cover laid over the top of the paste. The emulsified paint is absorbed back into the paste, which dries onto the cover and the lot (up to 30 layers of paint!) is peeled off. This is a great method, but very expensive.

Many firms in the UK now have special tanks of stripper in which they can strip paint from doors and larger, transportable items. This represents a great saving.

When a piece of work is stripped and neutralized it will usually require a light sanding before painting, as the neutralizer often raises the grain of the timber. Any paint applied without the timber being neutralized will not last.

Mechanical stripping

This is usually the last resort when stripping timber. There are many electric sanders on the market – huge roller sanders, belt sanders that will take 3 mm off the surface of a piece of timber before you know it, detail sanders, orbital sanders, circular sanders – along with many grades of different types of abrasive papers. None of these, and this includes hand sanding, will get through several layers of paint in anything like the time available to most busy people.

---

43 Painting timber

Any decoration job, either DIY or professionally done, is only ever as good as the preparation and thought that has gone into it. If, for example, you are going to varnish a surface, sanding the timber across the grain prior to varnishing will leave scratches, which will show through the varnish and ruin your work. As the painting itself is fairly straightforward, this project concentrates on the all-important preparation, followed by some top painting tips.

BASICS

▶ *Clean the surface before painting it. There is grease in the air in every home, from cooking and general cleaning. This grease settles on all surfaces and must be removed. Paint, if it is to stay where it is put, must have a stable base.*

▶ *For the best results, use the best brushes you can afford. Cheap brushes will not only lose bristles quickly but will leave brush marks much more easily in the paint.*

▶ *Sand new or bare timber and then prime it before you paint it. Sandpaper is available with different degrees of coarseness of the surface. These are called grades. The grades are measured in numbers and the lower the number the coarser the grit.*

New timber should be sanded with medium to fine paper of about 120 grade. For large areas, an electrical sander may be ideal. Using rolls of abrasive paper makes it easy to cut to length to fit in most power sanders.

> **Insight**
>
> Paint will always dry a different colour on wood filler to the colour on the timber so keep filler to a minimum on surfaces where this will show.

▶ *After sanding there may be little indents that need to be filled. Nail heads, etc. can spoil your paint finish. A very popular myth among DIY enthusiasts is that paint can fill holes. This is not true! All-purpose filler will usually do the trick or, for varnished surfaces, a wood filler should be used which matches the colour of the wood as closely as possible.*

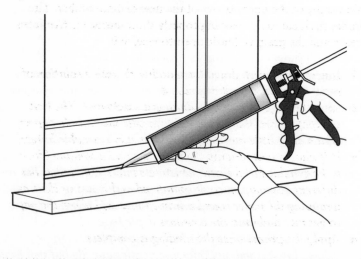

FILLING GAPS WHERE THE WOODWORK MEETS THE WALLS

Where the woodwork meets the walls there is often a gap. This gap can be filled very easily using flexible filler or decorator's caulk in a special application tool called a sealant gun.

1   *Cut off the sealed end of the tube and screwed on the nozzle.*
2   *This nozzle has a hole in the end which is often too small. Cut back the nozzle further to allow a larger bead of filler to be released from the tube, and at an angle to make application much easier.*
3   *Insert the tube into the gun and squeeze the trigger to apply the filler.*
4   *Once the gap is filled, run a wet finger down the joint to tidy it up. Remove surplus filler with a damp rag.*

PRIMING THE WOODWORK

Always apply a primer before painting. If an undercoat or topcoat of paint is applied to bare wood, the moisture is sucked out of it too quickly and the paint does not have a chance to soak into the timber. The paint therefore dries on the surface and will quickly peel. Primer is a thin paint that soaks into the grain slightly and takes some of the porosity out of the new or bare timber. The primer itself can only soak in properly if the surface is free from grease and the grain is a little open to receive it.

1   *If necessary, wash down the woodwork with a solution of sugar soap which will degrease it.*
2   *Sand the surface with a medium grit sandpaper. The best sandpapers are aluminium oxide or silicone carbide papers, which are a little more expensive but stay workable longer.*
3   *It is always best to wrap the paper around a sanding block to keep a flat surface with which to sand. If the timber has different contours, such as chamfered architrave or skirting, wrapping the paper round a firm sponge will allow the paper to get into and onto the contours.*
4   *Apply the primer once the sanding is complete.*

Tip

Remember to protect carpets and other soft furnishings with dust sheets. If there are any knots in the timber these should be treated with knotting solution which will stop the sap leaking out of the timber and spoiling your paintwork.

You do not need to remove all the paint on previously painted surfaces if it is not flaking and is in a stable condition. Simply clean thoroughly with sugar soap and then sand down with a fine paper to give a key for the new paint.

If the existing paint is not in good condition, it may be as well to remove it. This is usually easiest done using a paint stripper (see Project 42).

If only small areas of the paintwork need to be removed, sand them down as smoothly as possible, creating a very gentle slope between the existing paint and the wood underneath. Then spot prime the areas of new wood with primer and carry on painting with undercoat and gloss.

Wear a mask for sanding existing paintwork as older paints may contain lead which can be dangerous. The safest way is to use 'wet and dry' paper and keep it wet.

UNDERCOAT

When the timber is sealed and primed it can be undercoated. The undercoat provides a film of paint that forms a non-absorbent, flexible base for the top, decorative coat. The undercoat, ideally, should be as close as possible to the colour of the chosen topcoat.

An undercoat is always a good idea on previously painted surfaces as it will give you a much better finish and stops the paint 'dragging' on the surface.

PAINTING TIPS AND PROBLEM SOLVING

▶ **Topcoat** *The topcoat is usually a gloss, matt or eggshell paint that is suitable for the location of the work.*
▶ **Top-quality gloss finish** *To get a gloss finish that looks really good, wait for the first coat to dry completely, then use 600 grade 'wet and dry' paper with water over the surface. Wipe off the excess water with kitchen towel. The next coat will*

*look almost like glass. Do this again for a third coat that will
look like glass.*

▶ **Sticky door** *If you have just painted a door and are worried
about it sticking, as they all do, wait for it to dry and rub the
edges with a candle before closing.*

▶ **Colour match** *If you are decorating and intend to revamp the
room, touch the paint brush, with the various colours you are
using, onto a piece of paper. You can then drop this into your
wallet or purse and when you see an item of furniture you like,
you can check it against your colour palette.*

▶ **Keep your cool** *When painting the outside of your house, try
to avoid dark colours. They absorb heat very easily and are
much more prone to blistering as a result. Also try to paint the
walls in the following order: west facing in the morning, east
in the afternoon, and south and north when they are shaded
the most. Painting in direct sunlight can make the paint dry in
a patchy way and can give a poor finish.*

▶ **Old paint** *If you have half a tin of paint that you need to keep,
turn it upside down before storing it (making sure the lid is
fixed firmly!). This will remove the need for cutting away a
skin when you use it again. If you have not done this and find
you have bits in your paint, strain it through an old pair of
tights before you use it.*

▶ **Smelly paint** *To get rid of the smell of fresh paint, cut an onion in
half and leave it in the room. It will take away most of the smell.
Also, a teaspoonful of vanilla essence stirred into the paint helps
remove a lot of the odour without affecting the colour.*

▶ **Wall lights** *Cover wall lights with a plastic carrier bag when
decorating. It will save you hours of cleaning time.*

▶ **Easy stripping** *If you have any wallpaper to strip, go to the
chemist and buy some alum. Fill a bucket with water and add
two teaspoons of alum to each pint of water. Wet the paper
thoroughly and allow it to dry in. It should then lift off the
wall much more easily.*

▶ **Masking alternative** *Masking paper can be a pain to get off
glass and can easily leave marks that are worse than the paint
would have been. Spend some time cutting newspaper into
strips and damp each strip before using it as masking tape.*

The dampness will allow you to manoeuvre it into position
and keep it stuck to the glass long enough for you to paint
your frame. It falls off easily afterwards!

▶ **Roll it up** *If you have finished with your emulsion roller and*
brush for the day, but intend to carry on tomorrow or in a few
days' time, wrap them tightly in a carrier bag. They will stay
soft and usable for up to a month if wrapped properly.

▶ **Gloss over it** *To have the same effect with your gloss brush,*
keep it in a jar full of water, or at least so that the water is
over the bristles and retaining band. Shake it out the next day
and carry on.

▶ **Paint thinners** *Don't waste your thinners – cut the top from a*
plastic drinks bottle and use that for cleaning your brushes.

▶ **Old brushes** *Hard brushes can be rejuvenated after a spell in*
hot vinegar. Comb the bristles with a fork afterwards and keep
in shape with an elastic band until dry.

▶ **Old tins in the shed** *Keep track of the paint you have saved*
by sticking a piece of masking tape down one side of the tin.
When you have finished painting, mark a line on the tape to
indicate the top of the paint, and it might be handy to write
on the date as well. No more wrestling the top off to find you
haven't got enough paint for the job.

▶ **Messy roller tray** *Before you start painting, wrap your roller tray*
in cling-film and just roll it up and throw it away afterwards.

▶ **Painting chairs** *Stand your chair legs in saucers or something*
similar to avoid ground contact or balancing acts!

▶ **Messy handles** *Keep paint off door handles, hinges and locks*
by applying some Vaseline, on a piece of tissue, to them before
you start painting. The paint won't stick to this.

▶ **Putty mess** *If the putty you want to use is very oily and too*
soft, roll it around on a piece of newspaper first. This will soak
up the excess oil and make it ready for use. Keep it soft by
wrapping it in cling-film or silver foil.

▶ **Rejuvenating masking tape** *Put the tape in the microwave*
oven with a glass of water. Set the oven on full for about
1 minute. Switch off and check that the tape has become quite
warm (do not overheat). The tape will now peel off just as it
did when new. When the tape becomes cold, just reactivate it.

- ▶ **Sticky tin** *When you have opened and stirred a new tin of paint, tie a piece of string tightly between the two rivets where the handle connects. This will enable you to wipe your brush and rest it without getting paint all over yourself or the tin.*

Faults in painted surfaces
Faults in painted surfaces are a nuisance and can sometimes be avoided. Here are some common faults.

- ▶ **Grey/white surface haze** *Sometimes called 'blooming', this is a result of the paint being affected by moisture during drying. The moisture can be from condensation in an unventilated room or water from another source, such as rainfall.*
- ▶ **Blistering** *This is almost always caused by moisture in the timber, which has been painted over without being allowed to dry properly. The moisture tries to evaporate but cannot get through the paint. The paint will eventually crack and peel, allowing more moisture in. Windowsills are very prone to these blisters, sometimes because the ends of the sills have not been prepared properly, allowing the moisture in. This fault often occurs on metal surfaces as well, due to the surface not being properly prepared before painting, including rust removal and the use of a primer. The interaction between two different metal surfaces can cause 'electrolytic corrosion' which may also lead to blistering.*
- ▶ **Cracking** *Sometimes called 'checking' or 'aligatoring', this usually happens in regular cracking patterns on the surface of the paint. This is caused by applying the top coat of paint before the one beneath it is completely dry – the coats will dry at different rates, causing shrinkage.*
- ▶ **Peeling** *If areas of paint can be easily peeled off it is most commonly due to a contaminated surface or the use of the wrong (or no) primer.*
- ▶ **No shine to gloss** *This will happen if the primer used is too thin or if insufficient primer or undercoat has been used. The absorbent timber will soak the paint in too quickly and leave a poor finish.*

- **Slow drying** *This is generally caused by moisture contamination, old paint whose drying agent has evaporated, or low temperatures.*
- **Wrinkles** *Too much paint applied in one go on a vertical surface will cause the paint to run, drying with a 'wrinkled' appearance.*

10 THINGS TO REMEMBER FROM PROJECTS 38–43

1 *New plaster must always be allowed to dry properly and sealed before decoration.*

2 *Use proprietary paint for kitchens and bathrooms.*

3 *Use the best-quality tools you can afford. Cheap brushes leave bristles on the wall!*

4 *Water stains must be blocked before decoration. They will always bleed through even 100 coats of emulsion.*

5 *Always take time measuring and setting out wall coverings to avoid wastage and tiny cuts of tiles and wallpaper.*

6 *Always use tiles and wallpaper with the same batch number.*

7 *Allow enough additional material for wastage.*

8 *If you are unsure about the old paint containing lead, be on the safe side and use a chemical stripper.*

9 *More time spent preparing the job properly will result in a much better finish.*

10 *Priming and undercoating timber will give a much better finish to the topcoat.*

Index